THEM AND US

THE IRISH AT CHELTENHAM

JOHN SCALLY

MAINSTREAM
PUBLISHING

EDINBURGH AND LONDON

Copyright © John Scally, 1999

First published in Great Britain in 1999 by
MAINSTREAM PUBLISHING COMPANY (EDINBURGH) LTD
7 Albany Street
Edinburgh EH1 3UG

ISBN 1 84018 347 0

This edition, 2000

A catalogue record for this book is available from the British Library

Typeset in Berkeley Book and Stone Sans
Printed and bound in Great Britain by Cox and Wyman Ltd

Contents

This book is dedicated to everyone at Tully's Travel Ltd, Carlow, Ireland's premier racing-travel specialists and carriers of thousands of Irish pilgrims every year to racing's theatre of dreams and the memory of Oliver Mannion.

Acknowledgements

My thanks to Shane Broderick, Peter Bromley, John Cooney, Jim Dreaper, Paul Duffy, Seamus Farrell, Mary Finn, Mick Fitzgerald, Tom Foley, Ollie Hannon, HRH Princess Haya Bint Al Hussein, Cameron McMillan, Adrian Maguire, Ian Marimon, Cliff Noone, Vincent O'Brien, Micheál O'Muircheartaigh, Niall Quinn, Marie Sheehan and Norman Williamson for their help.

My deepest gratitude to Frank Tully and all at Tully's Travel Ltd, Carlow, for their sponsorship.

Special thanks to Charles J. Haughey, Archie O'Leary, Peter Woods, the wonderfully entertaining Ted Walsh and, for overwhelming kindness and generosity, the 'voice of racing', Sir Peter O'Sullevan.

Very special thanks to my good friend Noel Coughlan for his practical assistance and for putting the vast reservoir of his knowledge about racing at my disposal.

As always, I also wish to express my appreciation to Bill Campbell and all at Mainstream.

Introduction

Danoli nearly killed me.

The call of research had taken me to Tom Foley's stable in Banglestown to meet Ireland's favourite racehorse. I was like a child in a sweetshop as I patted this hero and drank in Tom's marvellous words. I loved listening to him because his stories were so full of warmth, of mystery and of hope. In particular I loved when he talked about Danoli because of the passion with which he spoke.

Reluctantly I bade farewell and faced an incessant stream of Friday evening traffic as I made my way back to Dublin. Monsoon-like rain was making music on the car roof. Suddenly I was entangled in the clinging cobwebs of memory. In the gloom, my mind drifted back to my darkest day. My mother's voice was fractured with emotion as she spoke down the crackling line. Although her voice was scarcely audible, her words are forever imprinted in my memory: 'Prepare yourself for an awful shock. Are you sitting down?' The blackest possible scenarios exploded through my brain. Except this one. 'Poor Oliver got a heart attack this morning and died in Bertie's shed. The ambulance came and took him away. Can you come home?'

Oliver Mannion was my best friend. My next-door neighbour. My cousin. My soulmate. He was the brother I never had. He was just 33 years of age. Two days before he died, his own horse had run its first race.

'How did he do, Oliver?'

'Second.'

'Wow! That's great.'

'Not really. He was second-last!'

He was a walking encyclopedia on racehorses, jockeys, trainers and owners. I recalled the glow on his face as he returned from the equine Holy Grail in March 1995. He had never taken a holiday: 'How would they manage without me?' he always said. Yet that day in Cheltenham, in the height of the lambing season, opened the door to the wider world for him. Up to then his horizons had been limited to the fields in Roscommon.

One of his sweetest legacies to me is an almost fanatical devotion to Danoli. Our last words together were about this sporting hero.

My reminiscences were abruptly terminated as I made sudden contact with the trailer of a tractor. A local farmer was transporting a load of fertiliser. Nothing wrong with that, except that it was now pitch dark and he had no back light. I suddenly rediscovered my devout Catholic faith and I heard myself say a passionate act of contrition. The force of impact sent the car hurtling across the road and somehow I ended up a quarter of a mile away via a zig-zagging motion that would not have been out of place in a James Bond film.

Numbed by pain and shock, I sat motionless until there was a sharp knock on the window. Then, in a strong Carlow accent, the farmer asked, 'Did you not see me?' Although he had eyes which looked more intimidating than Anthony Hopkins' in *The Silence of the Lambs*, I started to laugh, but it hurt too much. For a second I wondered if I had stumbled into a Monty Python sketch. Or was this 1 April?

Then my journalistic instincts took over and although the front of the car was a mangled wreck, I broke through the pain barrier to reach forward and check that my tape recorder was okay. Thankfully it was. I just wished I could have said the same for the car. The rest of the evening is a distant blur, though I remember the two gardai assuring me I would feel better in the morning.

I woke up the next morning not knowing who or where I was. The only thing I was aware of was a throbbing pain in my head and the fact that my back seemed to have developed a mind of its own when I tried to move.

As my memory returned, two questions presented themselves.

Was writing a book on racing worth this pain?

No.

Was it worth all this torture to spend a couple of hours with Danoli and Tom Foley?

Definitely.

PART ONE

The Players

ONE

Patriot Games

It's Them and Us

Two incidents sum up what Cheltenham means to the Irish racing public. In 1964 the 'voice of racing', Peter O'Sullevan, reached a decisive moment in his commentary of the Gold Cup: 'Mill House for England, Arkle for Ireland.' The Empire and its former colony, with centuries of turbulent history between them, represented by two horses. This was war without bullets. An old battle in a new theatre.

All Irish hearts willed Arkle to victory. Mill House's aura of invincibility was subjected to its most severe scrutiny. Although Arkle was an extraordinarily exceptional horse (characterised by his accurate jumping and his habit of overlapping his forelegs with his hind legs like a greyhound), he had two significant advantages which helped to carry his career to extraordinary heights: he was trained by the late Tom Dreaper, and he was ridden by one of the finest jockeys in modern times, Pat Taaffe. In the end it was Irish eyes that were smiling. In this world of hype, he remains one of the few serious contenders for the accolade of horse of the century.

Fast forward to 1996. The dynamic duo of Aidan O'Brien and Charlie Swan have just delivered Ireland's second winner at the festival, Urubande – O'Brien's first victory at the equine promised land. Ex-jockey and Channel 4's racing front-man Brough Scott advances with his microphone and asks the winning trainer, 'We have seen your statistics over here, well over 200 winners in one year – what is your secret?' Immediately a small Irishman sticks his head through a tiny gap in the circle of friends. 'Don't tell him.' His interjection provokes great acclaim from the onlookers. It would have been unthinkable to have shared 'our' recipe for success with the auld enemy.

Racing was not just sport for him, it was also about nationalism. The historical relationship between Ireland and Britain had always been one of inequality. Ireland had always had to play second fiddle, but on the racing track the position was reversed. These horses were not simply animals, they were Irish heroes. In winning the great races they were also putting the Brits in their place.

The man in question was not xenophobic but, like the majority of Irish people, he had a love-hate relationship with Britain. It was just one of the psychological scars of colonial oppression. He hated many of the things, though by no means all, the British had done to Ireland, yet he was grateful that England had opened its arms to offer employment and a home to so many Irish people.

When they bet on an Irish horse at Cheltenham, Irish fans are betting on national property, investing emotional as well as tangible currency. When a fancied Irish horse loses, the loss is more than just monetary. Any Irish win precipitates a show of national identity. Punters brush aside gatemen and crowd on their way to the winners' enclosure to roar every Irish victory as if each one somehow confers glory on them, personally submerging their individuality in the name of patriotism. The eyes have it, grown men blubbering like babies as they come back from the winners' enclosure. Cheltenham torments them in their waking hours and haunts them in their dreams.

This book is not a compilation of the stories of every Irish horse that has run or won at the Cheltenham Festival. Rather, it is an attempt to unravel a mystery: why is it that Cheltenham beckons and the Irish come?

TWO

One Woman and Her Horse

'I met with an accident on the way to the racecourse. I arrived safely.'

JOE E. LEWIS

The Irish love for horses is reflected in its rich canon of literature. The fourth part of Jonathan Swift's *Gulliver's Travels* takes us to the Houyhnhnms, the land where horses rule. Ireland's most famous literary opus, James Joyce's *Ulysses*, is set on Ascot Gold Cup day. However, one of Ireland's greatest poets of the twentieth century, Patrick Kavanagh, argued that since the reference was only to a punter speculating on the result of the race, Joyce was relegating the sport to peripheral status. He went on to claim that all sporting subjects are 'superficial' as 'the emotion is a momentary puff of gas, not an experience'.

The fact that Kavanagh's own sporting career was an unmitigated disaster may have fuelled his cynicism. Like Albert Camus, Pope John Paul II and Julio Inglesias, he was a goalkeeper – albeit in Gaelic football. In the early '30s he played for his local team, Inniskeen Grattans, succeeding Tom 'The Collier' Callan, who, in the words of his brother Peter, was 'so stiff from farm work that he could only stop a ball that hit him'. Kavanagh's most famous contribution was to wander off to buy either an ice cream or a drink, depending on whose version of events you listen to, while the opposition scored a goal between the deserted posts. The final ignominy came when he conceded the match-losing goal in the county final by letting the ball roll between his legs. His own supporters shouted, 'Go home and put an apron on you!'

His career as a sporting administrator fuelled even more venom. As club treasurer he kept club funds under his bed, which prompted some nasty rumours. Kavanagh's own response to the innuendo was, 'It is possible that every so often I visited it for the price of a packet of cigarettes, but nothing serious.'

Kavanagh's dismissal of racing is proof positive that he never went to Cheltenham.

In the Beginning

Cheltenham is situated on the river Chelt, a tributary of the Severn, against the backdrop of the Cotswold Hills and is steeped in history. It received the royal imprimatur when King George III visited the place in 1788 and proclaimed that drinking the waters did him good.

The first race meeting there was held 27 years later on Nottingham Hill, above Bishop's Cleeve. Miss Tidmarsh, a five-year-old bay mare owned by Mr E. Jones, has the distinction of being Cheltenham's first recorded winner at its first official meeting on Cleeve Hill on 25 August 1818.

By the mid 1820s, Cheltenham races were on a par with Ascot, Epsom and Goodwood. Then came a bolt from heaven. The evangelical Dean Francis Close fuelled a puritan revival in the area after he was promoted to St Mary's Parish Church. He stated, 'I verily believe that, on the day of judgement, thousands of that vast multitude who have served the world, the flesh and the devil will trace up all the guilt and misery which has fallen on them.' Racing was one of the sins of the flesh in this ascetic view of the world. As his views quickly gained popular currency, there were demons-trations on the course and the grandstand was burnt to the ground in 1830. As the moral majority could not tolerate the evils of betting, racing in the vicinity went into a steep decline.

By 1855 flat racing had died out entirely in Cheltenham. In the latter half of the nineteenth century, steeplechasing too was in decline throughout England. In 1902, however, the slide was halted when a new meeting was inaugurated in Prestbury Park, the current site of Cheltenham racing. The local community gave the reopening great support and Prestbury Park gradually consolidated its support base.

There were eight starters in the first Cheltenham Gold Cup in 1924. After the three-and-a-quarter-mile steeplechase, Red Splash emerged victorious from Conjuror II and Gerard L. The first Champion Hurdle attracted only four horses and the meagre first prize of £365 spoke volumes about the low standing of hurdle racing at the time. Cheltenham 1926 was also overshadowed to some extent by controversy over the betting tax. The Chancellor of the Exchequer, Mr Winston Churchill, had in his budget instituted a 5 per cent betting tax on every stake placed on a racecourse or with a credit bookmaker, to take effect from 1 November.

Many Cheltenham winners served their apprenticeship in Ireland. A case in point was Easter Hero, who went on to win consecutive Gold Cups in 1929 and 1930. He had raced for the first time in 1925, finishing unplaced in the Killeston Plate at Baldoyle. It was then that the great Irish horse Golden Miller brought new fame to Cheltenham by winning five consecutive Gold Cups. (In 1934 he also won the Grand National in record time.) In 1937 he was denied the opportunity to make it six when rain and snow caused the abandonment of the already once-postponed national hunt festival. The following year he made a great effort to win his sixth, only to be beaten by two lengths by Morse Code. It was effectively the final curtain call for a wonderful champion. Racing experts said at the time, 'We shall not see his like again.'

The same epitaph, in feminine form, could be applied to his owner. The Honourable Dorothy Wyndham Paget, with her imposing physical presence and old-fashioned clothes, was known by sight by everybody who went to Cheltenham. Born in 1905, she was the great-granddaughter of Henry Paget, 1st Marquess of Anglesey, who had commanded the cavalry at Waterloo. Her father was Lord Queenborough, owner of St Louis, winner of the 2,000 Guineas in 1922. Her mother Pauline Whitney belonged to one of the wealthiest families in America. An early indication of Ms Paget's temperament came when she was expelled in quick succession from six of the most expensive girls' schools in England. A quirk of fortune led her to racing. One day she was out riding when a horse called Bridget bolted with her on board. Afterwards Bridget was sent off to go into training and won a race. Having been bitten by the bug of gambling on a horse, Ms Paget decided to become a serious owner.

She normally had a very torrid relationship with her trainers. The statistics tell the story: in 30 years her horses moved to at least 17 different stables in England, and she also had trainers in Ireland. She was shy and usually spoke only to her immediate entourage and her trainers – though in the case of the latter it was usually via the telephone or one of her secretaries. She once said that the close proximity of strange men made her vomit! As if to illustrate the point, she once wrote to the Minister of Transport to enquire if the wartime ban on the reservation of railway carriages might be waived in her case. The Minister politely replied that while he regretted any inconvenience she might be subjected to, he was unable to comply with her wishes in the interests of the war effort.

After the war she was on her way to a race meeting when her car broke down. The only transport around was a butcher's van. She instructed her secretary to purchase it. The butcher sought and received £300. According to legend, Ms Paget arrived at the race meeting sitting between two carcasses. After that she refused to travel by car again, no matter how short the distance, without at least one car in tow.

Her passion for horses was almost matched by her passion for food. Once she ordered four steaks in a restaurant. When they were ready, the waiter asked if she would like them served immediately or if she would like to wait for her guests.

'Who said anything about guests?' she replied.

The Golden Touch

Ms Paget's initial choice of Basil Briscoe as her trainer was hugely influenced by the fact that he was training the most promising hurdler and steeplechaser seen in Britain in living memory, Insurance and Golden Miller respectively. Briscoe had been training them for Philip Carr, an astute judge of horses but a man whose health was in rapid decline. Towards the end of 1931, Ms Paget heard that he might be induced to part with them. She offered £12,000 for both. While that seems like small change today, it was a stunning price for national hunt horses at the time; the only opportunity she would have of recouping her money would be if one of them won the Grand National.

Briscoe himself held brief tenure of Golden Miller in 1930. That March he got a telegram from Ireland from Captain Farmer, best known for his partnership with prominent Northamptonshire trainer John Drage, offering him an unbroken three-year-old out of Miller's Pride for the tidy sum of £500. Briscoe was impressed by the heritage, having trained two successful horses out of the mare, so he responded, 'Yes, sending cheque.' The following week the three-year-old horse arrived – and Briscoe cursed himself for buying a horse he had never seen when he saw the state of his latest acquisition. The horse had been running in a field all his life and his former owner had not bothered to scrape the mud off him before sending him across the Irish Sea. Exhausted from his long journey by sea and rail, the horse stood in his box with his head down, a portrait of helplessness. He was no trouble as he was broken in – in fact, he was so apathetic that any hint of trouble would have been enthusiastically welcomed.

Briscoe's fading hopes for his horse could not have been boosted when he told his head lad that he had named the beast Golden Miller, only to be told, 'That's too good a name for a bad horse.' Briscoe countered, 'Well, he'll improve a lot.' He was told in reply, 'He's f**k all good now and even if he improves a thousand per cent he'll still be f**k all good.'

After he had been ridden for a number of weeks, the Irish horse was entered in a maiden three-year-old race at Southwell, where he put in a truly awful performance. However, Philip Carr saw some hidden potential in the horse and offered £1,000 for him. Briscoe could hardly believe his luck. He was making twice the sum he had paid for a horse that was apparently a total dud.

Yet within a short space of time Carr's opinion was vindicated. He ran Golden Miller in an all-age hurdle race at Newbury and, the only three-year-old in the field, he showed great promise when finishing third. His jockey, Bob Lyall, a leading light in the field, went so far as to describe him as one of the most promising three-year-olds he had ever mounted. Golden Miller went on to win his next two races at Leicester (the Gopsall Maiden Hurdle) and Nottingham by impressive margins, earning £83 and £88 respectively, and from then on his star rose spectacularly. By the time Ms Paget became his owner he was a household name.

Ms Paget reaped an almost instant reward from her investment at Cheltenham in 1932, when Insurance won the Champion Hurdle and Golden Miller the Gold Cup on the same day, netting their owner £1,340. When Golden Miller, as a five-year-old, took on the best steeplechasers in the country in his first Gold Cup, it was a mere three and a half months after he had made his debut as a steeplechaser. It seemed a bridge too far for a virtual beginner, but at 13–2 he romped home.

In 1934 Golden Miller won the Grand National, in the process beating the course record by eight seconds, seventeen days after winning the Gold Cup. Souvenir hunters pulled hairs from his tail. Cheltenham had never seen his like. They even had to take the unprecedented step of closing the gates. The following year roads to the course were blocked and trains were bursting at the seams with people desperate to see the Gold Cup duel between Golden Miller, ridden by Gerry Wilson, and Thomond II, ridden by Billy Speck. Golden Miller won by three-quarters of a length.

Golden Miller and Arkle made jumping every bit as popular as flat racing. Throughout his seven-season career, Golden Miller won 31 races valued at £15,176. None of his Gold Cups netted more than £670, but his Grand National win brought in £7,265.

Up to that point the most famous Irish-bred horse had probably been Troytown. A raging gale was howling and cold, slanting rain was lashing down as the horses went to the start for the 1920 Grand National. Not surprisingly, in the circumstances, the going was heavy. The winner in the two previous years, Poethlyn, started as 3–1 favourite, but the large Irish contingent were backing Troytown, the second favourite at 6–1.

At 17hh, with terrific bone, a great shoulder and substantial depth of girth, Troytown (by Cyllene's son Zria) cut an impressive figure. He was bred in Meath by his owner Major Thomas Collins-Gerrard but did not race until he was six. With Poethlyn falling at the first fence, Troytown led the field into the driving rain. His jockey, Jack Anthony, was severely disadvantaged when the reins slipped through his gloved hands, subsequently describing his mount as more like a steam engine than a horse and his Becher's jump as like taking off in an express lift.

There was almost a catastrophe at the last ditch when Troytown made his only error. He misjudged his take-off, slipped and ploughed through the five-foot-high obstacle, leaving a gaping hole. Somehow he managed to hold his feet, but now he was behind Harry Brown's mount The Bore. A spectacular leap at the third last took him from a length down to a length in front and to an incredible ovation from the Irish fans he raced to victory – one of only five of the twenty-four starters to finish.

He had won the Grand Steeple-Chase de Paris the previous year and was sent over to retain his title. He could only manage third. Five days later he ran in the Prix des Drags but fell and broke his leg above the knee. True to form, he heroically struggled to his feet and tried to continue, but he collapsed again after a few yards. There was no option but to put him down. He was buried at the animals' cemetery at Asnières, the first racehorse to be interred there.

The first Irish-bred horse to make a major impression at Cheltenham was Easter Hero, who won consecutive Gold Cups in 1929 and 1930. He had been purchased by a Mr Lowestein for the awesome price of £7,000. There had been much hype about the 1930 clash between Easter Hero (8–11f) and Gib (13–8), but in fact it ended as something of a damp squib as Gib fell two fences from home. He was remounted to finish third behind Grakle, who was beaten by 20 lengths by Easter Hero. It completed a memorable double for trainer Jack Anthony and jockey Tommy Cullinan, who also won the Champion Hurdle with Brown Tony in a thrilling finish.

Romeo's Twin

Ms Paget's vast collection of Irish-trained horses was under the careful stewardship of Charlie Rogers. Charlie was a man of unparalleled charisma, and so taken was she by his charm that she nicknamed him 'Romeo'. The name stuck. Although nicknames do not have the same popular currency in racing as they do in rugby, for instance, they are still an integral part of the sport. In the eighteenth century jockey John Mangle, who rode five St Leger winners, was known as 'Crying Jackie'. Two hundred years before Paul Gascoigne, he regularly burst into tears after losing a race.

Charlie had an eye for horses to match his charm and supplied Ms Paget with a virtually never-ending supply of winners like Albany Blue and The

Saint (the first winner trained by Gordon Richards). He managed her stud at Ballymacoll in County Meath, where she spent several months during the war. Her Irish connection was strengthened when Dan Moore, Ireland's top jockey for years, became her leading rider.

'Romeo' purchased all of her jumpers from Ireland until Fulke Walwyn became her main English trainer. He recommended that she turn her attention to France: as the French horses had been winning everything on the flat, he suggested that they were also breeding top jumping material. This led to the purchase of a four-year-old called Mont Tremblant who had won a flat race at Longchamp. So smitten was Ms Paget by the horse that she sent Fulke back to purchase his taller half-brother Lanveoc Poulmic, who instantly became her favourite. Despite his size, Lanveoc Poulmic was very agile and proved virtually unbeatable in maiden races. Ms Paget was convinced that her new discovery would match the achievements of Golden Miller, but although he won eleven races in three seasons, none of them was of much importance. His few outings at big races were less than successful, including a fall in the Gold Cup.

After a disastrous four seasons, the horse was sent to Ballydoyle to be trained by Vincent O'Brien. After a long rest he appeared on the threshold of rehabilitation and was given a run in Naas as a warm-up for the King George VI Chase at the Christmas meeting at Kempton. With two fences to go the big horse was a long way clear, but then he was pulled up. Vincent O'Brien wrote to Ms Paget, 'He broke down so badly that we had to put him down right away. It was very, very sad.'

Mont Tremblant went on to win the 1952 Gold Cup, giving Ms Paget her seventh triumph in the race following Golden Miller's five victories and Roman Hackle's success in 1940.

Ms Paget had little success in Ireland, though Golden Jack was once the best novice chaser there, winning the Galway Plate in 1942 and running Prince Regent close in the Irish Grand National. She brought off six doubles at six consecutive meetings. Towards the end of 1945, Housewarmer won three steeplechases and four of her Irish-trained jumpers had won eight races between them.

After the war ended, Ms Paget could not find immediate accommodation in England for her Irish-trained horses so they remained in Ireland and were dispatched to England to race whenever necessary. In a pre-air-travel era, this was a severe handicap. On the other hand, Irish-trained jumpers had a huge advantage over their near neighbours because jumping had not been disrupted.

In the early years of the war, racing had continued in Britain but was nonetheless affected. When Medoc II won the Gold Cup under Frenchie

Nicholson in thick fog, radio listeners were not informed about it by commentator Raymond Glendinning, who was fully aware that his commentary was being monitored by Germans who had a vested interest in knowing the weather conditions in England.

On 6 January 1945, after a gap of almost three years, jump racing resumed in Cheltenham. Ms Paget won three races in one afternoon at the Cheltenham Christmas meeting with Hamlet, Astrometer and Housewarmer, all trained in Ireland and ridden by Dan Moore.

In 1946 she made it a great day for the Irish at Cheltenham with a hat-trick of victories by Irish-trained horses. Distel won the Champion Hurdle, with an emphatic victory over Carnival Boy. Dunshaughlin won the National Hunt Handicap Chase despite the handicap of a 5lb penalty for a recent victory at Windsor. He was not, though, nearly as well backed as African Collection, another Irish raider, who started a good favourite. Dunshaughlin was splendidly ridden by Bobby Ryan and beat Silver Fame into second place. Ms Paget's third winner, Loyal King, defied a 10lb penalty in the Grand Annual Chase to beat another Irish horse, Keep Faith, by a couple of lengths.

A Laughing Matter

It is estimated that Ms Paget spent almost £3 million on racing up to her death, at the age of 54, in 1960. Her last words were, appropriately, 'We must get these entries off to Wetherby's first thing.' She had the final of her 1,532 victories on 30 January 1960 at Naas and was the only owner in racing history to win the Gold Cup and Grand National (Golden Miller), the Champion Hurdle (Insurance) and the Derby (Straight Deal).

In the final years of her life, most of her horses were with Sir Gordon Richards. Their relationship dated back to Royal Ascot in 1939, when he pulled off a feat almost as great as any of his illustrious achievements in the saddle – he succeeded in making her laugh! She had just lost a small fortune, even by her opulent standards, on her colt Colonel Payne, whom Gordon had ridden for Fred Darling's stable in the Cork and Orrery Stakes, as the trainer had informed her she could put her maximum bet on. As Richards unsaddled, Ms Paget marched up to him, forcefully demanding to know where Darling was. The jockey coolly replied, 'I wouldn't be quite sure, Ms Paget, but I've a pretty shrewd idea he's on the top of the stand, cutting his throat.'

THREE

The Master

'Do you remember how on a racing track every competitor runs but only one wins the prize? Well, you ought to run with your mind fixed on winning the prize . . . Our contest is for an eternal crown that will never fade.'

1 COR 9: 24–26

A man's reach should exceed his grasp, or what's a heaven for? Vincent O'Brien's rare and wonderful achievements cast doubts on the wisdom of this assertion, however. His crown as king of racing trainers will never fade. Of course, he has occasionally disappointed himself and others. In fairness, the perfect talent has never existed. But O'Brien learned speedily from his rare failures. Seeming to get his bearing from signs known only to him, his ratio of success to failure is incredible.

Vincent O'Brien was born on 9 April 1917 at the family home of Clashganniff, Churchtown, near Buttevant in County Cork. His father Dan's first wife, Helena, died during childbirth in 1914 and in 1916 he married her first cousin, Kathleen Toomey. The fact that Dan had two families, each with four children, invariably meant that any horses which showed promise had to be sold. Despite this he managed to win both the Irish Cambridgeshire and the Cesarewitch with Solford and Astrometer respectively.

In the 1930s the Irish economy was devastated by the economic war, but in the year of the Wall Street Crash, 1929, Dan O'Brien received a legacy of £30,000 from America which enabled him to stay afloat as many around him felt the chill winds of recession. Vincent started going to school when Ireland was busy at battle, first through the War of Independence and later the Civil War.

The relationship between a good teacher and a willing pupil is the stuff of myth but is also an essential part of the superstructure of civilised society. In 1987 American athlete Carl Lewis made an extraordinary gesture at his father's funeral when he placed his 100-metre gold medal from the 1984 Olympics in his father's hands. He told his astonished mother, 'Don't worry, I'll get another one.' The following year he did so, following winner Ben Johnson's disqualification for drug use. His gesture at the funeral had spoken volumes about how a sporting hero can owe almost everything to his father.

As a recent advertisement campaign reminded us, everyone remembers a great teacher. Sympathetic pedagogues with an authentic attachment to their charges are a pearl beyond price. As a boy, Vincent O'Brien went everywhere with his father and in the process gained an invaluable education into the world of horses. Ironically, though, Vincent's first 'touch' did not please his father. In 1941 an outbreak of foot-and-mouth disease forced the cancellation of the local point-to-point season, which was bad news for Dan O'Brien's top horse in this arena, White Squirrel. Vincent, though, continued to ride her and one morning tested her against some of his father's flat horses. He was pleasantly surprised by her form. He tested her a week or so later to confirm that White Squirrel could hold her own in higher company, then entered her in a bumper (a flat race for jumping horses) at Clonmel. He did not tell his father – because his father would only tell his friends, which would lower the odds – until he got to the changing-room. His father put a tenner on at 20–1 and Vincent put on everything he had in the world, £4, although by the time he made the bet the price had dropped to 10–1. White Squirrel came home first in a field of 27. Initially Vincent's father was delighted because he had never won so much money on a horse in his life, but as the full details of his son's touch became apparent he was furious that Vincent had not told him to bet on his own horse.

Dan O'Brien died from pneumonia in 1943 – a year before penicillin became available.

Rakin' It In

It was about then that his son took his first major step as a trainer. Great oaks from little acorns grow. In December 1943 Vincent visited Newmarket for the first time. There, for only 130 guineas, he purchased Drybob, a three-year-old with little apparent potential. He also met the Leamington Spa breeder Sidney McGregor, who had bred Derby winner April The Fifth and National winner Bogskar, who invited him to train a four-year-old with an unimpressive CV called Good Days. In his first year as a trainer Vincent brought off the Irish autumn double, as Drybob dead-heated for the Cambridgeshire and Good Days won the Cesarewitch.

In the summer of 1945, Dr Otto Vaughan from Mallow sent O'Brien a large, backward six-year-old gelding he had bred named Cottage Rake. The horse had run his first race the previous year – finishing unplaced on the flat at Thurles. On 27 December 1945, Vincent ran him in a two-mile maiden hurdle at Limerick Junction, which he won at 10–1. Two months later he won a two-mile bumper at Leopardstown by ten lengths. An attempt was made to sell the horse to the Yorkshire owner Cuddy Stirling-Stuart, but he failed to pass the vet's inspection. In common with many big horses, there were concerns about his wind. The horse was then sold to a Mr Vickerman on foot of a £1,000 deposit subject to a satisfactory vet's report. While the Rake didn't fail the vet's inspection, he didn't pass either. However, Dr Vaughan was unwilling to return the deposit and for approximately £2,500 Cottage Rake found a new, albeit somewhat reluctant owner. Yet by 1948 the horse had won the Gold Cup.

O'Brien's recollection of this triumph is very clear.

> I led Cottage Rake out on to the course and decided to go down to the last fence to watch the race. As they came to the last Martin Molony on Happy Home jumped it a length and a half clear of Aubrey Brabazon on Cottage Rake. There was no public address in those days and there was no use asking anybody around what had won. I made my way towards the unsaddling enclosure by way of the back of the stands and at this stage I dared not ask anybody what won. I was holding on to my wildest hopes. As I approached the winners' enclosure, Cottage Rake was coming from the opposite direction and I saw Aubrey touching his cap. The greatest moment of my life had just become a reality.

The run-up to the Cheltenham National Hunt Festival in 1949 was fraught with uncertainty as O'Brien's stable was struck with the cough. Vincent switched his three most fancied horses, Cottage Rake, Hatton's Race and Castledermot, and a lead horse, to a borrowed yard close by. Hatton's Grace avoided infection but both Cottage Rake and Castledermot suffered mild attacks. Irish racing was shrouded in the mists of tradition but O'Brien sensed that travelling to Cheltenham by plane would be easier on his horses than crossing by boat. He showed commendable pioneering spirit and organised the first flight from Ireland to England with runners. It was an epoch-making experience for racing fans of that generation.

Then fate took a hand. Atrocious weather forced the cancellation of the third day of the meeting and the Gold Cup was rescheduled for the following month. The gods were smiling on O'Brien, because Cottage

Rake's preparation for the big race had been hampered by a lingering cold and a runny nose. The extra month gave him time to return to his prime – and he needed to. Coming to the last he trailed Cool Customer by two lengths, but Aubrey Brabazon pulled out all the stops and the Irish champion won by two lengths in one of the greatest contests in the history of the illustrious race.

Eleven months later Cottage Rake pulled off the Gold Cup hat-trick, joining Golden Miller as the only horses to have won the Cheltenham Gold Cup three years in succession. Thanks partly to his jockey, Aubrey Brabazon, Cottage Rake (5–6f) won very easily by ten lengths from Finnure (5–4). It was the most facile Gold Cup victory since the days of Golden Miller, with Brabazon confirming his reputation as a jockey for the big occasion. It was a very poor gallop for the first mile and a half, and to the surprise of many Brabazon took Cottage Rake to the front with the other five bunched close up. Going away from the stands again, Cottage Rake was asked to pick up the pace, and he went into a six-length lead. At the final turn for home, he was about four lengths clear, but Brabazon moved into overdrive as they rounded the bend and came to the next fence in front of Finnure – with the race won. The victory was an anti-climax.

Aubrey's up, the monkey's down
The frightened bookies quake,
Come on, me lads, and give me a cheer
Begod, 'tis Cottage Rake.

In the early days there was some serious money to be made in the betting ring. Cottage Rake won his first Gold Cup at 10–1 and Hatton's Grace won the first of his three consecutive Champion Hurdles at 100–7.

Cottage Rake really put O'Brien on the map as a trainer *par excellence*. Sadly, the horse did not retire in a blaze of glory after he passed from O'Brien's nurturing hands. His final outing tells a sorry tale. With Dick Francis in the saddle he trailed in third, beaten by all of 25 lengths, in the Shrewsbury Chase at Cheltenham worth a first prize of £204, insulting to one of the all-time great horses.

One Irishman who was happy to see the end of Cottage Rake's dominance of the Gold Cup was the great Martin Molony. Racing was in his genes. His father, who had won the Military Cross in the First World War, owned and trained the Galway Plate winner Hill of Camas in 1915. Martin was second in the Gold Cup to Cottage Rake on Happy Home and Finnure, the first for Ms Paget and the second for Lord Bicester. In 1951 he finally claimed the Gold Cup on Silver Fame. Sadly, after a fall in

Thurles that September from a horse called Bursary, resulting in a fractured skull, Martin never raced in public again. Some shrewd observers say that his style of riding lives on today in Adrian Maguire.

The Brab

Vincent O'Brien has often spoken about the importance of Aubrey Brabazon in his early successes. For his part, 'the Brab' was equally complimentary about O'Brien. 'The mastermind of Vincent had it all planned. I really only obeyed Vincent's instructions.'

Aubrey was born into a racing family in 1920. Both his father, Cecil, and his uncle, Leslie, were successful amateur jockeys and after Cecil became a trainer Aubrey was apprenticed to him following a sojourn with J.T. Rogers. It was a happy arrangement for Aubrey to be able to enjoy the comforts of home at a time when most apprentices had to put up with Dickensian conditions. The Brab's potential was evident from an early age. He won his first race on Queen Christina in the Phoenix Park when he was just 13. In 1938 he really got a suitable vehicle for his talent when he linked up with King Caprice, and they formed a formidable partnership on the flat. In 1940, though, because of rising weight, Aubrey was forced to turn to steeplechasing. Vincent O'Brien has often argued that the reason why the Brab was such a polished jockey was because of his training on the flat.

Aubrey's hero as a jockey was the great Derby winner Steve Donoghue because he very seldom resorted to the whip, and only then as a last resort. Asked who was the greater jockey, Donoghue or Lester Piggott, the Brab replied, 'If I was an owner of a horse and I wanted to run him again in a big race I would definitely go for Steve, because he would give him an easier ride, but if I was a backer I would go for Lester.'

Despite his abhorrence of using the whip, the Brab had a tough streak. He once had a bad fall at Becher's in the Grand National in which he got a kick from a horse who had never been told not to kick a man when he was down. He broke his ribs but still competed in the last race on a French horse who had the habit of pulling hard. The strain on the broken ribs punctured his lung and caused him to bleed internally, which led to a stay in hospital.

In a radio interview, Aubrey revealed that he had once been offered £300 to stop a horse in Haydock, but because of his alliance with Cottage Rake he had plenty of legitimate ways to make a killing.

I suppose we were lucky that we never came up against either Golden Miller or Arkle when Cottage Rake won those three Gold Cups, but apart from those two Cottage Rake must rank as one of the greatest Gold Cup winners. The early Cheltenhams for us were very different from what it became at the end. The Irish contingent was minute in the early years, but the success of Vincent's horses really made the festival for the Irish racegoing public. Mind you, the English were a bit resentful the year that Vincent won the three plum races of the festival.

I was also very fortunate to win the Champion Hurdle on Hatton's Grace. Although he wasn't much to look at, he had a heart like a lion and you were never beaten on him – a bit like Monksfield.

Amazing Grace

In 1950 O'Brien gave Ireland a Gold Cup/Champion Hurdle double with Cottage Rake and Hatton's Grace winning the two blue-riband events. No Irish trainer has ever emulated this achievement.

Two days prior to Cottage Rake's hat-trick, Hatton's Grace, fired up from victories in the Irish Lincoln and Cesarewitch, had retained the Champion Hurdle, a triumph he would repeat in 1951 with Tim Molony in the saddle instead of Brabazon. That year National Spirit and Hatton's Grace came to the last hurdle almost together and with the race between them. National Spirit fell, leaving Hatton's Grace to win on his own from the French pair Pyrrhus III and Prince Hindou. In the process he became the first horse to win the Champion Hurdle three times, achieving the feat in successive years.

It was Tim's first success in the Champion Hurdle and a fortuitous ride for him, as his brother, Martin, would have ridden the 11-year-old gelding had he not been struck down by measles. Martin was champion jump jockey for five consecutive seasons from 1948 to 1952 and won the Champion Hurdle from 1951 (Hatton's Grace) to 1954 (three straight wins for Sir Ken). He rode a total of 726 British winners.

Hatton's Grace, who had once been sold for 18 guineas, won the Gold Cup that year by six lengths. He was once described by the legendary Michael O'Hehir as 'the ugly duckling of the parade ring', but perhaps handsome is as handsome does.

O'Brien's other famous victories included Castledermot's win in the National Hunt Chase, otherwise known as the amateurs' Grand National, with the celebrated Lord Mildmay in the saddle.

It is probably because Cheltenham is so important in the national psyche that Irish horses have not done as well in the Grand National, given that the race comes so soon after the festival. Nonetheless, Aintree too was a successful hunting ground for Vincent O'Brien. He had the distinction of winning three consecutive Grand Nationals with three different horses: Early Mist in 1953, Royal Tan in 1954 and Quare Times (who had won the National Hunt Chase with Bunny Cox in the saddle the previous year) in 1955.

Parting Is Such Sweet Sorrow

O'Brien ended up with 23 winners at the Cheltenham Festival between 1948 and 1959. The latter year represented his Cheltenham swan-song, and fittingly he marked it with two victories, York Fair and Courts Appeal winning the two divisions of the Gloucestershire Hurdle. The Gloucestershire Hurdle was a lucky race for O'Brien. He had first won it in 1952 with Cockatoo, but his most famous winner was Saffron Tartan, particularly as victory came against another top Irish-bred horse, Predominate – who went on to become a leading horse on the flat, winning at Goodwood in four consecutive years. When the Master of Ballydoyle went on to train on the flat, Don Butchers took over the training of Saffron Tartan and together they won the Gold Cup in 1961.

Every major player in racing needs a good back-up, hence Peter Scudamore's dependence in his latter years as a jockey on Joan Collins – the physiotherapist, not the former star of *Dynasty*! One of O'Brien's most loyal allies, himself a wonderful judge of a horse, was younger brother Phonsie, a noted amateur jockey who finished second on Royal Tan to Nickel Coin in the 1951 Grand National. Like Tony O'Reilly, Phonsie has a great reputation internationally as a wit and raconteur and numbers former American President George Bush among his close friends and fishing partners.

Having notched up an unrivalled national hunt record, winning three consecutive Grand Nationals, four Gold Cups and three Champion Hurdles, O'Brien made an even more sensational impact on the flat. He prepared champions such as Sir Ivor and Gladness, as well as his first star, Ballymoss.

Only the great Crepello prevented 33–1 Ballymoss from winning the Derby in 1957, but a month later, at 9–4 on, he romped home to win the Irish Derby. He was a late developer; as a two-year-old he had won only one race from four starts. On good ground he was capable of great performances, such as when he won the Trigo Stakes, defeating his stable companion, the wonderful mare Gladness, at 20–1.

His Achilles' heel was always believed to be heavy ground, as he turned in some abysmal performances in unfavourable conditions. That theory was revised slightly when, ridden by T.P. Burns, he was victorious in the St Leger on a wet Yorkshire day in 1957, winning by a length from Court Harwell. However, he followed up by losing the Great Voltigeur Stakes, where his defeat was again attributed to soft ground.

As a four-year-old Ballymoss came into his own, winning the Coronation Cup, Eclipse Stakes, and the King George VI and Queen Elizabeth Stakes. The Prix de l'Arc de Triomphe would round off a memorable year – but a serious spanner was thrown into the works. Ballymoss's outstanding form had tempted O'Brien to make a major ante-post bet. On the day of the race it poured out of the heavens, but O'Brien's efforts to cancel his bet ended in failure. No one was more surprised than his trainer when Ballymoss, ridden by Scobie Breasley, went on to gallop through the mud and win the race.

Ballymoss broke the UK record by winning £107,165 in stakes. The high point of his career as a stallion was that he sired one Derby winner in Royal Palace. Perhaps his greatest historical significance was that he launched O'Brien, known as a top national hunt trainer, on to centre stage as a classic trainer.

O'Brien's most famous horse is probably Nijinsky. In 1970 Nijinsky bestrode the world of racing like a Colossus. At 7–4 on he was the shortest-priced favourite for the 2,000 Guineas since Colombo in 1934 and duly obliged by two and a half lengths. He was immediately made firm favourite for the Derby despite the high-quality field which included the great chestnut colt Gyr (whom Etienne Pollet had postponed his retirement for a year to train), who had been considered unbeatable, and Stintino, who had made a big impression in his trial. Nijinsky won by two and a half lengths in the fastest time since Mahmoud in 1935.

After a facile victory in the Irish Derby, he had six lengths to spare when winning the King George VI and Queen Elizabeth Stakes. Then tragedy struck when he contracted ringworm, causing his hair to fall out and his skin to become raw. Despite Vincent O'Brien's wishes that he should have time to rest, his owner insisted he run in the St Leger. He won the race but at the cost of large weight loss.

The Arc would round off a perfect year. With 100 yards to go he led Sassafras but was beaten by a head. After the race his jockey, Lester Piggott, was blamed for his defeat.

Tracy Piggott is ideally placed to comment on the reasons for Nijinsky's failure in the Arc:

If anybody is serious about their sport one has to take it seriously, but particularly in racing. Think about the money at stake. In Nijinsky's case, the horse was going to stud and breed. The build-up to the race was hampered when he got a very bad attack of ringworm. It was an American strain and it took a lot out of him. My father still felt he wasn't over the top leading up to the Arc but there was a lot of attention on the horse in the paddock before the race and he was very highly strung. He was always temperamental; it's in his pedigree [his sire was Northern Dancer] to be that way. He got very upset before the race, and he had a very hard season, and that all contributed to the fact that he didn't do as well as normal.

Retired to stud, Nijinsky sired Golden Fleece, Shadeed, Caerleon and King's Lake. O'Brien's cast of racing legends included The Minstrel, El Gran Señor and Saddler's Wells. In all he won 44 European classics, in addition to the Prix de l'Arc de Triomphe three times. O'Brien formed the most successful partnership in the history of racing – and possibly the most economical with words – with Lester Piggott. A small illustration of this success is provided by the fact that jockey award ceremonies became known as 'the Lesters'.

The Irish RM

Peter O'Sullevan has strong Irish connections. He was born in Kenmare, where his father, Colonel John Joseph DSO, served as resident magistrate from 1918 to 1922. He describes his 'most fortuitous racing experience' as 'contracting pneumonia on the eve of an intended association with an equally unskilled partner in a wartime novices' chase at Plumpton – an excursion which neither horse nor rider could reasonably have been expected to survive'.

O'Sullevan is the expert's expert. Little wonder that Lester Piggott said about him, 'Compared with him, all the rest are amateurs.' His is a special gift. Close your eyes and listen to his mellifluous tones and the years roll back. He is ideally placed to evaluate Vincent's career – although he jokes about his age.

I'm so old that the only exercise I take is to walk down to the betting shop. Mind you, it's the only exercise I've taken in years. When you get to be as old as I am, three things start to go. The first thing you lose is your memory – and I can't remember the other two!

There are a lot of colourful personalities in racing. One need look no further than Channel 4's flamboyantly attired John McCririck, who makes no concession to sartorial convention. [O'Sullevan knows a thing or two about dress sense. 'I love shopping for clothes, even women's clothes. One of my very favourite programmes is *The Clothes Show*. I never miss it.']

Ireland has given racing some incredible characters. In the world of broadcasting there was the late Michael O'Hehir. Of course, his son Tony has taken on his mantle. In fact, Tony has relieved me of some of my money! After the Grand National that never was I was having dinner and I was enjoying a few glasses of wine – probably quite a few glasses, now that I think of it – when Tony joined me for a meal with one of his colleagues. I bet him I think it was £40 that there would be no racing on the Monday. However, the Monday arrived and the race went ahead. As soon as I saw Tony I put my hand in my pocket and handed him his money. I said, 'Don't be worried that you are taking advantage of an old man who was not in full possession of his faculties because of drink. The reality of the situation is that if I had been stone-cold sober I would have bet twice as much!'

In the world of racing I think back to Paddy 'Darkie' Prendergast. He was famous for talking up his horses. Bing Crosby once told me, 'After listening to Paddy talk about your horse for two minutes, you just had to feel real sorry for the opposition.' Come to think of it, Paddy was nearly as good a singer as Bing!

In 1954 he was banned from racing horses in England for most of the season and I went to visit him. I was surprised to see one of his classic hopes, Moonlight Express, working in a wide circle on the Curragh. He told me, 'They learn a lot more that way than galloping in a straight line.' Lester Piggott once told me that Paddy was a great trainer and that his horses, like Staff Ingham's, ran straight because they had been properly taught.

The only problem with Paddy was that he had an explosive temper. In fact, he once lost his cool with me. Back in 1965 I wrote an article which tried to explain his phenomenal success on the flat. I approached it in terms of describing Paddy as a wonderful chef and outlining the ingredients in his recipe for success. I asked the art department if they could put a chef's hat on a good picture of Paddy to go alongside the opening paragraph. It looked very well, or so I thought. But when I rang Paddy a week later he was fuming. He shouted down the phone, 'You made me look like a right blithering idiot!' I had no idea what he was talking about and told him so. It was the hat. He refused to accept that I was actually complimenting him. After I accused him of having no sense of humour, the conversation went from bad to worse. We didn't speak again for months.

That June, after he had trained Meadow Court to win one of the classics in the Curragh, I was rushing across to congratulate the owners, Bing Crosby and his partners, when I bumped straight into Paddy. Momentarily forgetting our dispute, I put out my hand to congratulate him. Before I could say anything, he grabbed me and said, 'If you don't come to the party tonight, I'll never speak to you again.' My reply was, 'I thought we weren't speaking now!'

'That was a green-eyed, jealous colleague of yours putting in the poison and saying you'd made me a laughing stock. I shouldn't have listened to the git. He'll not be entering my yard again.' He then told me to back Dandini in the last race but I didn't and missed a winner.

Noel Murless once told me that training is four-fifths experience and one-fifth intuition. And it's the last fifth that counts. If ever a trainer proved that, it's Vincent O'Brien.

I knew Vincent would effortlessly make the switch to flat racing. I remember writing in 1953 something like, 'It's not in accord with tradition for classic winners to be trained in Tipperary, but I'm developing the opinion that with Vincent, one of Ireland's youngest trainers, almost anything is possible.' Even I, though, didn't expect him to achieve practically every honour in sight.

Looking back to my visits to Ballydoyle, one of the most fascinating things was how the yard was an index of Vincent's fast-growing popularity and prosperity. I recall especially how quickly the personnel's bicycle shed became a carport.

In my opinion, Vincent and Paddy Prendergast did more than any other two personalities to put Ireland on the international racing map. Little wonder, then, that Lester Piggott once told me, 'In my opinion he [Vincent] was the best trainer of all time. I cannot think that Vincent's achievements will ever be matched by anyone.'

However, I have to tell a story against myself concerning one of Vincent's few failures – probably his most high-profile one, when Nijinsky was defeated in the Arc. A few people came up to me afterwards. They were pretty drunk and they asked me, 'Well, Peter, did Lester make a boo-boo?' I really lost it with them and in no uncertain terms told them to f**k off. I have to confess I felt much better after it.

The Horse Whisperer

O'Brien has the countenance and demeanour of a parish priest, which may explain why he has been described as 'the whispering doctor' (he received an honorary LLD from the National University in Ireland in 1983). Yet he also had style and class, riding the wave successfully and coming again and again to the winning shore. It was oddly appropriate that his daughter, Elizabeth, married James Bond film producer Kevin McClory.

O'Brien scaled virtually every height that a trainer could aspire to. The hallmark of his catalogue of triumph had always been his unassuming professionalism and his unparalleled eye for a horse. His genius lay in his ability to look at an unraced horse and evaluate it, imagining its likely development. Then, when the horse moved to the training stage, he displayed an almost mystical intuitive understanding of a horse's psychology.

He consistently picked the pockets of racegoers at Cheltenham with more skill than the Artful Dodger, often bringing the worst of the Irish weather but always the best of horseflesh. Any horse who wins three Cheltenham Gold Cups must be considered exceptional. Cottage Rake was such a horse. Yet this achievement warrants only a tiny chapter in the incredible success story that is Vincent O'Brien, the young man from North Cork who became master of Ballydoyle largely because of his talent to spot greatness from the most unpromising of beginnings. Cottage Rake is just one of a litany of great names that constitute a virtual *Who's Who* of racing who came under O'Brien's stewardship.

When it comes to horseracing, nobody knows more about winning than Vincent O'Brien. He is unquestionably Ireland's, if not the world's, greatest ever trainer. Asked by this writer to select his all-time greatest Irish racing horses, he came up with the following choices:

Jumpers
1. Prince Regent
2. Arkle
3. Cottage Rake
4. Hatton's Grace

Flat
1. Ballymoss
2. Gladness
3. Santa Claus
4. Sir Ivor

5. Nijinsky
6. The Minstrel
7. Roberto
8. Golden Fleece
9. Assert
10. El Gran Señor
11. Saddler's Wells
12. Secreto

FOUR

Simply the Best

'And it is Arkle who leads as they come to the last fence. Both jockeys are absolutely all out now. Arkle is the leader. Arkle has taken the lead off Mill House and Mill House has no answer to Arkle's speed. As they come towards the last fence it's Arkle for Ireland. Both riders are hard at it. Here they come into the last. Arkle over first. Mill House over second in the run-in with 150 yards to go. It's Arkle for Ireland. A great shout goes up from the stand as Pat Taaffe has Mill House's measure. The Gold Cup is going to go to Ireland. With 100 yards to run it's Ireland . . . Gold Cup to Arkle. Arkle is the winner. Mill House is beaten. The champion is dethroned . . .'

This was the BBC radio commentary of the finale of perhaps the most famous race in history. Listening to the commentary, it is not immediately obvious whether it is the race between the two horses or the two countries they represent which is the most important issue at stake. What might not have been foreseen at the time, though, was that as 'the champion was dethroned', not only was there a new champion but the most enduring legend in racing history had begun.

Arkle was trained by the late Tom Dreaper, but he was not Dreaper's first great horse.

The Equine Artist Formerly Known As Prince

It was only after Arkle had won his second Gold Cup that Tom Dreaper admitted he might possibly be a better horse than his last ride (whom he also trained), Prince Regent. Yet Prince Regent, owned by J.V. Rank, never earned the plaudits his talent merited because of the Second World War. Prince Regent's first race came when he was unplaced on the flat at Baldoyle. It was a case of third time lucky for the horse, as he won a bumper in Naas on his third outing with Dreaper in the saddle.

Were it not for the acquisitive tendencies of Adolf Hitler, Prince Regent would certainly have a more prominent place among the racing immortals. Had there been a Cheltenham Festival in 1942, when he won the Irish Grand National, and in the next three years it is open to speculation whether he could have emulated Golden Miller's achievement and won five consecutive Gold Cups. In 1939 he was on the brink of greatness, but by 1945 his star was waning. Restricted to racing in Ireland, the horse clocked up a succession of big races, notably the Irish Grand National in 1942 when carrying 12st 5lb, and became a national hero.

One story told which highlights his popularity concerns the day Dreaper was leading a string of his horses on foot to a major crossroads. He asked a garda to stop the traffic. The garda is reputed to have asked if Prince Regent was present. When told he was, he said, 'I'll stop all the traffic on both sides for you so!'

With the end of the war, Prince Regent finally had the opportunity to show his talent on a bigger stage. Tom Dreaper's horse was 11 when he comfortably won the Gold Cup in 1946; with Tim Hyde in the saddle he won by a clear five lengths from his closest rivals Poor Flame and Red April to claim the £1,130 prize.

His next assault was on the Grand National, where he made a series of errors on the first circuit: at the fourth, at Valentine's, at the second open ditch and at the 17th, where he actually fell, only to regain his footing and gallop on. He had learned his lessons by the second circuit and incredibly jumped the last two fences in the clear lead, but on the cruel 494-yard run-in he ran out of steam and was passed by Lovely Cottage and Jack Findlay.

Sir Peter O'Sullevan was a huge fan of the horse.

> Prince Regent was Ireland's outstanding chaser of the war years. In my view he was one of the two outstanding horses not to have won the Grand National in my time. The other one was Crisp. I recall that Tom Dreaper had a special affection for the horse, who was his last winning ride in a bumper. As a son of My Prince he had great depth of girth and was vastly superior to the majority of his contemporaries.

The Belvederian

Belvedere College has given Ireland and the world some of the all-time rugby greats including Karl Mullen, Tony O'Reilly and Ollie Campbell. It has also produced one of the giants of racing, Pat Taaffe. He rode his first winner while still attending the school on Merry Coon at a point-to-point at Cabinteely. Within months he had won his first winner under rules at the Phoenix Park. He should have been on the highly rated Curragh Chase but the horse was sold on the morning of the race, so he got a spare ride on Ballincorona, which won at 20–1.

Over the following few years Taaffe established himself as a leading amateur rider. All his Christmases came at once in 1949. Tom Dreaper's stable jockey, Eddie Newman, was injured, so Pat stepped into the breach for the plum rides at the Leopardstown Christmas meeting. He saddled four winners over the two days, which prompted the stewards to insist that either Pat turned professional or he would have to restrict his riding arrangements. Tom Dreaper solved the problem by offering him a job, paving the way for one of the most famous partnerships in equine history.

Unusually tall for a jockey, Taaffe was a reluctant hero. Anyone who met this unassuming man would have been shocked to discover that he had 26 winners at Cheltenham, including four Gold Cups. Yet it all almost went horribly wrong. In 1956, a few months after his marriage, he fractured his skull after a horrific fall from a horse called Ireland at Kilbeggan. He lay unconscious for five days and it was touch and go whether he would recover. As he made his first tentative steps on the road to recovery, he doubted if he would ever be able to perform to the required standard and told Tom Dreaper to look for someone else. His trainer replied, 'If you don't ride them, I won't run them.' No further discussion was necessary.

Taaffe's attitude to life was probably best summed up in his reaction to the accident which cost him the tips of the second and third fingers of his right hand when they were jammed between a wall and a falling drum of treacle: 'It was a nice clean job. I didn't even have to have the ends trimmed away.'

Taaffe had all the talent a jockey could have wished for. But natural talent is not always enough. One of the most gifted Irish jockeys was Ben Dillon, one of the giants of the turf at the turn of the century because of his hugely successful partnership with the wonderful mare Pretty Polly. Dillon, though, had horrific problems with his weight. His biography in the National Racing Museum in Newmarket euphemistically describes him as 'somewhat unreliable'. As his racing career collapsed through his self-destructiveness, the very charming Irishman became a 'kept man', living with the music-hall star Marie Lloyd, drinking all her money away too. Tragically he died in obscurity as a night porter at South Africa House. Pat Taaffe had no such character flaws. He was made of the right stuff.

Born to Run

Arkle was a wonder horse and an Irish national hero. He was foaled on 19 April 1957 at the Ballymacoll stud in County Meath and was bought as a three-year-old by Anne, Duchess of Westminster, for only 1,150 guineas. The previous year she had met Tom Dreaper at Leopardstown and had asked him to train one of her horses. Her wish was granted. That evening Dreaper went home and told his wife that they had another horse coming. She asked him if he liked the look of the horse. Dreaper replied that he hadn't see him. When asked if he liked the horse's pedigree, he responded, 'Not much, but I like the look of the girl!' Dreaper went on to train 97 winners for the Duchess, of which Arkle was easily the most famous. His other famous owners included Gregory Peck, whose Owen's Sedge won the 1963 Leopardstown Chase.

Arkle was bred by the Bakers in County Dublin. Anne Baker's memory of Arkle is of 'a very intelligent horse, who carried his head beautifully right up to his death, who was very curious'.

His sire, Archive, was a 48-guineas stallion, while his dam, Bright Cherry, was by no means an outstanding two-mile race mare. As a foal Arkle got a bad knock, which left a lump about his hind hoof, while being transported in a horse box. As a yearling he ran into a hedge and required 14 stitches.

Arkle got his name from a mountain facing the Duchess's home by Loch Stack in Sutherland. His early appearances on the racecourse gave no indication of his future greatness. His genius was cultivated by his trainer Tom Dreaper and perhaps the greatest natural jockey of all time, Pat Taaffe. Yet it was not love at first sight. Taaffe famously said of his partner, 'You could have driven a wheelbarrow between his hind legs.'

In December 1961 Arkle could do no better than third and fourth in bumper races at Mullingar and Leopardstown respectively. On both occasions he was ridden by Mark Hely-Hutchinson – a man with a nice line in self-deprecation. He subsequently stated that his claim to fame was that he was the only jockey to have ridden Arkle without winning.

The following month Arkle, under Liam McLoughlin, made a winning debut over hurdles at Navan at 20–1, defeating Pat Taaffe's mount Kerfero. His owner's husband turned to her after the race and said, 'I think we might have something here.' From then on Taaffe donned the yellow jacket and black cap of Arkle's owner the Duchess of Westminster. The pair won all four hurdle races and 22 out of the 26 chases – and a staggering £78,821 in prize money. Their long association saw only one fall, during a schooling at Dan Moore's in Fairyhouse.

The horse can make the man. When the Russian crowds saw Trotsky on a horse they said, 'What a man!' but when Lenin rode one they whispered, 'What a horse.' Arkle and Taaffe were made for each other.

Taaffe had come close to the Gold Cup in 1962 on Fortria but he lost to Fred Winter (who had won his first Gold Cup on Saffron Tartan) on the French raider Mandarin. A decade and a half later, with Winter firmly established as a successful trainer, his close friend Dave Dick persuaded him to spend £15,000 on an up-and-coming chaser in Ireland called Midnight Court. As a virtual novice he won the Gold Cup.

The story of the Irish's winning connection with Cheltenham could be significantly added to if we invoked the same parentage rule that has enabled so many soccer players to wear green shirts. A case in point is Fred Winter. His mother, Ann, was an Irish Catholic and Fred took the faith he inherited from her so seriously that each Sunday he took around the collection plate at first Mass at the Oratory of St Francis de Sales, in the Kentish village of Hartley. In addition, 1997 Gold Cup winner Mr Mulligan was trained by an Irishman, Noel Chance, and the 1998 Gold Cup winner Cool Dawn was bought by trainer Robert Alner from the Costello family in County Clare after failing to win in four Irish point-to-points.

Run of the Mill?

Until 7 March 1964, Mill House seemed destined to become the greatest steeplechaser ever – or at least since Golden Miller. Enter Arkle in the Gold Cup, one of the classic steeplechases in the post-war era. The script had to be drastically rewritten.

Mill House was bred in Ireland by the Lawlors of Naas and got his name from Mrs Lawlor's private house. As a three-year-old he was sent to the care of Tom Taaffe. Ironically, he was schooled and ridden in his first two races by Pat Taaffe, the man who more than anyone else was responsible for consigning him to the role of also-ran.

When he was sold and sent to train in England, Taaffe told his new jockey, Willie Robinson, 'You will soon be on the best horse in Britain, and quite possibly the world!' Taaffe's prophecy seemed well founded when Mill House won the Gold Cup in 1963 as a six-year-old after just five steeplechases.

The following November Mill House had his first clash with Arkle, in the Hennessy Gold Cup. Arkle was little more than a novice despite having won each of his six chases. Mill House had 12st, Arkle 11st 9lb. The bookies went with 15–8 Mill House, 5–2 Arkle. Mill House won by eight lengths, although Pat Taaffe claimed that Arkle would have won but for a slip at the last ditch.

The following year Arkle exacted retribution in the mist, demolishing the course record by four seconds to win the Gold Cup. Trotting serenely down towards the start, Mill House's ears cocked with the grace of a ballet dancer and the constitution of a tank. Beside him Arkle almost seemed diminutive – but as tough as nails and superbly fit.

From the start, Willie Robinson cruised into the front at a deceptively easy pace. Arkle, pulling hard, contested second place with Pas Seul ahead of King's Nephew and jumped the first few fences, like all the rest, with an impressive combination of accuracy and boldness. In marked contrast, Mill House 'fiddled' more than once and after the first full circuit drew a startled gasp from the crowd by getting right under the open ditch in front of the stands. But then, as if to redeem himself, he stormed off down the hill, opening up a six-length gap over his pursuers. For a horrible moment for the Irish fans in the stands it seemed as if the race might be decided there and then. What kind of wonderhorse could live with those giant strides?

But turning past the farm, Pat Taaffe and Arkle gave the perfect answer. The Irish in the crowd echoed loud and clear across the course and even a mile from home the crowd's murmur became a roar as the Duchess of Westminster's yellow jacket drew closer with each passing stride. Arkle was ridden throughout with tactical genius. The plan of using one decisive burst worked like a charm.

As Mill House turned towards the last three fences, anything seemed possible. Arkle had moved up easily to a length behind the favourite and, hearing him come, Willie Robinson must have known the game was up. Three fences out, with Arkle at his quarters, Mill House threw one final, almost despairing, leap, but it did not yield him one yard and in a dozen strides the 'challenger' was level.

Long before this, a crescendo of noise had exploded from the stands. Then, as the Irish eyes saw the hallowed prize within their grasp, it rose to a fearsome yell of triumph. And suddenly, going to the last, as Robinson drew his whip, it was game, set and match. With a decisive injection of pace, Arkle rocketed clear. He jumped the last a length in front and pulled away up the hill to win by five lengths. To his great credit, Mill House never faltered and never conceded defeat. Forced by circumstances to lead from the start, he was merely compelled to yield to a better horse.

Willie Robinson said afterwards, 'Coming to the third last, I thought to myself I had the better horse. At the time we were prepared to take Arkle on again to put my theory to the test. Mill House was the perfect chaser, the kind of horse that everybody in Ireland had been trying to breed for two centuries. Arkle, though, was the perfect athlete. He had more speed than Mill House at any part of the race, beginning or end.'

It was almost too exciting for the Duchess of Westminster. 'Every time I opened the papers that year it seemed that they were full of who was better: Arkle or Mill House? The English thought Mill House, the Irish went for Arkle. Three fences from the end, my husband turned to me and said, "I think we have it." I was so tense I snapped to him, "Shut up!"'

There was more than the Gold Cup and national pride at stake in the race. The two jockeys, close personal friends, had a bet with a difference: the jockey who lost the race won the bet. Their personal duel had begun in the Hennessy and Taaffe had won a new suit. Although Robinson lost the Gold Cup, he won a honeymoon trip.

Mill House would never beat Arkle again. They met three more times including at the 1965 Gold Cup, when Arkle left Mill House in his wake by a staggering 20 lengths. In winning his second Gold Cup Arkle equalled another record, his 20-length margin having been matched in the race only by another Irish-bred horse, Easter Hero, in both 1929 and 1930, but Easter Hero had had no challenger of Mill House's calibre to compete against.

Their final clash was in the Gallagher Gold Cup at Sandown in November 1965. Mill House's superb jumping gave him a four-length lead at the bottom turn before Arkle switched gear and beat not only Mill House but also his course record, by 17 seconds.

Arkle made St Patrick's Day in 1966 a truly great day for the Irish by winning his third consecutive Gold Cup. The victory was not the hard-fought epic his great tussles with Mill House in the previous two Gold Cups had been. The victories came despite a blunder at the 11th fence, which did not perturb the horse or his jockey, Pat Taaffe. He won by 30 lengths – the biggest winning margin in Gold Cup history – without ever really having to be at full stretch. He had hacked along for the first mile, allowing Dormant and Snaigow to lead, then at the eighth fence he jumped his way to the front of the five-strong field. Arkle's mistake at the end of the first circuit was probably a lapse in concentration. He hit the fence hard, but the ever-calm Taaffe barely shifted in the saddle. As if to atone for his past sin, Arkle stood well back at the following jump – a ditch – and cleared it with plenty to spare. Dormant (second, 20–1) and Snaigow (third, 100–7) were allowed to keep within reasonable distance until racing down towards the third fence from home. Arkle (1–10f), still on a tight rein, accelerated into top gear and the contest was effectively over.

New Year's Day 1962 was a watershed in Irish society, with Ireland getting its first television service. The first television sets had begun to trickle into the country by a few months later. These 'picture boxes' installed by the wealthier farmers were the latest of the never-ending miracles of science. They held children from their play and adults from their memories beside the fireside. The poorer families, who could not initially afford televisions, would almost beg to spend their evenings in those fortunate houses where the images flickered and came and went. The tenth commandment 'Thou shalt not covet thy neighbour's goods' had never been broken so often as when the televisions first came to Ireland.

Unlike Golden Miller and Prince Regent, Arkle's enduring hold of public consciousness was ensured because of television. Apart from his class, one incident at Ascot turned him into a media darling. His regular work rider, Paddy Woods, was unable to travel, so the much smaller Sean Barker stepped into the breach. It was thought the substitute was too tiny to saddle Arkle, particularly as the horse had a habit of stretching himself as he was being saddled. However, Arkle's much-talked-about intelligence came into play and he bent down to let the little man saddle him. The English papers had a field day with the story.

High-Flyer

In Gaelic football they talk about the greatest players never to have won an All-Ireland medal. In racing they talk about the greatest steeplechasers never to have won the Gold Cup. At the top of that list is Flyingbolt.

In the early 1980s, many people wondered how a small country like Ireland could have thrown up two such prodigious rugby talents as Ollie Campbell and Tony Ward in the exact same position at the exact same time. A similar situation arose in the mid-1960s with the emergence of Flyingbolt and Arkle. The coincidence is heightened when one considers that not only were they contemporaries, they were also stablemates!

As in the Ward–Campbell case, they had contrasting temperaments. Their jockey Pat Taaffe observed, 'In character they were like night and day. A small child could walk into Arkle's box with absolute safety. Flyingbolt would kick the eye out of your head!' In fact Arkle had a special relationship with children. Part of his legend is that he retrieved for young Valerie Dreaper a ball which had found its way into his box and dropped it at her feet like a dog. Valerie's brother Jim, himself a Gold Cup-winning trainer, confirms that the story is completely true.

> As children we were all warned that although Arkle was an absolute
> pet, Flyingbolt was the exact opposite and that if the ball went

anywhere near him in the yard we were to leave it there. He was vicious in the extreme.

My father once said about Arkle and Pat Taaffe that even for the greatest of horses it was a privilege to be ridden by such a man. Arkle was not always foot-perfect, though. He could be a bit flippant about the occasional fence. He was a marvel, and his record supports anyone who calls him the greatest, but it is foolish to think there can never be another steeplechaser to match him. In fact, there may well have been one in the yard with him. Who can say how brilliant Flyingbolt might have become if he had not contracted brucellosis? Pat Taaffe said that if Arkle and Flyingbolt had met in soft going, he would have stuck by Arkle but wouldn't have been sure he was right.

In his first season (1964) over hurdles Flyingbolt was undefeated, with his biggest win coming in the Gloucestershire Hurdle. Switching to chasing in the following season, he was unbeaten once more, including a runaway success in the equivalent of the modern SunAlliance Chase at Cheltenham. As a six-year-old, comparisons started to be made between him and Arkle. This trend continued when he won the Massey Fergusson Gold Cup by 15 lengths.

As Arkle won his third Gold Cup in 1966, Flyingbolt won the Two-Mile Champion Chase by 15 lengths and completed a remarkable season by winning the Irish Grand National under 12st 7lb whilst conceding a huge weight advantage to the runner-up Height O'Fashion. It was Tom Dreaper's tenth winner in the race, having previously won with Prince Regent (1942), Shagreen (1949), Royal Approach (1954), Olympia (1960), Fortria (1961), Kerfero (1962), Last Link (1963), Arkle (1964) and Splash (1965). The public demanded a race between the famous stablemates but neither trainer nor jockey would agree to it. The reason for their reticence can be found in Taaffe's autobiography *My Life and Arkle's*, which recalls how both horses had been hacking upsides when Flyingbolt had taken off. Arkle had responded in kind, leaving Taaffe helpless, and the two wonderhorses had flown neck-and-neck, flat out over schooling fences. Their jockeys could only hang on for dear life. No harm was done but they were never allowed even to be schooled together again.

In his last major radio interview, Taaffe praised Arkle.

> He was easily the best horse I've ever seen or hope to see and he was the most gentle horse. He was very easy to ride and actually he ran most of his races himself. I always had great confidence in him and if he got himself into trouble he always got himself out of it again

very easily. He was a showman, like a human being. He knew he was a champion and thought more or less everybody should look on him as a champion. The more cheering that went on for him, the better he liked it. Mill House too was a great horse, though a hard one to train. He was unlucky to be on the go at the same time as Arkle.

Taaffe's only failure as a jockey came on a young Foinavon, who subsequently came to prominence in 1967 when he bypassed incredible mayhem at the 23rd fence to win the Grand National at 100–1. 'He fell with me at Ballydoyle, and when I looked around to see if he was all right, he was lying there eating grass!'

Sadly, Foinavon had passed through Tom Dreaper's stable before he won the Grand National, as had Early Mist, the 1953 winner. Dreaper never won Aintree's Grand National, though his Prince Regent, Vulture and Black Secret were all placed there.

Captain Fantastic

Surprisingly, Peter O'Sullevan's abiding Cheltenham memory of Pat Taaffe is not of Arkle.

Mill House and Arkle was pure theatre. It was the best of English versus the best of Irish, the subject of poetry and song. Pat Taaffe was my long-time friend but the Cheltenham victory of his that meant the most to me was not one of Arkle's but his Gold Cup triumph with Captain Christy. What made that win so special was the emotional level generated by Bobby Beasley staging a fairytale comeback.

Captain Christy was the Jekyll and Hyde of racing. On his day he was unbeatable, but consistency was not one of his salient characteristics. Initially he was owned, trained and ridden by Major Joe Pidcock, who as a 62-year-old rode him in the three-mile hurdle at Cheltenham. That summer the five-year-old was bought by Mrs Jane Samuel and entrusted to the stewardship of Pat Taaffe. Almost immediately the Captain struck form, winning five of his seven races including the Sweeps Hurdle and the Scottish Champion Hurdle the following season.

The first season of his steeplechasing career was packed with incident: unseating his rider two out in the Black and White Gold Cup at Ascot, falling when coasting in the Wills Premier Chase final at Haydock, and winning the Cheltenham Gold Cup as a relative novice.

The win really belonged to Bobby Beasley in one of the greatest human-interest stories in racing's history. Beasley had looked like the typical 'has-been' two years previously because of a combination of alcoholism, increasing weight and a succession of bad falls. But he pulled himself together and 15 years after his first Cheltenham Gold Cup success on Roddy Owen rounded off a distinguished career with Captain Christy's win.

1974 continued to be a good year for the Captain when he won the King George VI by eight lengths from the luckless Pendil, who had been brought down when in a strong position in the Gold Cup. There was to be no repeat Gold Cup victory the next year, though, when the horse made no impression in the soft ground and was pulled up.

The Captain's most awesome performance came the following season in the King George VI Chase, when he defeated his nearest challenger, Bula, by an astonishing 30 lengths. Two months later tendon trouble caused his career to go into sharp decline.

A Nation Mourns

Arkle was only nine years old when he broke a pedal bone in his hoof in the King George VI Chase on 26 December 1966. Although he was giving away 21lb, Arkle was leading at the last but was pipped at the post by Dormant. Despite vigorous efforts to get him returned to fitness, there was to be no fairytale comeback and Arkle was retired the following October.

Lottery, the first Grand National winner, ended his days pulling a cart in Neasden. Arkle endured no such humiliation. The old Irish half-crown coin had a horse on its imprint and when Arkle got injured, a sharp entrepreneur managed to convince some gullible racing fans to fork out ten bob for them, four times their face value, on the basis that they were medals for Arkle. As his fame spread, fan letters addressed to 'Arkle, Ireland' found as direct a route to him as one of Robin Hood's arrows. He appeared at the Horse of the Year Show in 1969 and appropriately the band played 'There'll Never Be Another You'.

At the height of Arkle's popularity, his trainer's wife was interviewed on television about the hordes of unexpected visitors who were dropping into the yard to catch a glimpse of him in the flesh. Mrs Dreaper jokingly remarked that she would have to introduce a visiting hour and she jocosely suggested Sundays between four and five. At four o'clock the next Sunday the yard was besieged by sightseers! The following day a notice appeared in all the papers saying that in fact Arkle did not have visiting hours.

Jim Dreaper remembers the attention from his childhood days.

> When I was seven years old I was sent to a boarding school in Kells so I missed out on a lot of the excitement. My master there, Jack Sweetman, was a great racing man and he kept me informed about all the happenings in the racing world. His son Alan is now a journalist for such publications as *The Racing Post*. The only problem then was that the headmaster, an Englishman, considered racing folk the lowest of the low. I remember Jack kept me informed about the build-up to the first Gold Cup between Arkle and Mill House and the Irish–English thing was very strong – even though Mill House was an Irish horse with an Irish jockey. They even held the race on a Saturday that year, which all added to the interest.
>
> Arkle's popularity caused some problems for us as a family. It was a hell of an imposition. People seemed to forget that we had a professional yard and a farm and it was a bit of an inconvenience. Sundays back then were supposed to be a day of rest and most people took that belief seriously. In our yard, though, there was a constant stream of visitors and countless knocks on the door with people looking to see him, to get their picture taken with him and to put their children up on his back. As a lot of people knew, he could be seen from the road, so we had a lot of gawkers.
>
> The strange thing was that there was very little talk about Arkle in our house. The conversation was dominated by the horses that were no good. What was wrong with them? What could be done to turn the situation around and turn the horses with no form into winners?

A nation mourned when, in an act of mercy killing, Arkle was put down because of chronic stiffness. The *Pall Mall Gazette*'s tribute to the greatest cricketer of them all, W.G. Grace, was, 'He has drained the language of eulogy and it is no use applying superlatives to him any more.' The same might be said for Arkle. Perhaps the most fitting epitaph to this peerless horse comes from Peter O'Sullevan.

> Comparisons between horses are invidious. I wouldn't endeavour to interpret racing history and list in order of preference the greatest horses of all time. Mind you, I have broken my own rules a few times and ventured to suggest that Arkle was the best over jumps

and Ribot and Sea Bird II the best I had seen on the flat. In one of my commentaries from one of his Gold Cup triumphs I said something like, 'And it's Arkle who is the champion, probably the best we've ever seen.'

Cheltenham Conqueror

Two years after achieving his hat-trick of Gold Cups with Arkle and 22 years after his first win with Prince Regent, Dreaper was back in the winners' enclosure for the fifth time in the Gold Cup with Fort Leney. He was led over the last by The Laird but fought back like a tiger up the hill to win by a neck.

Dreaper went one better in the Queen Mother Two-Miles Champion Chase, winning with Fortria (1960 and 1961), Ben Stack (1964), Flyingbolt (1966), Muir (1969) and Straight Fort (1970). 1970 also saw Dreaper winning the SunAlliance Chase for the third time with Proud Tarquin. His previous winners in the race were Arkle (1963) and Arkloin (1965). The following year Arkloin (by the same sire as Arkle, Archive) won the National Hunt Handicap Chase. It was Dreaper's third victory in the race; he had previously won with Sentina in 1957 and 1958.

It is noteworthy that only one of Dreaper's 26 wins at the festival came over hurdles (Flyingbolt in the Gloucestershire Hurdle in 1964), as he regarded hurdling as almost nothing more than education for chasing proper. Fittingly, Dreaper's last win at the festival came in the Arkle Challenge Trophy Chase (formerly the Cotswold Chase) with Alpheus, ridden by Eddie Wright. He had previously won the race with Fortria (1958), Mountcashel King (1961), Ben Stack (1963) and Flyingbolt (1965).

The Swinging '60s

Racing was very poor in Ireland until Sean Lemass dragged the Irish economy kicking and screaming into the twin track of modernity and prosperity; the Irish Derby was worth a mere £6,387 in 1955, which was no better than a modest English condition race. The tradition of large numbers of Irish racing fans travelling *en masse* to Cheltenham began in the '50s, prompted by a run of four Irish victories in the Gold Cup between 1946 and 1950. At this time, with post-war rationing still in place in England, the tourists earned favour with the locals by bringing with them bountiful supplies of eggs, steaks and sausages, which they were able to use for bartering. From their early days the Irish were associated with partying around the clock. Relations between the Cotswoldians and the Irish have since been marked by friendly rivalry and mutual affection.

The mood of optimism that had marked the swinging '60s still beat strongly in the early 1970s. Ireland was about to take her place in the EEC and move into the fast lane. The possibilities seemed limitless. The census returns of the previous year had painted an optimistic, even rosy, picture of a nation at last boldly taking its rightful place among the world's élite. New factories and schools were springing up everywhere. The scourge of emigration had not just been halted, it had been reversed, as thousands of people returned to the Emerald Isle from England, America and Australia.

It was a time of extraordinary change. A variety of factors came together like converging lines to produce a social, economic and cultural revolution. Ireland had ceased to be a predominantly agricultural country; industry and commerce had become more important than farming. As a consequence of this, Ireland had become an urban society, with the majority of people living in towns and cities instead of on the land. Whereas in the 1950s emigration had resulted in most of the country's finest and brightest leaving the country, by the early 1970s Ireland had become a country of young people. For the first time since the Great Famine, the Irish population recorded an increase. The cancer of emigration had abated. And for the first time since the Middle Ages, the vulnerable Irish economy was showing promising signs of being able to support itself.

Other changes were less tangible but no less significant. Educational standards were much higher. The introduction of free secondary education in the late '60s by the Minister of Education Donogh O'Malley had far-reaching effects. The most obvious manifestation of this was the myriad yellow school buses which populated country roads as they ferried armies of schoolchildren from the country into the towns. However, better education brought new expectations, new ways of thinking and doing, and in many cases a sharp questioning of what had gone before.

Ireland had now entered the era of the global village. At the flick of a switch the world was at the viewer's fingertips. No picture was more dramatic than the sight of Neil Armstrong walking on the moon in 1969. The sounds of the Beatles were as well known in Longford as they were in London. Although no Irish band could emulate their success at the time, a host of showbands like Larry Cunningham and the Mighty Avons, Eileen Reid and the Cadets, Brendan Bowyer and the Royal Showband, whose famous dance number 'The Hucklebuck' became an anthem for a generation of Irish jivers, attained extraordinary popularity. Radio Luxembourg became more important than Radio Eireann to many young people.

The deep silence of the Irish countryside swallowed up the music of change hungrily. It was a time to dream, and every dream seemed achievable. As economic and educational standards increased and more people travelled, the number of racing pilgrims to Cheltenham rose accordingly.

FIVE

Magic Moments

'My horse was in the lead, coming down the home stretch, but the caddie fell off.'

SAMUEL GOLDWYN

In 1997, in an effort to counteract the decline in public interest in the Derby, the powers that be in Epsom recruited the services of Vinnie Jones. Vinnie's main claim to fame came when he tested the private parts of the young Paul Gascoigne in a match between Wimbledon and Newcastle, momentarily making Gazza an honorary member of the Bee Gees. As a publicity stunt the Epsom authorities engaged Vinnie to grab hold of a less tender part of Frankie Dettori's anatomy and lift him in the air. There is no need for the Cheltenham Festival to resort to such cheap stunts. Its hold on racegoers comes from its assembly line of magic moments – with Irish horses very much at the forefront.

American Raymond Guest had a dream – to win both the Derby and the Grand National. In 1962 and 1968 he won the Derby with Larkspur and Sir Ivor respectively. The Grand National was to prove more problematic, even though he made several attempts – often with two horses. His prayers were finally answered with the emergence of an Irish horse, L'Escargot.

Dan Moore trained L'Escargot to win both the Gold Cup and Grand National. As a top jockey Moore had enjoyed a good-natured rivalry with Aubrey Brabazon. As a joke he had once painted the sleeping Aubrey's toenails with red nail varnish! In 1968 L'Escargot won the Cheltenham Gloucestershire Hurdle. Two years later, starting at 33–1, he beat French Tan by a length and a half to win the Cheltenham Gold Cup. The following year, in his only success of the season, he retained the Gold Cup. He galloped doggedly home through the deep mud to finish well clear of five opponents who passed the post in clear exhaustion.

The race, like that of the previous year, spawned great debate as to whether L'Escargot would have beaten the horse who had fallen when leading three fences from home. In 1970 it was Kinloch Brae; a year later it was Glencarraig Lady who crumpled on landing. Tommy Carberry, L'Escargot's rider on both occasions, is certain that his mount would have won both races regardless. L'Escargot (7–2jf) escaped interference from Glencarraig Lady's fall, but Leap Frog (7–2jf) and The Dikler (15–2) were rather less fortunate, The Dikler in particular being forced to check and swerve to avoid her. When L'Escargot slowed up approaching the last fence, it still appeared that Leap Frog might catch him. Leap Frog, however, was jaded and L'Escargot forged clear again to win by ten lengths. It was then that the decision was taken to train him for the Grand National. The Irish hold on the Gold Cup was maintained the following year when the Francis Flood-trained Glencarraig Lady, ridden by Frank Berry, won the great race.

In 1972, following a fourth place in the Gold Cup, L'Escargot made his first Grand National appearance. Despite carrying top weight and being 17–2 favourite, he was knocked over at the third fence. The following year he finished fourth again in the Gold Cup and came a distant third to Red Rum and Crisp at Aintree. With the help of blinkers he finished second to Red Rum the following year. The margin between them was seven lengths.

In 1975, at the age of 12, L'Escargot came to Aintree having won only one race in the past four seasons and as a consequence had dropped to 11st 3lb in the handicap. Even Red Rum could not afford to concede him 11lb, and L'Escargot, with Tommy Carberry in the saddle, emerged victorious with 15 lengths to spare – in the process becoming the first horse since Golden Miller to win the Gold Cup and the National. Guest's dream fulfilled, he retired L'Escargot on the spot, giving the horse to Dan and Joan Moore who had trained him so well. In Carberry's words, he was a 'hell of a horse'.

Carberry's great Cheltenham moments are not confined to L'Escargot. Apart from his Gold Cup triumphs, his most popular Cheltenham win was perhaps on Bill and Tony Durkan's mare Anaglog's Daughter to claim the Arkle Chase in 1980.

Bum Deal

Sporting memories provide one of the steadily diminishing links with the past as the exploits of the heroes of our youth are linked together in a chain of bonding with those of the next generations, more real to many than the events of political history. The name Carberry needs no introduction to Cheltenham because of Tommy's association with Dan Moore.

Tommy's son Paul inherited his father's genes. Not even an accident to his brother Thomas, who was knocked unconscious by a fall and suffered periodic fits afterwards, prevented Paul from following in his father's footsteps. He became champion apprentice in Ireland under the expert tutelage of Noel Meade before taking up the prestigious post of retained jockey to Robert Ogden, one of the most powerful owners in the north of England, before returning to Ireland to begin an epic duel with Ruby Walsh for the position of champion jockey. He has a long way to go, though, to emulate the feats of his father.

Paul has managed to equal one record already. As the gloom descended on a miserable second day for the Irish in 1993, Carberry on Rhythm Section left the field in his trail to claim the Guinness Festival Bumper. Like his father (and another Irish jockey, Jason Titley, who also realised the impossible dream of winning the Grand National with Royal Athlete on his first ride in the race), Paul won on his first ride at Cheltenham.

There is a big difference between father and son in terms of style. In the classic tradition of Irish jockeys, Tommy rode with a deep seat and long reins, whereas Paul favours riding as short as many jockeys on the flat. This has not always been to his father's liking – after a race in Dundalk, Tommy told his son that his backside was too high!

At the 1999 festival Paul pulled off a major coup to claim the Royal and SunAlliance Chase on the Noel Chance-trained, Irish-bred Looks Like Trouble. The race, though, brought huge disappointment for the Irish fans because the Edward O'Grady-trained favourite Nick Dundee, who had appeared to be cruising to victory, fell at the third last.

The Moores too have their own unique place in the Cheltenham roll of honour. Dan's son Arthur knows what it's like to enter the winners' enclosure as a trainer. Klairon Davis, having won the Arkle in 1995, was an impressive winner of the Queen Mother Champion Chase the following year, pounding the last ditch before streaking past Viking Flagship and Sound Man. Arthur Moore had previously won the race with Drumgora in 1981, whilst his father had won the first running of the race with Quita Que in 1959 and 14 years later had had a second winner with Inkslinger.

With 15 winners at the festival in his career, Dan Moore shares equal-third rating with Eddie O'Grady behind Tom Dreaper and Vincent O'Brien as Ireland's most successful trainers at Cheltenham. In the aftermath of his father Willie's death in 1972, O'Grady had to forsake his veterinary studies in University College, Dublin. Initially owners were wary of his youth but after two difficult years he struck gold when he had his first Cheltenham winner, Mr Midland, with Mouse Morris in the saddle. Other winners included Staplestown, Mr Donovan, Mountrivers, Ventana Canyon and Time For A Run. Probably his most notable win was with Golden Cygnet in the 1978 Supreme Novices' Hurdle. After his victory Fred Rimell was moved to say, 'Never have I seen a horse win at the festival meeting so easily.' Tragically, the horse was fatally injured when falling at the last in the Scottish Champion Hurdle at Ayr with Night Nurse and Sea Pigeon beaten. On his death he was described as the best Champion Hurdler that never was. O'Grady had no festival winner between Northern Game in 1984 and Time For A Run ten years later; had he not spent most of that decade concentrating on the flat, his Cheltenham tally would probably have been higher.

Ten Up

Tommy Carberry steered Ten Up to a narrow victory over Glandford Brigg to win the 1974 SunAlliance Chase. The following year the Jim Dreaper-trained horse won the Gold Cup, with Carberry again in the saddle. For County Meath-based Dreaper it was a case of following the family tradition, his father, Tom, being Ireland's most successful ever trainer at Cheltenham with 26 wins. Whereas his father's parents, prosperous farmers, had had no interest whatsoever in racing and Tom had been well into his twenties by the time he rode his first point-to-point, Jim was in the opposite environment. He acknowledges that becoming a trainer was an inevitable career move for him: 'Being the only boy, it was predestined, I suppose, that I would take on my father's business. My parents were happy when I took it on and it was great for me to step into a ready-made business.'

It was as a jockey, though, that Dreaper first made his mark, notching up about 60 winners. He is probably best remembered as an unfortunate loser of the 1971 Grand National on the 20–1 shot Black Secret. Sandy Sprite, Bogweeno, Black Secret and Astbury came to the last fence with Specify trailing narrowly behind. Black Secret took the lead and held it until the final few strides, when John Cook passed him on Specify. With typical modesty, Jim admits that he was only aboard Black Secret because the deal made when the horse was sold to a schoolfriend of his mother's stipulated that the price would be £1,000 if young Dreaper were the regular jockey and £1,500 if the task went to Pat Taaffe. 'Being a good Quaker lady, she decided to take the cheaper price and put up with me.'

Like his father with Arkle and Flyingbolt, Jim had the good fortune to have two great horses at the one time. He was not too phased when Ten Up struck Cheltenham Gold.

I was only 24 then and I was only three years training. My father hadn't got married until he was 47. Round here they say a man shouldn't marry until he's fit for nothing else! I was young and foolish enough to take it all in my stride. In the build-up both Ten Up and Brown Lad won big races handsomely in Ascot and there was a lot of talk that if everything went well and we got the right conditions we could do very well. Ten Up was always a promising horse from his first race, a bumper, which he won. Like Brown Lad, though, it took him a long time to learn to be a good jumper.

I would say it is easier to win the Gold Cup than to win a Grand National because there are even weights. In the Irish National you could be giving a stone to a good horse. I would also say Ten Up is an ordinary horse in terms of Gold Cup winners but we had the luck with him. I have no doubt but that Brown Lad was a better horse, but he was unlucky because he didn't get the weather he needed. The year he should have been in his prime he lost out with injury.

My best year at Cheltenham was in 1975 with three winners: Ten Up, Brown Lad [in the Bonusprint Stayers' Hurdle] and Lough Inagh [in the Queen Mother Two-Miles Champion Chase – a race his father won no fewer than six times]. The strange thing is that the one that probably gave the greatest pleasure was Lough Inagh because he was what I would call a hit-or-miss horse. By that I mean when he was good he cleared the fences no problem, but he was very erratic and when he was bad he didn't clear the fences. For that reason most jockeys didn't want to take him on. He was ridden by Sean Barker, who died last year. Sean was what people might describe as a journeyman jockey. So it was wonderful to see him having his day in the sun.

Cheltenham is the ultimate for racing people. To me it's like the Leaving Cert. You do all the homework but it's only when you do the exams that you discover if you're a top student or not.

Dreaper has no doubt why this is the case.

The English–Irish thing is absolutely vital to the meeting, and if you ask manager Edward Gillespie he will confirm that for you. Without that it would just be an ordinary meeting. That's what gives it its bite.

Unfortunately the intervening years have brought nothing but disappointment to Dreaper, especially with the 17.3-hands-tall Harcon, Merry Gale and, most famously, Carvill's Hill, who was taken from his stewardship and transferred to Martin Pipe. His verdict on the horse who flopped when favourite for the Gold Cup is that he had 'a magnificent engine and a faulty chassis'.

Gentleman Jim identifies two great Irish personalities in Cheltenham.

> One of the great Irish characters is Tommy Carberry because he has such a marvellous record there, not just with me but with Mr Moore's horses. Mick O'Toole is the other great character for no particular reason other than that he is Mick O'Toole!

Golden Days

O'Toole trained another Gold Cup winner for Ireland in 1977 in the shape of Davy Lad, though Lanzarote's death cast a tragic shadow over the race. It was a massive disappointment for trainer Fred Winter, as owner Lord Howard de Walden's 1974 Champion Hurdle winner had begun the summit of steeplechasing as if to the manner born. (Lord de Walden has an interesting history. On a visit to Germany in 1931 he knocked down a man whilst driving a car – it was no less a person than Adolf Hitler!) Lanzarote (7–2) had held third place to Tied Cottage and Fort Devon when his hind legs gave way beneath him two strides after the ninth fence and he slithered to the ground. Summerville overtook Tied Cottage with four fences left and appeared destined for victory. He faltered suddenly between the last two jumps but battled on bravely to finish third before pulling up lame. Tied Cottage (20–1) and Davy Lad (14–1) passed Summerville (15–1) approaching the final fence, where Davy Lad made a fine leap and drew steadily clear to win by six lengths.

Davy Lad, who had won the SunAlliance Novices' Hurdle in 1975, was one of four Irish winners that day along with Meladon, Kilcoleman and Rusty Tears, taking the Irish total for the festival to seven – only one short of the 1958 record. It was a fitting reward for the Irish invaders who had been denied flights from Ireland because of an Aer Lingus dispute and had been forced to take the boat.

Mick O'Toole began his training career not with horses but with dogs. His record at Cheltenham from 1975 to 1981 was exceptional, clocking up nine winners as trainer, seven of them with Dessie Hughes in the saddle – although Chinrullah, which won the 1980 Queen Mother Champion Chase, was subsequently disqualified for a technical breach.

Chinrullah had triumphed in the Arkle Challenge Trophy Chase the previous year.

In 1976 O'Toole won the SunAlliance Novices' Hurdle with Parkhill. That same year he took the Stayers' Hurdle with Bit Of A Jig after an epic tussle with the Fred Winter-trained Simon's Pace, snatching victory by three-quarters of a length. He also twice won the Supreme Novices' Hurdle, with Mac's Chariot in 1977 and Hartstown in 1981, and in 1978 he emerged victorious in the National Hunt Chase with Gay Tie.

O'Toole is a big Cheltenham fan.

> I've found myself in tears a few times after winning there. Even when Irish horses don't do that well, like the late 1980s and early '90s, the Irish fans never lose any interest in it.
>
> The thing that makes Cheltenham from an Irish point of view is that everyone has a dream of having a winner there. I'd say a lot of Irish horses go there without realistic chances. Their owners live in a fantasy world. Racing is a game of make-believe. If people didn't think they had horses that were better than they really were, national hunt racing would collapse. A lot of Irish horses have gone there as favourites but have flopped, while some have gone as no-hopers and won at 20–1.
>
> I've had good years there and bad years. I had a great run after I won my first winner at the festival when I won seven years in a row. Some of the bad years I hadn't got my money back until Ascot.
>
> One of the most exciting places to be is at the gallops on Tuesday morning because there is so much tension, not to mention John Mulhern in his colourful jacket! John was notorious for changing his mind about whether or not to send horses to Cheltenham. At that stage it's all down to the horses. It's all finished for the trainers. There's real magic in the air at about a quarter to seven in the morning. You'll see every top jockey there. If you say to a jockey like Richard Dunwoody, 'I'd like you to be there at 6.55 in the morning to give the horse a last run out,' he'll be there.

'Monkey'

Cheltenham 1977 was a bumper festival for jockey Dessie Hughes. Not only did he ride Davy Lad to win the Gold Cup, he also rode Tip The Wink to win the Arkle Challenge Trophy and Mac's Chariot to victory in the Lloyds Bank Champion Novices' Hurdle. Hughes, though, is probably best remembered for partnering Monksfield to win the 1979 Champion Hurdle.

'Monkey' had an inauspicious beginning. He was unsold in the yearling sales in 1973 because he looked too small, ugly and unsound. The following year he was bought by a virtually unknown trainer, Des McDonogh, for 740 guineas. Although he sold Monkey a few months later for £1,125, one of the most famous relationships between horse and trainer had begun. Up to then McDonogh had been best known as an actor, particularly for his starring role in *Charley's Aunt*.

When Monksfield (bred by an astronomy expert called Peter Ryan) ran his first race on the flat, his first-time owner Dr Michael Mangan, a radiologist working in Newfoundland, asked his mother-in-law to bet £10 for him on the Tote. Despite having the benefit of expert advice, she never placed the bet. Starting at Tote odds of 647–1, Monksfield won.

Although he was destined never to win again on the flat, he went on to become a top-class hurdler, beginning with the Irish Benson and Hedges Handicap Hurdle and the Huzzar Handicap Hurdle in 1976. He really established his reputation at Cheltenham in 1976 when finishing second to Peterhof in the *Daily Express* Triumph Hurdle.

In 1977 he finished a battling second to Night Nurse in the Champion Hurdle after a mistake at the last, and a few weeks later the pair dead-heated in the Templegate Hurdle at Aintree in an epic race. That November, however, Monkey stared death in the face. McDonogh was so desperate that he enlisted the services of the local soothsayer. However, a course of folic acid did the trick and the horse recovered full fitness.

The following year Monkey stormed up the hill to beat Night Nurse and Sea Pigeon to claim the Champion Hurdle, to the predictable chorus of Irish tears and cheers. His jockey was 44-year-old Tommy Kinane. Kinane's age has attracted almost as much comment as his riding – a trend fuelled by the fact that at one stage he had three different dates on his birth certificate: 3, 11 and 21 October 1933. He was a formidable opponent and not a man to yield to anybody. Even the great Pat Taaffe felt his wrath when he allegedly barged into Kinane in Navan. Tommy promised him he would 'do' him in return. The opportunity to return the compliment came at Tramore a few days later. Kinane passed Taaffe as he went down the hill and yelled, 'Now, Pat, do you remember Navan?'

'Ah, Tommy,' replied Taaffe, 'you wouldn't!'

'I would not. Good luck,' responded Kinane as he kicked away to win.

In the build-up to the 1979 Champion Hurdle, the pundits in England suggested that Monksfield had lost his enthusiasm. It would be a case of eating humble pie for all who had predicted his demise. Forced to make almost all his own running and headed by Sea Pigeon before the last flight,

Monksfield landed on the flat with this title seemingly slipping away. But no horse ever refused more stubbornly to yield to defeat, and his fightback up the hill for a three-quarter-length victory was truly heroic. It was tough luck on Sea Pigeon, who was running on ground far softer than he liked as he produced the race of his life.

Dessie Hughes took Monkey straight to the front and led him boldly wide in search of the best ground. Both Sea Pigeon and Kybo, who sadly slipped on landing over the second-last fence, followed his path, and those who foolishly took the conventional shorter route were all beaten a long way from home. Monksfield gave a perfect exhibition of efficient, flawless hurdling. He constantly saved ground and energy in the air. (Incidentally, naming horses is a curious business. Isidore Kerman named his most famous horse Kybo after the initials of the advice his mother had once given him: 'Keep Your Bowels Open!')

Controversy had dogged Monksfield's build-up to the Waterford Crystal Champion Hurdle when 46-year-old Tommy Kinane was replaced as his rider by Dessie Hughes – much to Kinane's chagrin. In the event the race was one of the finest ever seen, with Monksfield and Sea Pigeon coming to the last flight stride for stride – but Sea Pigeon was cruising while the tiny Irish horse was struggling. Three cracks from Hughes's whip saw Monkey conjure up an incredible jump before his most remarkable quality, courage, was clearly demonstrated and he started to claw back Sea Pigeon's advantage. Against the odds he stuck his head in front 100 yards from the finish to secure victory. It was his will to win which had pulled the big race out of the fire. He never flinched, no matter how tough the going got – the embodiment of equine character. It was right and fitting that he should become the first Irish jumper since Arkle to become horse of the year.

In 1980 Monkey sought to win the Champion Hurdle for a third time, a feat achieved by only three horses: Hatton's Grace, Sir Ken and Persian War. However, Sea Pigeon (13–2) beat Monksfield (6–5f) to become the oldest winner of the race for 30 years. This was the sixth time the two horses had met, with Monksfield having won all of the previous battles. But following this victory, Sea Pigeon, whose flat-race triumphs included the Chester Cup and the Ebor Handicap, could legitimately claim to be one of the great all-rounders.

Tied Up

The 1980 Gold Cup was a bitter-sweet moment in the history of Irish racing. Tied Cottage won the race by eight lengths and in the process provided Tommy Carberry with his fourth Gold Cup victory. Second in 1977 and a last-fence faller when fighting for the lead with Alverton in 1979, Tied Cottage (13–2) finally went on the Gold Cup's winning roll with a powerful display of stamina and jumping. Carberry took him into a clear lead before Diamond Edge (5–2f) closed the gap with a mile to go, but the Irish veteran was merely taking a breather. Diamond Edge suddenly ran out of steam racing down the hill and Approaching then emerged as the most serious challenger, but Tied Cottage's gallop had worn him down entering the straight. Mac Vidi (66–1) kept up a brave confrontation, but the mudlark Master Smudge (14–1) came through to deprive him of second place.

Sadly, Tied Cottage was later one of three Irish-trained horses disqualified from their Cheltenham races after routine tests revealed an irregular substance believed to come from a consignment of equine nuts delivered to their stables in infected containers. No suspicion of skulduggery was directed at the trainers, but this proved to be irrelevant to the disqualification rules.

The race had given Dan Moore his 15th and final festival winner. His wife, Joan, was in charge that day because, as the world of racing knew, Dan was in the grip of a terminal illness.

The Moores figure prominently when Peter O'Sullevan is asked to name the great Irish characters of Cheltenham.

> Gosh, there are so many. Mick O'Toole had great success there and was a very flamboyant character. John Mulhern is a wonderful personality, as was Willie O'Grady. His son, Eddie, has carried on that family tradition admirably – but in a quieter way. Arthur Moore represents Ireland in the best possible way, just as his father did. I remember Dan very well. He did so tremendously well. I almost hate to use the word about him because it sounds too old-fashioned these days, but he was such a gentleman.

Tommy Carberry was a big fan of Tied Cottage.

> He knew his way around Cheltenham blindfolded. He was a good ride around Cheltenham, very free. The only thing you had to do was drop your hands and let him off. The fences are so well presented that they are easier to jump than Ascot, Fairyhouse or Leopardstown. If the horse makes an effort he'll jump them, and Tied Cottage only fell there when he was very tired. The Cheltenham fences do find horses out but I wouldn't mind

schooling a novice horse there. It is easy to get a horse to jump there.

Forgiven Not Forgotten

In the hostelries, stories of Irish horses' triumphs in Cheltenham are intertwined with heartwarming stories of owners, jockeys and trainers who overcame tremendous setbacks. A case in point is Forgive 'N' Forget and his Tipperary-born trainer Jimmy Fitzgerald. The horse was owned by Manchester-based Tim Kilroe, who had bought him for the bargain price of £45,000 from Barney Curley.

In 1983 the gelding by Precipice Wood won the Joe Coral Golden Hurdle Final at 5–2 with Ashbourne man Mark Dwyer in the saddle. An Irish-trained horse, Eliogarty, made history that year when Caroline Beasley became the first woman to ride a winner at the festival in the Christies Foxhunter Chase. Her win posed a few problems for race commentator Michael O'Hehir, who had to correct himself when using the word 'man' about Eliogarty's jockey.

A dislocated shoulder saw Dwyer losing the ride on Forgive 'N' Forget in 1984 to John Francome when the horse finished second to A Kinsman in the SunAlliance Chase. Despite this, Fitzgerald promptly backed his star pupil to win the 1985 Gold Cup at 33–1. The eight-year-old Burrough Hill Lad had furnished Jenny Pitman with her first Gold Cup triumph in 1984 and was a raging ante-post favourite to emulate the achievement in successive years but was ruled out by injury.

Following a shoulder operation Mark Dwyer was ready to bid for Gold Cup glory once again. The 22-year-old Meath man bided his time and took up the running at the last with Righthand Man and Earls Brig challenging strongly, Forgive 'N' Forget winning by one and a half lengths from Righthand Man. Dwyer won a second Gold Cup on Jodami in 1993.

Fitzgerald's promising career as a jockey, with 225 winners including seven with the 1964 Champion Hurdle winner Magic Court, had been cut tragically short when he suffered a horrific fall at Doncaster in 1967 which left him with a fractured skull, complete deafness in his left ear and dizziness for 12 months. It took a year for him to find his balance again, though he would never recover hearing in his damaged ear. He purchased a large farm in Malton and forged a training career for himself. The road to glory was fraught with pitfalls, however – his first Gold Cup prospect, Fairy King, broke his back at a race at Kempton.

Forgive 'N' Forget finished third in the 1986 Gold Cup behind Dawn

Run and Wayward Lad, beaten by three and a half lengths. In 1988, though, tragedy revisited Fitzgerald when his prize horse, running in the festival for his sixth consecutive season, broke his leg at the top of the hill with a second Gold Cup in the offing. The race was won by David Nicholson's Charter Party.

Primrose and Blue

In 1993 Montelado became the first horse to win consecutive races at Cheltenham. He had closed the previous year's festival by winning the bumper, the national hunt flat race, and in 1993 won the first race, the Trafalgar House Supreme Novices' Hurdle, for jockey Charlie Swan and trainer Pat Flynn. It was a fairytale story for the Roscommon-based syndicate who owned him, led by Ollie Hannon, whose poultry company is one of the biggest employers in the area.

> The horse was owned and bred by Donal O'Rourke from Castlerea and his son Gerard. Brian Neilan, a solicitor from Roscommon, and the late John Joe Fallon, a famous Roscommon footballer from the early 1950s, were also involved. Poor John Joe was diagnosed as having cancer and expressed interest in selling his share in the horse. I came on board. Part of the deal was that I got to name the horse and that he would run in the colours I inherited from my father. They are the Roscommon colours, primrose and blue. I got involved when he was a yearling or a two-year-old.
>
> Initially the horse was trained by Dermot Weld but then Pat Flynn took over. Pat is a great man and very easy to deal with. I could ring him at three in the morning. I've had a horse in training with Aidan O'Brien, but I don't think I'd have the nerve to ring him at three in the morning!
>
> We ran Montelado in his first bumper in Thurles in 1991. He won, and he repeated the performance in December. After that we were going into the bar at Limerick to celebrate when Pat Flynn said to us, 'I suppose you want him to go and run in the bumper in Cheltenham.' We told him that there was no bumper in Cheltenham. But he knew better than us, because the bumper was run for the first time in 1992.

The horse was ridden by Philip Fenton in his first two races but Richard Dunwoody was in the saddle for Cheltenham. All the hype in the build-up to the race had been about the John Magnier-owned Tiananmen Square, ridden by Tim Hyde, who had impressed with his two previous wins, notably the second victory at Fairyhouse, when he absolutely annihilated the opposition which included a number of previous winners. But it was to be Ollie Hannon and not Magnier who was laughing.

> We hadn't any concept of how it would pan out but we were all backing our own horse nonetheless. We certainly weren't confident we would win but we thought we had a chance. The excitement was intense when we won. It was a real fairytale. Here I was with my first horse and I was a winner in Cheltenham. I had never known what it was like to be a loser. When we got to the parade ring the crowd sang 'When Irish Eyes Are Smiling'. The trophy was presented by the late Lord Wyatt, who said, 'Bring in all the village with you.' As it was the last race of the festival, everybody was very relaxed and it was easygoing. It was the next year when all the security concern took over. When we got back to the hotel there were a lot of telegrams waiting for me. One of them was from Albert Reynolds, who was Taoiseach at the time. There was one hell of a party when we got back to Roscommon.
>
> We ran Montelado again in the bumper in Punchestown at the end of April and Tiananmen Square beat him. We rested him for that summer and his comeback was in the Babs Babes race, which he won. That was on a Thursday and he won a maiden hurdle on the following Sunday. Although we were beaten in the First Choice Novices' Hurdle in the Christmas meeting at Leopardstown, we were almost ante-post favourites for the Cheltenham Supreme Novices' Hurdle. We were under a lot of pressure with our jockey situation, as Richard Dunwoody couldn't take the ride because he had just signed up with Martin Pipe, so we got Charlie Swan to take the ride. Pat sent Montelado over to Cheltenham a week early to get him acclimatised to it. We had a great contingent supporting us from Ireland.
>
> The night before the race we bumped into Peter O'Sullevan. He told us that he fancied Buro Eight to win our race because he had won his previous race by 20 lengths. But we did to him what we had done to Tiananmen Square the previous year! We broke the course record and won easily [by 12 lengths]. It was a lot more formal than the previous year. It was the BBC's last year to have the rights to the festival so they interviewed us, and after that every Tom, Dick and Harry interviewed us.

That evening we were celebrating in the Arkle Bar and although there were a lot of us there, we hadn't taken it over. We had this bath full of ice and champagne in the middle of the room and this English woman tripped over it and fell into it. As she got up, dripping wet, she said, 'I've heard of magnums of champagne but I've never heard of a bath of champagne before!'

That evening at the vigil Mass in Roscommon, the priest said, 'I'm not going to keep you this evening because we're all out to celebrate the Cheltenham victory.'

A tendon problem ruled Montelado out of action until 1996, when he made a winning return in Listowel and went on to win the Irish Cesarewitch with Mick Kinane in the saddle. In 1997 he finished ninth in the Champion Hurdle and the decision was taken to retire him. He now resides in the Charlie Swan Equestrian Centre. Ollie Hannon's only regret is that he never got a chance to race against Danoli on good ground when Montelado was in his prime.

Fergie

1996 was the year of Imperial Call and Fergie Sutherland, the old Etonian who had come to Ireland 30 years previously. Born into a soldiering family, he took a commission in the British Army and in 1952 he lost a leg in the Korean War. Going up a hill, one of the four troops he was with tripped the wire of a land-mine and set off the blast. The man who would be adopted by Ireland as one of her own was the only one badly injured. According to legend, he used to visit friends with a bootful of spare legs: one for shooting, one for riding and one for dancing! Fergie, though, was uncomfortable with the media interest in this aspect of his life. His regular response to questions about his military career was, 'Old hat, cold potatoes.'

Imperial Call was purchased from the legendary Tom Costello's yard in Clare. His victory would give the Costello academy of equine genius one leg of a hat-trick of Gold Cup winners in six years, with Cool Ground and Cool Dawn (purchased by owner Dido Harding for a mere £7,000) the other victors. Sutherland had been promised £20,000 for a couple of horses but the asking price for Imperial Call was £23,000. Fergie's power of persuasion came into play and he convinced his buyers to part with the extra money.

In his novice year Imperial Call had been overshadowed by the likes of

Sound Man, Strong Platinum and Klairon Davis. Subsequent victories in Clonmel and in the McCain Handicap Chase, interspersed with a fall at the first in the MMI Stockbrokers, had not revealed his true potential. The fall at Punchestown was a very anxious experience; after falling, he carried on into nearby fields, jumping two barbed-wire fences along the way.

It was only in 1996, in the Hennessy Gold Cup, that the first indication of his exceptional talent was given. The bookmakers fancied Master Oats and Monsieur Le Curé, particularly as the soft ground suited them. Charlie Swan had triumphed on Imperial Call at Leopardstown, defeating Conor O'Dwyer on Strong Platinum in the process. For the Hennessy, though, Swan was loyal to Life Of A Lord and O'Dwyer stepped into the breach. Despite a bad mistake at the last the combination performed very well. The sceptics wondered if they would last the extra two furlongs for the Gold Cup, if he had the experience and if his jumping would be up to its most severe test.

In the Gold Cup, Imperial Call was always travelling well. The much-lauded English grey One Man, ridden by Richard Dunwoody, was also moving well. It was the old battle of Ireland and England. Couldn't Be Better and Rough Quest were also looking dangerous, but the Gold Cup is never won until the horse has cleared the last and sprinted away from the rest of the field, up that forbidding hill. From the home turn, Imperial Call's combination of stamina and acceleration saw off all the competition. At the age of seven he became the youngest winner since Little Owl in 1981. It was a testimony to his achievement that the horse that came second, Rough Quest, went on to win the Grand National three weeks later.

Fergie displayed great reserve during and after the race – his hardened face was motionless when Conor O'Dwyer romped home on Imperial Call with a super sprint. When he threatened to be swamped by a sea of ecstatic Irish punters after taking the Gold Cup, Fergie barked at them, 'Let me see my hoss – he's the only reason I came back to this country.'

According to William James, the world is a theatre for heroism. Fergie's victory was Cheltenham at its most magical: the small stable triumphing in the sport of kings, rendering sport what it truly is – life at its innocent best, the world as it ought to be, the ideal realised for a moment. Sport is an expression of optimism. Such a victory enshrouds sports lovers with a redemptive feeling, melting away depression, pain and bitter disappointment, hinting at a bygone age of innocence and values that no longer obtain.

In 1998 23-year-old Raymond Hurley took over the training of the Callnerish gelding after Fergie's retirement. By then Imperial Call's career had been dogged by injuries and marred by his fall at the last at Punchestown at the end of 1997 and an abysmal performance in the Hennessy at Leopardstown the following February.

But 1996 had seen Irish punters in seventh heaven. Apart from Imperial Call Ireland had victories with Klairon Davis, Urubande, Loving Around, Wither Or Which, Elegant Lord and Ventana Canyon. It was a 'greenwash' for Irish tourists more accustomed to returning to Erin's Shore with lean wallets.

SIX

The Gallant Jonjo

'Rutherfords lost a bit of ground there but he's all right and they're turning now to the fence after Becher's, and as they do the leader is Castle Falls with Rutherfords alongside . . . and Rutherfords is being hampered and so is Castle Falls. Rondetto has fallen, Princeful has fallen, Kirtle-Lad has fallen, Norther has fallen, The Fossa has fallen, there's a right pile-up . . . Leedsy has climbed over the fence and left his jockey there, and now with all this mayhem Foinavon has gone off on his own . . . he's about 50 . . . 100 yards in front of everything else.'

Michael O'Hehir's description of the chaos at the 23rd fence of the 1967 Aintree Grand National which led to victory for the 100–1 no-hoper Foinavon is probably the most famous piece of commentary in the racing archives. But anybody who heard Dessie Scahill's passionate commentary of Dawn Run's Gold Cup victory will probably agree that he comes a close second. As Red Rum, the horse who turned the greatest lottery in racing into something approaching a certainty, had done a decade earlier, Dawn Run captured the hearts of racing fans everywhere.

In March 1986 Dawn Run made history by becoming the first horse to win both the Champion Hurdle (in 1984) and the Gold Cup. Three months later she lay dead. According to Phil Bull, racing is 'the great triviality'; Dawn Run's death in a race disproved that.

The outcome of that Cheltenham Gold Cup is part of steeplechasing folklore, as it saw Dawn Run come from behind to secure a last-gasp win in a course-record time, bringing her earnings to an all-time national hunt record. Wayward Lad finished second, with Forgive 'N' Forget third. After the race, John Francome described it as 'one of the most exciting races I've ever seen'.

One test of fame is when the multitudes know you simply by your first name. For instance, Garret, Gay, Cliff, Packie and Jack: no further introduction required. Racing has its own élite who are instantly identified by a Christian name: Lester, Frankie – and Jonjo.

Born in County Cork in 1952, Jonjo O'Neill served his apprenticeship with Michael Connolly at the Curragh and rode his first winner, Lana, when dead-heating in a flat race at the local track in 1970. When he moved to England in 1973 he joined Gordon Richards's stable. He became champion jockey in the 1977–78 season, winning a then record total of 149 races. He repeated that achievement two seasons later.

Eighteenth-century author Charles Colton remarked that there were three hurdles to be crossed in authorship: 'To write anything worth publishing, to find honest men to publish it and to get sensible men to read it.' Dick Francis succeeds on all three counts and makes his unique imprint on the landscape of the imagination. Every year since 1964 he has written an equine thriller and his books have been translated into 34 languages. Since 1992 he has resided in the idyllic Cayman Islands with a lifestyle marred only by the fact that the racing coverage on local television is limited to the Breeders' Cup and US classics. His second son, Merrick, has followed him into the world of racing. A former trainer, he lives in Lambourn, where he runs Europe's largest horse transport company LRT. Despite being champion jockey in the 1953–54 season, riding 76 winners and quitting three years later with a career total of 345, Dick Francis is known as 'the man who didn't win the National'. Riding Devon Loch for the Queen Mother in 1956, Francis was 20 lengths in front and just 50 yards from the winning post when the horse inexplicably spread-eagled and lost the race. Francis had more success at Cheltenham – including a winner two days after he fell there and the horse stood on his face, an injury which necessitated 32 stitches.

Jonjo never won the Grand National either. Worse still, he never completed the race. Nonetheless, he has the not-inconsiderable consolation of having twice won Cheltenham's big two: the Champion Hurdle, on Sea Pigeon in 1980 and Dawn Run in 1984, and the Gold Cup, on Alverton and Dawn Run. (He won 15 races on Sea Pigeon, though injury cost him the ride in the horse's Champion Hurdle triumph in 1981, when John Francome deputised.) In 1979 Jonjo won the Gold Cup with Alverton, who the same year broke his neck and was killed while trying to jump Becher's in the Grand National, which was won by its first Scottish winner, Rubstic, at 25–1.

Dawn Run's first victory was with her owner, Mrs Charmian Hill, then in her sixties, in the saddle. Almost immediately the stewards of the National Hunt Committee refused to renew her licence to ride. However, the mare came into her own when winning the Champion Hurdle in 1984 with Jonjo O'Neill as her jockey. In Jonjo's own words, the Irish 'went crackers' after the victory. A lengthy injury, however, meant that her owner's conviction that she would win the Gold Cup would not materialise until 1986.

Jonjo had first ridden Dawn Run in the V.A.T. Watkins Hurdle at Ascot in November 1983, defeating Amarach by a short head. She had then been beaten by Boreen Deas at Naas when conceding a lot of weight. Next came a narrow defeat to Gaye Brief at the Christmas Hurdle at Kempton Park, but honour was restored when she beat Cima to win the Champion Hurdle.

Shadow of a Gunman

Jonjo had a number of bad injuries in his career. At one point he had to have an extensive metal plate and several screws inserted in his right leg to help bind the bones. Years later he would joke, 'When I was struggling with cancer and not earning, the metal out of my legs got me a few bob as scrap.'

He was injured on the first day of the Grand National meeting and Tony Mullins stepped in to ride Dawn Run to victory in the Aintree Hurdle on National day and followed it up with victories in the Prix la Barka and the Grande Course de Haies at Auteuil. Dawn Run had travelled to Auteuil to attempt to become the first winner of the British Champion Hurdle to take the French equivalent, the Grande Course de Haies. The rumour was that she was going to be murdered at one of the early bends. As if to make a pre-emptive strike and ensure the best possible insurance policy, Tony Mullins took her past the stands on the long run to the first flight, leaving the other nine runners at least ten lengths behind. From then on it seemed as if the only real danger was a fall and she went on to easily justify her status as 6–5 favourite.

An incident in South Africa provided a good reason to take the threat seriously. In June 1966 Sea Cottage, who was hotly fancied to win the upcoming July Handicap in Durban, was shot and wounded in the leg by a gunman who was subsequently convicted for his crime. Astonishingly, the horse managed to recover in time for the race – though the fairytale result that everyone longed for did not materialise, as Sea Cottage only finished fourth.

The following season Dawn Run went chasing, winning her opening race at Navan. An injury relegated her to the sidelines for the rest of the season, but with Tony Mullins still in the saddle she won chases at Punchestown and Leopardstown in December 1985.

Run for Home

Controversy raged before the Gold Cup following the owner's decision to sack Tony Mullins, the son of her trainer Paddy, as Dawn Run's jockey after he was unseated by the horse at Cheltenham in the pre-Gold Cup race in January 1986. O'Neill was booked in his place – though Jonjo subsequently admitted that the horse ran more sweetly for Tony than for him.

In racing, success and defeat are always shared. Paddy Mullins was a huge part of Dawn Run's success. His first winner as a trainer was Dress Parade at Fairyhouse in 1953. In the early '60s he won 12 races with Height O'Fashion, but he lost the mare after a disagreement with the owner. From his base in Doninga he became Ireland's most successful national hunt trainer in the 1980s. One year he was champion trainer while his sons, Tony and Willie, were champion professional and amateur jockeys respectively.

Jonjo went over to school Dawn Run at Gowran Park but was dismayed by her jumping. The legacy of jumping hurdles for so long was that she was struggling over the big fences – to the extent that Jonjo said she 'couldn't jump a twig'! Asked about her chances of winning the Gold Cup, Jonjo replied that she shouldn't even have been entered.

As the other designated pre-Cheltenham races were lost to the weather, it was decided to take her to Punchestown for further schooling with a stablemate – to consider the tactics. Dawn Run did not perform well when trailing the other horse but leaped out of her skin when ahead. The message was clear: if the Gold Cup was to be won, it would have to be won from the front.

Danny Blanchflower once said, 'The business of luck is all part of our tactics. Irish luck is a highly specialised art that our people have cultivated for many generations. It needs an understanding of the little folk and it's an instinct for being in the right place at the right time.' Before the Gold Cup, Jonjo, resting on a bedrock of intimate knowledge, had decided that he needed to get to the inside at the start to keep an eye on the other front runners. When he couldn't get there, he cleverly let Dawn Run stand side on across the starting tape, telling the starter that he couldn't get out and that he would have to send the other horses back. The starter agreed, and as the other horses retreated, Jonjo stole into the inside.

Cheltenham's final furlong is a place of truth. Superior stamina at the end of the race paved the way for Dawn Run to beat Wayward Lad, lowering The Dikler's 1973 Gold Cup record by almost two seconds in the process. Dawn Run (15–8f) had an epic tussle for the lead with Run And

Skip. Both looked beaten at the last fence, which Wayward Lad (8–1) jumped slightly in front of Forgive 'N' Forget (7–2, third). Wayward Lad's string of defeats at Cheltenham looked destined to become mere bad memories, but then he started to tire and edged to his left up the final hill. Dawn Run, answering questions that others would rather were not asked, dragged up some hidden reserves of energy and, ridden with great determination by Jonjo, caught the fading Wayward Lad (on which Jonjo had taken third place in the Gold Cup of 1983) in the last 100 yards, beating him by a length.

Kerstin and Glencarraig Lady were the only other mares to have won the Gold Cup since the war. Incredibly, Dawn Run did so with the experience of only four steeplechases behind her.

Every facet of Dawn Run's race brought back memories of the glory days of Arkle. Indeed, scenes reminiscent of the Arkle era greeted Dawn Run's triumph before a crowd of 42,000 as she clipped 1.9 seconds off the record time for the three miles, two furlongs and 22 fences of steeplechasing's ultimate test.

Jonjo O'Neill displayed his sportsmanship immediately after the race when he grabbed Tony Mullins, hoisted the younger man on his shoulders and carried him to the presentation area.

Sweet Dreams Are Made of This

Shortly afterwards a special challenge race was arranged for £25,000 between Dawn Run and the two-mile champion chaser Buck House at Punchestown, which she won comfortably. Buck House, owned by Seamus Purcell, trained by Michael Mouse Morris and ridden by Tommy Carmody, had won the Queen Mother Champion Chase that year.

Against her trainer's wishes, Dawn Run was then taken to France to compete in the Grande Course de Haies at Auteuil, where she was ridden by the veteran French jockey Michel Chirol. At one fence she somersaulted and broke her neck in two places, dying instantly.

After winning 885 races in Britain, Jonjo retired as a jockey in April 1986 and switched to a career in training, where he has had success on the flat – his Gipsy Fiddler won the Windsor Castle Stakes at Royal Ascot in 1990 – and over fences. He returned to the winners' enclosure at the Cheltenham Festival in 1991 with Danny Connors, claiming the Coral Golden Hurdle Final. Like Bob Champion in the pantheon of all-time greats, Jonjo's courage not only served him well on a horse but also saw him fight cancer and win.

Dawn Run's legacy is a glorious tapestry of memories, but there remains a deep, gnawing feeling of regret that this horse that had evolved so quickly in the white heat of Cheltenham into a national hero had stood on the verge of further greatness, only for her mission to be sabotaged by tragedy.

During festival week in 1996, for once the eyes of the world were not on Cheltenham but on a small town in Scotland as Thomas Hamilton put Dunblane on the map in the most grisly way imaginable. If nothing else, it helped to put the word 'tragedy' into perspective.

History never stops, but racing enthusiasts are always happy to bask in the glories of yesteryear. Tradition is an essential ingredient of the Cheltenham Festival's sporting dish. Who will ever forget Norton's Coin, who won the Gold Cup in 1990 at 100–1, trained by Welsh dairy farmer Sirrell Griffiths, or Michael Dickinson, who saddled the first five in 1983? For many, though, an abiding memory of Cheltenham will always be Jonjo O'Neill with his arm raised aloft in triumph after conjuring a performance of exceptional class and turning defeat into victory. Ted Walsh is one of those people.

I have to be honest and say that the wins I had myself are the races that stand out most in my memory – though not in anyone else's! I think Arkle probably spoiled us by winning the Gold Cup three years in a row, because after that Irish Gold Cup winners were not that common. As a kid I remember a lot of stories about his great win over Mill House. I was too young to appreciate L'Escargot's win but Captain Christy's victory really got to me, especially because of Pat Taaffe's involvement, and that's one that certainly stands out. All the Irish Gold Cup wins since I remember fondly, like Imperial Call's victory. Other than that, I really got a great kick out of Monksfield's victories.

Probably the one that stands out the most, though, is Dawn Run's great win with Jonjo. I think it was because there was so much speculation before the race about who was going to ride her. She went to Cheltenham as a sort of novice and Paddy Mullins did a great job to get her there. She looked beaten, well and truly stuffed, when she got to the last. If she'd fallen then, people would have said she would have been third or fourth. Somehow she made a renewed effort. The fact that Jonjo had just come back from breaks and everything else made it all the greater for him. Jonjo is a north Cork man like myself. I rode my last winner, Attitude Adjuster, that day in the first race, so I was in great form. It's a day I'll never forget. If ever I hear replays of Dessie Scahill's commentary of the Dawn Run race, the feeling of the moment comes back to me. It brings me out in goosepimples. I was only sorry Dessie wasn't old enough to have commentated on Arkle's great win because of the giz he would have put into it.

SEVEN

The People's Champion

'Racing is the best fun you can have with your clothes on.'
ANDY ORKNEY

In the womb of racing history, from the most improbable of impregnations, a star was born. The farmyard at the end of a small and winding road in Aughabeg, County Carlow, appears like a haven, a hideaway even for a larger-than-life super-hero. Not that Danoli deliberately keeps a low profile. The mantle of celebrity fits him like a glove. He has starred in a car advert: 'In a perfect world we'd all travel as sweetly as Danoli.' In 1997 he featured in a Eurovision song contest postcard sequence. The previous year he had literally left his mark when making a guest appearance opposite Gay Byrne on *The Late, Late Show*.

The picturesque setting of his home beneath the snow-splattered Blackstairs Mountains belies its elevated status in the racing world. The yard is a mirror to its own reality: a fledgling stables slowly shaking off its former existence as a humble dairy farm. It has stopped drizzling and there is a faint aroma of moss from the unsown earth. The music of spring can be heard in the raindrops falling from leaf to leaf and from the leaves to the ground, as if there was no winter, as if winter had never been. In the distance the miracle of new life is evident in the faint bleating of a new-born lamb. The birth is a language of hope, lyrical yet maddeningly inarticulate, alive to the resonances of everyday life. In this moment of mystery and revelation, I marvel at the beauty which surrounds me in this land of gentle mists, where hurry is an alien concept and the ordinary kisses the extraordinary.

On arrival I am ushered into a room that is a shrine to Ireland's most famous horse. Photographs of Charlie Swan victorious in the SunAlliance at Cheltenham and Tommy Treacy winning Ireland's answer to the Gold Cup, the Hennessy Cognac Gold Cup, claim pride of place. If Paul McGuinness is the fifth member of U2, Danoli is the fifth member of the Foley family.

I am bombarded with hospitality from Tom Foley's wife Goretti. Tea is offered with Mrs Doyle-style enthusiasm. I understand immediately why, apart from a win in Cheltenham, what Tom likes most in life is a quiet evening with his family. He muses that the only gap in the wall is a photo of Danoli winning the Gold Cup. He is a long way from what Brendan Behan memorably described as the 'horse-arse Anglo-Irish' from Kildare and Meath. Intelligent, reflective and perpetually engaged, he speaks with shiny-eyed enthusiasm. Horses, and Danoli in particular, it seems, are not part of his life; they *are* his life.

In 1586 Sir Philip Sidney – wit, scholar, poet courtier, *preux chevalier* of the Elizabethan Age – was mortally wounded on the battlefield of Zutphen. As he lay dying, he handed his water bottle to a dying private soldier, saying, 'Thy necessity is yet greater than mine.' This is the type of heroic gesture one visualises Foley making for his horse. The images of Danoli's victories are pinned hard to the wallpaper of his trainer's brain.

Despite competing in the sport of kings, he has as much time for the 'small man and woman' as he does for merchant princes. Foley is utterly without artifice, very much from the 'what you see is what you get' school. The half-open newspaper contains a splendid photo of David Beckham. It is difficult to imagine a greater contrast to the Manchester United star than Foley, especially if the story from the World Cup in 1998 is true – that the real reason Posh Spice was allowed to visit him for 'morale purposes' was not because he was upset about being dropped for England's opening match but because he had missed the Armani summer sale in Bond Street!

Image, which is neither crucial nor irrelevant, depends largely upon winning. Foley has won and lost, usually heroically. He was not in the least phased when *The Times* said of him, 'He has an accent that causes cultivated Home Counties voices to ask if they are listening to Urdu.'

A Different Corner

Danoli's triumphs warmed his supporters' hearts. But the style in which they were achieved captured the public imagination and brought out a sense of national identity. Such victories are, of course, not confined to racing. No sociologist can ignore the power of Gaelic games to harness the communal values of loyalty, self-discipline and sacrifice – and all for the glory of the parish. They epitomise the importance of respect for place, memorably captured in Anthony Daly, the captain of the Clare hurling team, and his victory speech in 1995 after the Banner County had emerged from decades in the wilderness to claim the Munster title: 'We are no longer the Whipping Boys of Munster.'

Foley grew up in an era when Michael O'Hehir was at the height of his extraordinary career, in the days of wet batteries and communal radios. For hundreds of thousands of Irish people he was the only mediator. A phenomenon never to be emulated, he alone had the power to bring Gaelic games to the people. And he did.

Foley's late mother won a place in Carlow's Hall of Fame for her exploits in camoige. A former player himself, he is imbued with the ethos of Gaelic games. At grass-roots level they are based far more on giving than taking, though whether time and the corporate boxes in Croke Park will sustain that remains open to question. They are rooted in a sense of community which enables so many to give so much for, in purely material terms, so little.

Most of Foley's life has been spent in farming. In a classic mid-life taking of stock, he decided a change of career was needed.

> We gave up farming and started in racing because we couldn't make any money in farming! We couldn't possibly do any worse than we were. My mother often told me about uncles who were very tied up in horses, so I must have picked it up from them.
>
> I started off with a horse for Paudge Gill, Rua Batrick, and she won a nice race for me and from then on, thank God, we never looked back. It took about two years for us to establish ourselves. The pity of it was that any horse that was promising was always sold. Danoli wasn't, and that made a big difference.

Son of a Preacherman

'The proudest moment of my life' is the phrase used by Foley to describe Danoli's spectacular Cheltenham win in 1994. When Foley talks about the horse he trains, it is evident that his passion for Danoli knows no limits. When did this love affair begin?

> I got him as a three-year-old because I liked the look of him. He was a nice, relaxed horse and like every really good horse he had the head of a champion. The following June we brought him to his first race, a bumper at Naas. We knew before that race we had a goodish horse and were all set to back him, but when we saw the calibre of the other horses we got cold feet and he ran without any of our money on him.

Danoli won at 16–1!

The DNA cocktail that is Danoli's pedigree is not all that impressive. The son of The Parson, he was born in Willie Austin's yard in Cloughjordan, County Tipperary. His mother, Blaze Gold, won twice over hurdles and once at a point-to-point. Two of his half-brothers, Barronstown Boy and Creative Blaze, won over hurdles.

> I knew then this was the sort of horse you only dream about getting. We ran him after that in a number of smaller races but it was not until Christmas '93, when he won the Irish Champion Hurdle, that the racing public in Ireland saw what an outstanding horse he was. After Cheltenham the whole racing world could see what a great horse he was. Danoli was rightly considered to be the Irish banker of that Cheltenham and I was delighted that he repaid the loyalty of the Irish racing fans.
>
> I will never, ever forget the unbelievable reception he got after winning the race. It was not that people made a lot of money out of him because his odds were so poor, but it seemed to 'make' the meeting, especially for the Irish. We get loads of people visiting us, especially from England, just to see Danoli. He has put Carlow on the map. More prayers have been said over him than you would hear in any church.
>
> There was a charity auction not too long ago when Danoli's shoes were up for sale side by side with Michael Flatley's dancing shoes. I think some people billed it as the clash of the People's Champion versus the Lord of the Dance. When the hammer fell, the score was horse £1,000, dancer £800. But you know what the best part was? Flatley's shoes were nearly new and Danoli's were worn out!

Cheltenham was followed by another great victory at Aintree. However, Danoli's Midas touch would temporarily desert him when he lost at Leopardstown at the Christmas meeting in 1994.

> I didn't want to run him in that race because in my heart of hearts I knew that he wasn't just right, but I found it hard to get through to the vet that there was a problem, even though he had been coughing. The tests said he was fine but I knew different. In the end, the only reason we let Danoli run in that race is that people wanted him to run. It was a mistake and one that I will never repeat. What people probably don't realise is that Leopardstown is an unlucky ground for him. It was then the only racecourse in Ireland where Danoli had been beaten.

The Champion Hurdle at Cheltenham was set to be Danoli's greatest triumph, but the fairytale finish that all Ireland was hoping for did not materialise when, shackled by the chains of expectation, Danoli came third. With the benefit of hindsight, why did he lose?

> Because of the bad weather he hadn't run for three months before the Champion Hurdle. The horse was very anxious before the race because of his lay-off and got very worked up again in the parade. We had to try and simmer him down, which is not good preparation for such a big race and a class field.
>
> He made a bad mistake at the third last. I always like to see a horse getting a good straight run. But Danoli almost came to the ground – his head hit the ground. People say we wouldn't have won anyway. Maybe not, but he battled back bravely and finished third. While it was disappointing to lose, people had to remember he had at that point run 14 times, winning ten, coming second twice and coming third twice.

Panic

Normal service was resumed a month later when the horse with a wonderful heart had his second consecutive victory at Aintree. His resolve was evident to all and sundry. For Foley, though, there was a heart-stopping moment immediately after the race when he noticed that Danoli had sustained a serious injury during the race but had continued and held out against the odds, surely one of the finest rearguard actions in the long history of the sport.

> I saw straightaway that he was in trouble. The ground was firm – not that we minded firm ground – and the worst ground was by the rails. I said that to Charlie [Swan] and told him to come out maybe three yards from the rails. Charlie kept the horse on the best of ground but still we ended up getting hurt. Where it happened we don't know.
>
> I couldn't wait to get him out of the winning enclosure and get his shoes off so that I could see what was wrong with him. I was terrified that he had broken down. I rushed out of the parade ring and went up to take off the boot. His tendon couldn't have been better but you could see the joint swelling up. It was coming up as quick as could be and he was trembling something shocking. It was

hard to believe the pain he was in. They gave him an injection there to kill the pain – you couldn't give them enough credit for the way they did it. They bandaged him up and did a great job on him.

We had to wait until the racing was over until we could get to the veterinary clinic with him. But the minute the racing was over there were two policemen there on motorbikes and I can tell you they did some job. All traffic in every street was stopped and we got a clean drive through. Not one second was lost. I still can't believe it, the way they did that.

It was the very same as when the President of America was in Ireland. It wouldn't have happened here, though, for Danoli, and there is no point in saying otherwise. If I was to ask for the same thing here it would be to Mountjoy jail they would send me!

How was his blood pressure at the time?

It was pretty high! The way I looked at it was that even though they didn't know the horse or anything, watching them dealing with him gave me a lot of satisfaction. Had we been driving and getting stuck in traffic and losing time I would really have been wired up, but everything that could possibly have been done for him was being done.

When the X-rays showed the damage I was actually relieved, because although things were serious, it was not fatal. Then I had the fear of how he would react to having the pins in his leg. Vets are like doctors – they'll never give you a definite answer and they'll tell you all the things that can go wrong, so they were not a lot of assistance in helping us figure out if he would race again.

Danoli was in the hospital over there for two months. The vets looked after him better than any human being could have been looked after. Chris [the vet] rang us every second day to give us a run-down of what was happening. He never gave us a promise that he would come back racing. It was hard to get back and get going afterwards.

There's the risk of arthritis but you'll always have that, even when a horse enjoys perfect health. Our hope then was to get him back into shape and hurdle him for another season if we could and take it from there.

A small scar is the only visible sign of surgery, though Jenny Pitman's comment on Gold Cup winner Burrough Hill Lad could equally apply to

Danoli: 'He's had more operations than Joan Collins – and maybe more men working on him!'

> A few white hairs down alongside the joint and a little piece of swelling at the joint where the actual fracture was are the only signs left of what happened in Aintree. You'd have to be looking very hard to see the scars. It was very well done. You wouldn't have to be looking very hard to see the lump that is on the joint where it happened, but they claim that won't do him any harm. They claim that if anything it could be an advantage, as it will strengthen the bone.

Danoli's injury was not the only disappointment that befell Foley that year.

> It's a long ladder and you go up one step at a time, and it's definitely hard to go up that one step. Yet you can fall from whatever height you're up to to the very bottom in the one go.
>
> I had another great horse that year called Moon Man, who had shown great promise in his few races. I rated him very highly and I was looking forward to the Irish Champion Hurdle with him. But he went to race in Navan and broke his leg and had to be put down. That put the finishing touches to the year for us. I was hoping he would have achieved very much the same as Danoli and I was laying out the same plan for both. He'd have achieved very much the same.

Didn't the twin disappointments make him despair?

> It doesn't encourage you to keep going. When you are out racing and you are meeting people, everybody wants to ask you about your good horses. It's terribly disheartening when anything happens to them. To have two great horses and to have one killed and the other laid up is heartbreaking. The evening after Navan I just wished someone would come and take all the horses away. When I got back I was hoping all the stables would have been cleared. That Monday morning, though, I just got on with it.

A Leap of Faith

After he had enthralled the racing public for three years, the decision was taken to switch Danoli to the fences. The beginning of this career change took place in October 1996 at Ger Hourigan's schooling grounds. Three times Danoli effortlessly popped a set of three fences. For his anxious trainer, it was crucial that the first day at school was behind closed doors. Foley blends passion with perception, an adamant will to win with astute management.

> It was very important to get it just right. Danoli had never been brought up and showed a fence before. The ground hadn't been right up to then and we just hung on. When he schools, I always want him to relax and really concentrate on what he's doing. He has a tendency to get all excited even when there's only a handful of people around him. They just get to him. I just wanted him to walk up to a fence, look at it, go back and pop it and then think about what he'd done without disruption.
>
> I never had any doubts that he would make it over fences. Actually, I always felt he'd be a lot better over fences than he was over hurdles. When he first started hurdling, it was obvious that he had a great eye. He just measured them and never, ever missed one at home. He wasn't always so careful on the track because he sometimes looked around a bit. If I had any fear it was that he might overjump. That's one of the reasons why I didn't want to take unnecessary risks in his preparation.
>
> I suppose I took a few chances with him over hurdles but I was determined to wait until I got the right ground. That meant a change of heart for me because I had to be patient and sit back till I was sure everything was right. I wanted to be sure he had soft ground to land on.
>
> The funny thing was, I was happier with him in the autumn of 1996 than I had been the previous 12 months – even though he wasn't in as good a shape. The previous year he had begun the season looking ready before we even started working with him. When we started in 1996–97, though, he looked only three-quarters right. We had him in from the end of July and he did a lot of work for us. He looked like a Charolais bull, in perfect condition and very strong. I knew that we'd have a good idea of his ability as a chaser.

There was no masterplan as such. The priority was to get as much practice over fences as possible for the novice. Nowhere does the old adage that there is no substitute for experience apply more than in jumping over fences. Yet Foley was determined not to run before he could walk.

> My plan was to take it one race at a time. If he won one, then the idea was to think about moving up a step, but not till then.

Danoli's debut over fences came at Clonmel on Friday, 1 November. The meet drew a huge crowd and the atmosphere was charged with emotion. Immediately tongues started wagging about Danoli's clash with his old rival Dorans Pride in the Chiquita Drinmore Chase at Fairyhouse on 1 December. Yet many people were not convinced. So what was Foley's verdict?

> I was pleased with the performance and the win but I didn't get carried away. I knew much bigger tests lay ahead. Clonmel was a good start but nothing more.

A £7,000 race at Naas, the 2.30 Quinns of Naas Novices' Chase, was the setting for Danoli's second outing over fences on 9 November. The 2–7 favourite won, but most fans went away feeling that more questions had been raised than answered. Danoli had seemed to be struggling, especially at the second-last fence home. Tommy Treacy had then raised the horse into top gear and switched him to the far side on the approach to the final obstacle, and he had stayed on well to beat long-time leader Crossfarnogue on the run-in.

> We wanted to let him see his fences and at least he only made the one mistake, at the fifth from home. It was nice to see him come from a good bit back and still win.

Every time Danoli runs at Cheltenham, his trainer feels the weight of being Irish, of being the representative of the hopes and dreams of the Irish nation. A bad fall on live television shook the nation's faith in the horse but Danoli hysteria was restored with an emphatic win in the Hennessy Cognac Gold Cup, burying a class field in a race which showcased Foley's tactical nous as well as Danoli's physical conditioning. True to form, Ted Walsh did not mince his words about the fickleness of Irish punters: 'Every bastard in the country was knocking him the last day.'

Few events have the power to send a tingle down the spine of racing fans like an Irish Gold Cup winner being led into the Cheltenham winners' enclosure. In 1997 Danoli had to make do with the small lawn to its right. His body language said it all. His head was buried sadly in his chest, the muck from where he had hit the turf at the second last like a war wound on his shoulder, specks of blood dripping from his foot. Like Imperial Call he had started promisingly, but the ground had suited neither of them and neither had made it to the finish. The following year injury deprived both of them of the chance to redeem themselves, giving the festival something of a Hamlet-less feel for the Irish despite the best efforts of Dorans Pride. Injury would deprive Danoli of another crack at Cheltenham in 1999.

Dressed for the Occasion

Standing proudly in his stable, Danoli seems to be dressed up for visitors because he is wearing a brand new 'jacket'. When I remark on his sartorial elegance, I stumble on to an insight into the people's champion.

> They like being warm. It's important to have just one jacket or rug rather than two because one slips one way and one another. A good one will generally stay in the one place. He looks after his fairly well. There are other horses here and they'd have their jackets ruined by the next day. They'd turn around and bite them or something. He's a good horse and looks after his very well.

Does this suggest Danoli is a very intelligent horse?

> Yes, I always put him down as being as smart as an awful lot of people. Sometimes Goretti shows him his photo in the paper and he whines back at her.
> He always knew what he wanted to do and when something went wrong he wasn't too happy afterwards. When he got beat you wouldn't have to go down and find out if he had lost. The horse would let you know himself.

So can Foley communicate with his most famous horse like a latter-day Dr Dolittle?

> Yeah. You know him very well and you know his moods. One day we were asked to bring him to Gowran Park and parade him around. We paraded him in the ring, then brought him back to the stable. He was like a bold child. He sulked in the corner because he wasn't getting out to race that day. He wouldn't do anything because he just sulked.

Search for the Hero Inside Yourself

In the unforgiving world of boxing, there is a term of endearment for quitters. A fighter who turns his back in the heat of combat is labelled a dog. And, as the old sages will say, when the going gets tough, the dog will out. Even the most cynical could never describe Danoli as a dog.

As the late Enoch Powell famously observed of politicians, so one might say of racehorses: every career is bound to end in failure, or, if not failure, at least not complete satisfaction. Mainly because of injury, Danoli has not savoured complete satisfaction.

Yet when he performs well, *do lioigh an laoch san uile dhuine* (the hero in all of us is exulted). From the dawn of time, identification with heroes has been an integral part of the human condition. Great sporting performances have always grabbed the imagination of people of all ages as they fantasise about emulating the glorious feats of their heroes. Thanks in no small part to television, sports heroes now occupy an even larger part of the imagination than in earlier generations. The fear that we had lost Danoli to injury generated a sense of loss which far exceeded anything that would have been felt for any politician or media personality. Even the most casual fans took vicarious pride in the horse's style, craft, courage and character that fired the imagination.

A few flaws have been revealed along the way, notably in undignified falls. But perhaps this adds to rather than detracts from Danoli's popularity. George Michael, in a moment of exceptional, perhaps surprising, psychological insight, once said that a star is not a person who has a little bit extra but someone who has a little bit missing. It is significant that Ireland's favourite sporting hero over the last generation has been Paul McGrath, a footballer of sublime skill and a wonderful human being – with a few blemishes.

Danoli's story would have made Aristotle leap about in his sandals, it is such a brilliant illustration of the classic precepts of tragedy: the hero with his flaw and the audience torn between awe and pity. He has become Ireland's favourite equine hero because in some ways he is a mirror of our inner selves – but for that very reason the odd vulture has tried nailing him like they have nailed all others.

Foley's other horses have included Go Now, who announced his arrival on the scene with a 25-lengths win over heavy ground at Clonmel in March 1996 and confirmed that promise with success over hurdles the following October. However, Foley's life as a trainer can be defined in terms of two periods of time: BD and AD (Before Danoli and After Danoli). With Danoli he was able to become a David in the world of racing Goliaths. Even as the horse's achievements are still fresh for the savouring, Foley is speaking wistfully of his appetite for greater glory. Who was it that said ambition is a vicious mistress?

> From the day he won his first race the horse was never, ever for sale. I remember after he won Cheltenham I was asked whether he was for sale. I said no, a million pounds wouldn't buy him. I apologised to Danny [Danny O'Neill, Danoli's owner; Danoli's name is an amalgam of Dan O'Neill and his daughter Olivia] afterwards, saying it wasn't up to me to say, but he agreed with me!

Foley is not worried about people being where they should not be unless it means they are getting too close to the horse. Witness the speed with which Danoli was taken out of the parade ring after his Hennessy triumph. But he admits that having so many fans is not necessarily a bad thing.

> It's all part of the package. Danoli has the following and it's worse to try stopping it. Racing needs heroes who can ensure the sport's continued popularity. If these are people Danoli has brought into the sport, then well and good.

Racing already owes a great deal to the horse and trainer who injected an exhilarating new dimension into the sport. Few could then have anticipated that the excitement Danoli's Cheltenham win generated would be sustained, if not surpassed, in subsequent years in a series of contests marked not only by intense emotion but by high tension, pulsating finishes, inspirational performances and, above all, bravery.

Foley's relatively small stable in Banglestown in Carlow is a million miles away from the stereotype of the sport of kings and is a confirmation of the adage that small is beautiful. Danoli is on a pedestal with all of Ireland's racing greats and has earned the nickname 'the people's champion'. Why have the public taken him to their hearts?

> I think he's done a lot for racing and obviously he's done a huge amount for me. Journalists are always sticking microphones in front of me. There are many times I wish they'd just leave me alone, but it's much better to have one star in the stable than 100 also-rans. I do loads of talking but it's Danoli who answers the questions. The horse runs his heart out every time. No matter what the odds are, he's never afraid to try. He's such a great, gutsy horse, he would run his heart out with just three legs!

EIGHT

Shane's World

'*What kind of life would it be if I let myself go and become just a depressed hulk in a wheelchair? All of this takes effort on my part, because it's still very difficult to accept the turn my life has taken, simply because of one unlucky moment.*'

CHRISTOPHER REEVE

Sport is agony and ecstasy. It does not lend itself to grey areas. A number of sports personalities have experienced at first hand the 'slings and arrows of outrageous fortune' and discovered just how quickly glory becomes anguish. Fate is not kind. Take the case of former Arsenal, Liverpool and England star Ray Kennedy. He played a prominent part in Arsenal's first double in 1971, scoring 26 goals that season. Now, because of Parkinson's Disease, bliss for him is the 45 minutes' relief he gets from taking three pills. He is forced to take his medication to control his shaking every 90 minutes, though the side-effect is hallucinations. From time to time this necessitates a stay in a psychiatric hospital. Given his condition, it is unsafe for him to drive, which means that he must spend £12 on a round trip to pick up a prescription – a major expense for a man who lives alone in Newcastle on his pension from football and a meagre £60 a week disability allowance.

Most tragic of all is the story of Justin Fashanu. Following early success at the age of 17 when he made the Norwich City first team and the England Under-21s, he scored a stunning goal which deservedly won BBC's Goal of the Season award and as a consequence he featured prominently in the opening credits of *Match of the Day*. However, he lost the plot when he became obsessed with money, clothes, cars and Christianity. Brother of the much less talented but more successful John, Justin was also the first football star publicly to admit his homosexuality. In his own words, he 'was shot down in flames' by his footballing fraternity. After being implicated in a sleaze scandal, he committed suicide on 2 May 1998.

Adversity is the true testing ground of heroic status, as only a true hero can smile through a veil of tears. After his horrific fall on Another Deadly at Fairyhouse on Easter Monday 1997, Shane Broderick proved to be such a person. The injury came just weeks after he had finished third in the Gold Cup, a convincing assertion of his right to be considered as one of the radiant stars in the equine firmament.

The Sound of Silence

For many, the memory of the day in Fairyhouse will be the profound silence which descended on the racecourse after the accident, broken only by the faint rustling of trees in a light breeze and a quiet chorus of gasps of horror. From initial dumb disbelief, feelings around Fairyhouse heightened, feeding on fresh emotions as wave after wave of punters heard the chilling news. The sheer volume of bereft men and women standing awkwardly was startling; the only thing stringing all of them together was the feeling of loss. Everyone wanted to do something. Anything. But all they could do was pray in the hope that it would make time run backwards and everything could be as it was before. News of Broderick's injury cut a swathe of desolation among racing fans everywhere. This is a side of racing that can only make you wince.

Shane's fall resulted in a severe spinal-cord injury and associated disability. Initially his days streaked past in a blur and he was unable to move, reliant on a life-support machine. But he steadily progressed in the National Rehabilitation Hospital from a revolving bed to a normal bed, and then to a wheelchair and daily physiotherapy. There were difficult times along the way, notably when he was weaned off the ventilator and had to breathe on his own, and his problems were compounded by a chest infection and a loss of appetite. Shane also suffered from depression. But as his breathing improved, so too did his voice, his strength and his mobility. Physiotherapy helped him to improve the movement in his shoulders and the upper part of his right arm. He had to get to know his body again.

Tender Hands

A milky fog has risen outside the National Rehabilitation Hospital in Dun Laoghaire. It barely comes to my knees, but it is so dense that it hides the terrain and it feels as if I am wading through a swamp. Inside is nothing like the ER scenario I had visualised. Rather than high-tech machines,

Shane's bed is surrounded by a bizarre amalgam of religious icons and racing magazines. There is evidence too of the deluge of letters he receives from every corner of Ireland and beyond.

There are no George Clooney types in evidence, just a handful of health-care professionals who radiate a sense of calm and warmth. Shane presents a brave face to the outside world, though the introvert in his personality is a strong suit. What is striking is the contrast between his language and his content: a cheerful voice relates a sad story of extreme pain. Any despair his story might generate is relieved by the spunk of the narrator. Nowhere is the truth of Hugh McIlvanney's observation more apparent: 'Sport, at its finest, is often poignant, if only because it is almost a caricature of the ephemerality of human achievements.'

There is also a deep gratitude that his brush with mortality did not deny him the opportunity to finish off important business. A contrast between Shane and the Busby Babes in 1958 springs to mind. Many of those who were left behind are left with a legacy of guilt. Over 40 years on, Eddie Colman's mother is still tortured by her refusal to let the former Manchester United star have a bike when he was a boy because of the dangers on the road, and by the fact that she had a cold and didn't let him kiss her goodbye before he left for Munich. The great Duncan Edwards's mother, Ann, is still haunted by all that was left unsaid between them. Although she thought there was no one in the world like him, she had never told him she loved him. Neither Shane nor his family is cluttered with any such baggage.

Shane is taking heart from some recent events in the racing world. His partner Dorans Pride was given only a 5 per cent chance of recovering from colic and did so, whilst jockeys Declan Murphy and Walter Swinburn were living proof that it was possible to recover from serious injury and return to a full and active life. In fact, so severe were Murphy's head injuries after his fall from Arcot at the final flight of the Crowther Homes Swinton Hurdle on 2 May 1994 that *The Racing Post* had the headline MURPHY KILLED IN HORROR FALL set up in case the worst happened. But miracles do happen. Murphy rallied while in intensive care in Walton Hospital and within a few days was back home in Newmarket. Declan's recovery caught the imagination of the racing public. He had his comeback ride in October 1995 on Jibereen in the annual Flat vs. Jump Jockeys Challenge at Chepstow, for which riders were allotted mounts through a pre-race ballot. Although he won, the gloss was taken off his victory by ungenerous innuendo that the balloting for the rides might have been rigged. A month later he announced his retirement.

Shane was also very grateful that the trust fund for his future care and treatment had been so well supported. The target of £1 million had seemed a little ambitious. Within a fortnight it was reported that at least £300,000 had been raised during the Galway races and within a year the fund topped the target of £1 million. In keeping with both his legendary generosity and his status as Irish jump racing's greatest patron, J.P. McManus was said to have been one of the first to contribute.

Shane seems to have coped remarkably well with his tragedy. Looks, of course, can be deceptive. A case in point is Walter Swinburn. After he won the 1981 Derby on Shergar at the age of 18, his charm and good looks earned him the nickname 'The Choirboy'. Yet the Golden Boy had the devil in his tail. The innocent façade masked a taste for activities not normally associated with choirboys which culminated in Walter assaulting the owner of Il Piccolo Mondo restaurant on Newmarket's High Street in January 1997 and trashing the establishment to the tune of £600, prompting Swinburn to realise that the end was nigh unless he again got teetotal, fit and slim. To his credit he did, and now the bubbles in his glass are more likely to be of water than champagne.

Shane tells a story of two halves: first, the glory days with Dorans Pride and Cheltenham, and then the dreadful, unimaginable climax to an impressive career. Indeed, the evocation of the happier times that went before is so vivid that the disaster that followed seems all the more grotesque. Yet there is a vulnerability about him, a sadness that clings to him and a sense that his mind often travels in a land uninhabited by the rest of us. It is not difficult to imagine voices which run through his head like silver bullets, screaming memories into the caverns of his mind. Like a wasps' nest, he is glued by something so powerful that it withstands the storms that whirl outside. But, like the nest, if anybody probes too closely, the memories fly out and sting him: regrets, sadness and, above all, a sense of overwhelming loss.

Racing had been Shane's life since he had won the Dingle Derby as a schoolboy. However, it was his hugely successful partnership with Dorans Pride which catapulted him into the limelight and carved out lasting memories. In 1995 Dorans Pride gave Shane his first taste of that unique mixture of sweat and slap that constitutes the winners' enclosure at Cheltenham. Although a solitary victory cannot herald a new dawn, it looked on this evidence as if he was on the threshold of a glittering career, particularly bearing in mind the ruthless manner in which he slayed all-comers at the start of his new 'reign'. He deserved all the plaudits heaped upon him following a performance as captivating as the sport can offer. Opposing him in top form was like trying to defy a succession of breaking waves. Whenever danger lurked, he responded like a wounded lion.

He had learned that the top jockey's life mixes glamour with wet early mornings, days of being black and blue with bruises, frequent visits to the physiotherapist, long hours driving up and down inhospitable roads, unending tedium in the sauna and, worst of all, days when the thrill of victory yields to the sour taste of a bad fall and a mouthful of turf. The world of the jockey depends on minutiae: split-second decisions that mean the difference between winning and losing, landing on your feet or on your head.

A Question of Sport

Sky 'expert' and former jockey Gee Armytage, twice a winner at Cheltenham in 1987, showed her lack of general sporting knowledge when she asked Bryan Robson which sport he was involved in during an appearance on the quiz show *Sporting Triangles*. Shane is not of that ilk and speaks knowledgeably about other sports, hurling in particular, although it is only when the talk turns to Cheltenham that our conversation really takes off.

> It was great to even be in Cheltenham, never mind ride a winner there. It's great to be on top of the hill looking backwards. On the telly Cheltenham looks very big but in fact it is quite tight. You're nearly always on the turn and in a big field it can be tricky.

He describes the festival as a place where there is relatively little place for luck. Tactics count, but only rarely do they manage to turn a race more than talent or temperament. He describes the final hill as one of the most revealing tests of courage and determination ever devised for horse or jockey. So what does it feel like to have your first win at Cheltenham?

> It's hard to put it into words. A lot has happened since. Cantering back past the stands after a race is a great feeling. Everyone else is finished. It's all over for them, but it's not for you. Everyone is looking at you. People who see me now will say I was very unlucky, but I was very, very lucky to win a race at Cheltenham. Nobody can ever take away that feeling or that memory from me.

Lying in bed, there is a lot of time, too much time, for reflecting on what might have been. Norman Williamson once claimed that to win a Gold Cup you have to have courage from the horse, judgement from the jockey and determination from both. Shane and Dorans Pride met those criteria perfectly.

Pride without Prejudice

From his base in Patrickswell in Limerick, Michael Hourigan (himself a former jockey, having won nine races on the flat before making the move to the jumps) had nurtured the burgeoning talents of Adrian Maguire and Timmy Murphy before Broderick. A progressive man, one of the few Irish trainers to have his own horse swimming-pool, he bought Dorans Pride – or Padjo, as he is affectionately known – as a two-year-old for £6,000. The horse won a point-to-point as a four-year-old before opening his racecourse account in a bumper in Ballinrobe. Hourigan sold him on to Tom Doran, a London-based builder and a native of Bangor Erris, for £15,000.

One of a family of 14, Doran left his local tech at an early age. Initially he worked with Dublin-based builder and fellow Mayo man, Bill Durkan. At the age of 19, Doran moved to London with practically no money in his pocket. Although he didn't find that the streets were paved with gold, he started his own building firm and soon left his mark, notably when laying the tracks for the Channel tunnel. As his business flourished, Doran started to look for other mountains to climb. Dorans Town Lad was his first horse and was good enough to travel to Cheltenham, where he finished a creditable fifth. Then came Dorans Pride.

This horse was made for Cheltenham. He was running a blinder when he fell at the last in the 1994 SunAlliance Hurdle. Nonetheless, there were valuable lessons to be learned from the first Cheltenham experience. There are tricks to be uncovered about handling the course, like how to manage the hurdle track. The trick is to avoid being caught on the inner at the top of the hill when the early leaders and pace-setters start to tire and press back. For this reason, the longest way round is sometimes the shortest way home.

Dorans Pride won the 1995 Stayers' Hurdle. The race was a real fable of Cheltenham, the equine version of David and Goliath. Racing down the hill, Dorans Pride tracked the leader Bokaro, with Halkopus in their slipstream. Bokaro was owned by Tony O'Reilly, president of the Heinz Corporation and one of Ireland's wealthiest men. Halkopus was owned by the very wealthy Greek-Cypriot Athos Chistodoulou – and Dorans Pride was owned by the builder from Mayo.

A horse requires class to win the Gold Cup but as important in a three-

and-a-quarter-mile race is the ability to stay. Dorans Pride has no stamina worries and came back from colic to run third in the Gold Cup in both 1997 and 1998.

Having missed out on Cheltenham in 1996 when recuperating from his operation, Dorans Pride returned to action with a vengeance the following season and enjoyed a successful novice-chasing campaign before taking his chance in the Gold Cup. The only fly in the ointment was that the horse lost a vital 11 days' work in the month before Cheltenham after taking a horrific fall at Thurles.

That seemed a bad memory when, thundering down the hill approaching the second last, Dorans Pride appeared the most probable winner of the blue-riband event of steeplechasing, but he couldn't manage to stay with the renewed burst of pace Tony McCoy dug out from Mr Mulligan. Dorans Pride was just run out of it for second place by Barton Bank. For Shane it was an incredible achievement, particularly on the hard ground he hated – which had almost caused the horse to be pulled out of the race.

> He loved it there. Why wouldn't he? It's a brilliant venue. For a novice he didn't put a foot wrong. He was spot on, inch perfect all the way. The only pity was that there wasn't a bit of cut in the ground.
>
> It was an exhilarating experience. God, they went so fast! Every time you looked up you were on top of a fence. I swear I've been in cars that wouldn't go that fast. I thought we'd have got second but it wasn't to be. It was great to get even third, because it is the greatest race in the world.

Part of his incredible story can be attributed to vet Ned Gowing, who operated on Dorans Pride following his near-fatal bout of colic in the winter of 1996. Twice the vet took out his 'engine' and twice he put it back again, enabling the born-again horse to make a Lazarus-style comeback.

Hurdler on the Ditch

As he watched Dorans Pride take third place in the Gold Cup in 1998, Shane was not the only Irish jockey to miss out on the delights of Cheltenham because of premature retirement. Trevor Horgan, Francis Woods and Mark Dwyer also had similar misfortune. A car accident left Woods unable to lift his arm, and although Mark Dwyer won the Gold Cup twice, an elbow injury ended his career, leaving him unable to bend his arm fully.

Dwyer, though, achieved the distinction of being the first jockey and one of only two to ride an English-trained winner of the festival's bumper when he won on the Malcolm Jefferson-trained Dato Star in 1995. In 1999 Brendan Powell became the second jockey to break the Irish trainers' monopoly when he rode the Mark Pitman-trained 50–1 outsider Monsignor to win the bumper. Monsignor, though, is an Irish horse and is another product of Tom Costello, and Powell was one of the Irish jockeys who won all seven races on that day.

Dorans Pride's successes under Richard Dunwoody are carefully scrutinised and savoured, notably the Hennessy Cognac Gold Cup at Leopardstown in 1998, five weeks after arguably the most consistent national hunt performer of the 1990s had run a uniquely bad race to finish last of five at Naas. As a good judge of horseflesh, Shane's opinions and observations must be taken seriously.

> Winning the Stayers' Hurdle in 1995 and getting third place in the Gold Cup were two of the best moments of my life, but things change. When Dorans Pride runs now there is no one who wants him to win more than me. I have a great love for the horse and I expect him to win big races because I know how much ability he has.

Michael Hourigan was back in the winners' enclosure after the National Hunt Chase in 1999 with Deejaydee, with Tony Martin in the saddle. Historically, this race has been a minefield for gamblers, but Hourigan trained Deejaydee especially for this race, the horse having finished fourth as a maiden the previous year.

It was hoped that this victory would be an omen for Dorans Pride to finally win the Gold Cup, but he could only finish eighth after jumping upsides with Double Thriller for most of the race.

Superman

Shane and his mother, Mary, have taken comfort from a telegram of encouragement he received from former *Superman* actor Christopher Reeve. A keen horseman with a particular interest in Irish horses, Reeve was jumping on his horse Buck when suddenly the horse came to a dead stop. When Reeve went over he took the bridle, the bit, the reins, everything off the horse's face. He landed on his head because his hands were entangled in the bridle and he couldn't get an arm free to break his fall. His helmet prevented any brain damage, but the impact of the landing broke his first and second vertebrae. Like Shane, he is now hoping for great advances in medical research into the nervous system. Reeve dictated the telegram to Shane at his bedside. It reads:

Dear Shane,

I was very sorry to hear of your recent accident. I am sure that at the moment everything is very confusing and overwhelming. It certainly was for me . . . Most importantly I hope your family and friends are gathering round you. Their support is more important than any treatment. Even though you are probably experiencing moments of terrible anxiety and depression, I urge you not to lose hope because tremendous progress is being made in spinal-cord research and I'm absolutely convinced that neither of us will spend the rest of our lives in a wheelchair.

While the immediate situation is bleak, the future is not.

I send you my very best wishes.

Christopher Reeve

Shane produced more than his fair share of memorable victories and epic performances which ignited the imagination of racing fans. The craft and courage of this young man added another marvellous chapter to the already richly garlanded history of a sport that demands skill, speed, strength and character. The fervent hope is that he can continue to improve. With his trademark determination and staggering dignity, his progress to date offers an accurate portent of things to come.

NINE

Up Front

'Did you see me on the radio?'
DELIGHTED JOCKEY TONY DOBBIN TO HIS CHANGING-ROOM VALET
AFTER HIS FIRST CHELTENHAM WIN

Cheltenham can be the making of a young Irish jockey. In 1978, for example, 22-year-old Tommy Carmody really put himself on the map, riding a superb double on Mr Kildare and Hilly Way at the festival. This was in no small part responsible for his subsequent move to the prestigious Michael Dickinson's stable – the man who made the Gold Cup his own in 1983 by saddling the first five home, led by Bregawn.

The doyen of racing commentators, Peter O'Sullevan, has no doubts about the place of Irish jockeys at Cheltenham.

> Jockeys are a funny breed. They are very competitive, and one moment they are killing themselves to beat the other but the next they are the best of friends. I recall back in 1958, when I was ghosting Rae Johnstone's life story, he told me a nice story about his friendship with the great Jack Molony. Poor old Jack, who wasn't too hot at the reading stakes, would pass the paper which he had been studying earnestly to his neighbour in the Turkish baths, explaining that he had left his glasses with his clothes and asking, 'Would you ever tell me what it says here?' Rae was much too considerate to let on that Jack had been holding the paper upside down!
>
> Cheltenham to me shows the competitiveness and camaraderie of jockeys at their best. It's amazing to think of how Irish jockeys have dominated the festival, from Aubrey Brabazon to my old friend Pat Taaffe and, of course, the remarkable Jonjo O'Neill. In recent years, Irish jockeys have had something of a closed shop at Cheltenham between Charlie Swan, Richard Dunwoody, Norman Williamson, Adrian Maguire and the new kid on the block, Tony

McCoy – though soon Tony will probably be spoken of as a veteran. He's done so much, so quickly.

To win at Cheltenham you need brains. Some horses that have won there are a long way from the brightest. The brains have to come from the men on top. Those guys have plenty of them. They are not the sort of men to follow standards. They set them. They have given the festival a form of immortality.

King Richard

On 18 January 1964 Richard Dunwoody was born in the Royal Victoria Hospital in Belfast, weighing in at 7lb 2oz. Like Frankie Dettori, whose father, Gianfranco, was 13-times champion jockey in Italy, Dunwoody has an impressive pedigree. His father, George, was a successful amateur rider and trainer in Ireland. His mother Gillian also came from racing stock. Her father was the Epsom-based trainer Dick Thrale, who had been leading amateur during the 1920s. Then in 1930 at Lingfield, on Friday 13th, riding number 13 on the card and at the 13th fence, he suffered a terrible fall and badly fractured his skull. He remained unconscious for three weeks and his wedding to Leonora was postponed for six months. She too was a horsewoman of note with a wonderful eye for a horse and was a pioneer female bloodstock agent. She bought the 1959 Champion Hurdler Fare Time as a yearling.

On 4 May 1983 Richard Dunwoody rode his first winner in the promised land of national hunt racing: Game Trust, in a hunter chase at Cheltenham. An indication of his single-minded determination to be number one had come the previous year when he rode four winners at Hereford. He was travelling home with Brendan Powell, who enthusiastically remarked that the young Irishman must have been happy with his successes. Dunwoody's response said it all: 'I shouldn't have lost the last one.'

1990 saw Dunwoody capture the third of his 'big three': the Grand National in 1986 on West Tip (a race he also won in 1994 on Miinnehoma, owned by the *bête noire* of hamsters Freddie Starr), the Gold Cup in 1988 on Charter Party, and finally the Champion Hurdle on Kribensis. He became only the fourth jockey since the war to accomplish the triple crown, joining Freddie Winter, Willie Robinson and Bobby Beasley. It was as partner to Desert Orchid in two King George VI Chases (in 1989 and 1990) and an Irish National (in 1990) that Dunwoody really moved on to an élite plane. He would subsequently admit that the reception he received on the Irish-trained Montelado in the 1992 bumper had virtually surpassed his Gold Cup and Champion Hurdle triumphs.

In July 1993 Woody celebrated his championship (173 winners) with a large party at a restaurant near Oxford. As if to emphasise his Irish roots, the music was provided by the popular group from Tuam, the Saw Doctors.

The following year he was immersed in a tense and frenzied tussle with the young pretender Adrian Maguire for the title of champion jockey. He was taking no prisoners. As the contest between the two reached its climax in March, both men approached the second last in a Nottingham selling hurdle with the race between the two of them. As they approached the flight, Dunwoody swerved his mount Raggerty sharply left, almost forcing Maguire and Mr Genealogy off the course. It was out of character, but it did say something about his make-up. From his perspective, the end probably justified the means. Dunwoody won the duel with three to spare.

Top jockeys have to battle against the odds. Amateur Frank Wise wore an artificial leg when riding Alike to win the Irish Grand National at Fairyhouse. He had also lost the tops of three fingers from his right hand during the war. Some jockeys are bigger than the norm and have a perpetual struggle to make their weight. Richard Dunwoody is a case in point. As a consequence he is condemned to 'wasting' in the sauna, and for that reason he has been compared to Lester Piggott. What prompts a man to give up so much over such a long period? Lester was 56 when he won his 30th classic, making a mockery of Father Time's fabled sickle. Lester's daughter, Tracy, is ideally placed to describe her father's success and the make-up of a top jockey.

> I've no idea why he made the sacrifices. He's his own man. It's very difficult to describe why people put themselves through so much but I think it's been slightly exaggerated about his 'wasting away'. Yes, he definitely did have a problem keeping his weight down because he's one of the tallest jockeys, but as his body became used to that type of regime it wasn't too bad.
>
> He's a man who loves competition. You are on an animal, in a pack of other animals, with other men on the animals. The blood gets going, especially when there is a lot at stake. There's a lot of physical drive there. People love to win. I don't know anybody who doesn't like to win. I know I do. My father loves to win. He loves riding. He loves the horses and all the ingredients which accounted for his success. I think the main thing is absolute and utter

dedication. Any of the top jockeys today like Richard Dunwoody need that kind of dedication.

As Ronald Reagan said, 'It ain't easy, but it sure is simple.'

A Stable Environment

A man's size is sometimes in inverse proportion to his stature. Such a man is Adrian Maguire. He claims he became a jockey because 'I was too small to be a window-cleaner and too big to be a garden gnome'. His size, though, is to his advantage as a jockey. He has no need to get up to the bend-around contortions other rivals require. Born into a family of ten children in Kilmessan, County Meath, the son of a greenkeeper, like many jockeys he has been deprived of what some would call a 'normal' adolescence and education, though it does not seem to have done him any harm.

The sports star Maguire comes closest to is Martina Navratilova, because of her ferocious commitment. She often used the analogy of bacon and egg to describe the difference between involvement and commitment in sport – the hen is involved in the process through laying the egg, but the pig is totally committed. Commitment could have been Maguire's middle name. In 1994, his first season for David Nicholson, he travelled the Queen's highways and rode a record 915 mounts as part of his famous duel for the championship with Richard Dunwoody which went down to the very last fixture of the season at Market Rasen. Maguire's tally of 194 was the highest ever recorded by a jockey who did not win the title. The commitment is matched by ability, as is evident in David Nicholson's comment, 'I have only been in racing since 1945 but he's the best I've seen. That's not an accolade – it's the truth.'

Maguire's successes as a jockey came after the tragic death of his younger brother Vinny in a hit-and-run accident in Coachford, County Cork, in 1990. A promising rider, Vinny had been very close to his more famous brother. Adrian sensed Vinny's presence during his proudest moment.

Cheltenham is second to none. It's the Olympics of racing. Everything is geared to Cheltenham. If you are riding winners at Cheltenham, they are winners which will always be remembered.

I got my first race at the festival when Martin Pipe booked me to ride Omerta at 10 p.m. the night before the Kim Muir Chase. He had planned to use a French jockey but at the last minute he had to change his plans. The owners knew Homer Scott, who used to train the horse, and they rang him up looking for a jockey and I ended up falling in for the ride.

That was my first visit to Cheltenham. I had to ask directions to the weighing-room! I remember watching it on television as a young fella and I couldn't believe the size of the place – it was so big. You learn things quickly during your first race, like the fact that the course at Cheltenham is undulating. Most people thought Omerta was, I suppose, a 'has-been'. He had raced for a full year after being pulled up on his last outing. I knew, though, he was trained by Martin Pipe so I was certain he wouldn't be a bad horse. We took the lead at the second last and won by 12 lengths. The following month we won the Irish Grand National.

The 1992 Gold Cup held out the promise of glory for a horse with strong Irish connections. Paul Green and his two partners, Gordon Gray and Liam Marks, transferred one of Ireland's leading and most enigmatic chasing prospects, Carvill Hill, from Jim Dreaper to Martin Pipe. The fact that Pipe had transformed the fortunes of other fading stars like Beau Ranger and Omerta was probably the decisive factor in this decision. Pipe was unable to weave his magic with Carvill Hill, though, and his subsequent performances led one wag to describe the animal as 'the only horse which could take thousands of people for a ride at the same time'.

It was to be an Irish jockey, though, who grabbed the headlines. The passing of the years has not done anything to diminish Adrian Maguire's memories of that race.

Cheltenham has given me the best moment of my career when I won the Gold Cup on Cool Ground in my first ride in the race. Before leaving the weighing-room, I went over to Scu [Peter Scudamore, Carvill Hill's jockey] and wished him well. I didn't believe my horse had a chance of winning and I would have liked Scu to have done it. I thought they would.

The owner [Peter Bolton] was very keen to run but the horse wanted soft ground and it wasn't really as soft as he'd have wanted. They were excited just to have a horse in the race. The best I was hoping for was a third place. Nobody expected better. I never once thought I'd win.

I especially remember the buzz in the crowd. My guvnor then, Toby Balding, told me to jump off behind the others, alongside The Fellow, and take it from there. From the moment I got into the saddle I knew Cool Ground was right. He had a spring in his walk, his head was bouncing. There was a lot of noise and we could hear the band playing. It was as if he knew it was a special day and he wanted to get on with a job.

Cool Ground has a high cruising speed but I was worried he might struggle to hold his own on the first circuit. But he was always comfortable until, coming up to one fence, King's Fountain moved slightly to his right, The Fellow drifted to his left and suddenly Cool Ground couldn't see the fence. He put the brakes on, put his head down and snapped the reins out of my hands. I was knocked out of the saddle. I was certain I was gone but I scrambled for something to hold on to. I caught the reins and managed to hold on. I was very lucky, looking back on it.

It was very close but I was pretty sure I had won and Adam Kondrat on The Fellow leaned across and congratulated me. I threw a kiss to the heavens because I knew Vinny would be looking down on us.

As I drove back from Cheltenham that evening, I rang my mother on the car phone. She was so pleased for me. She told me everyone was thrilled for me.

The win came with a price tag attached. Maguire was banned for four days for excessive use of the whip.

Tragedy cast a cruel shadow in 1995 when his mother, Phyllis, died on the eve of the festival and a grieving Adrian had to rush home to Ireland. Twelve months later he was confined to the role of spectator after he broke his collarbone in a fall at Newbury 11 days before the festival. The following year he missed out again after breaking an arm in a fall at Leicester.

In 1998 there was more trouble as Maguire was catapulted to the ground in a fall from Zabadi in the Grand Annual Chase. Having missed out on the three previous festivals because of injury and bereavement, he sustained a broken left collarbone, head injuries and knee damage. He was initially knocked out but eventually regained consciousness and was fitted with an oxygen mask before being stretchered off the track back to the ambulance room and was later taken to Cheltenham General Hospital. The media had a field day with talk of his Cheltenham jinx.

It's absolute nonsense. It's just a run of bad luck. The three years I missed were very disappointing and then when I made my comeback last year it was very unfortunate that I had such a bad fall. Yet there is another way of looking at it – I was very lucky not to have been more seriously injured after that fall. I know a lot of people watching thought I had sustained life-threatening injuries.

What people forget is that Cheltenham has been in many ways a very lucky ground for me. Back in 1991 I was only 19 but I was lucky to make a big breakthrough at Cheltenham on Omerta. The next year I won the Gold Cup. Two years later I had a championship race double at Cheltenham with Mysliv on the Triumph Hurdle and Viking Flagship in the Queen Mother Champion Chase. This is not the record of somebody with a jinx at the festival.

Although he did not have a win in 1999, at least all the talk of a Cheltenham jinx was suspended as he escaped any injury and was driven home by his wife Sabrina rather than leaving Prestbury Park in an ambulance.

Stormin' Norman

Mallow-born jockey Norman Williamson landed a famous double at Cheltenham in 1995 with Champion Hurdle winner Alderbrook (his first ever win at the festival) and Gold Cup winner Master Oats, on his way to the Ritz Club Trophy for leading jockey at the meeting. He used every inch of toe to hand to elbow to galvanise the horses beneath him in a pageant of bravery, grace and nerve-tingling excitement. John Francome has indicated one of the secrets of Williamson's success: 'Norman sees a stride further away than anyone.'

Like Graham Bradley, Richard Dunwoody and Mark Dwyer, Williamson has scaled the twin peaks of the festival in winning both the Champion Hurdle and the Gold Cup. Dwyer, who won the Champion Hurdle on Flakey Dove in 1994, is the only member of this fab four to ride a winner on the flat. He served his apprenticeship with Liam Browne, and rode his first winner at the age of 15 on 9 June 1979 on Cloneagh Emperor at Limerick Junction. He was Ireland's champion apprentice in 1981, the year he saddled Dara Monarch to win the Group Three Anglesey Stakes at the Curragh at 66–1. The battle of the bulge caused him to switch from the flat to jumps, and in October 1982 he moved to Malton to link up with Jimmy Fitzgerald. His first winner in England came on Phoenix Prince on 16 October 1982 in a handicap hurdle at Market Rasen.

A farmer's son, Williamson ended his academic career in the Christian Brothers at the tender age of 12. He served his apprenticeship as an amateur rider for Dermot Weld, riding his first winner, Jack And Jill, at Clonmel on 19 May 1988. In 1989 he moved to England as stable jockey for John Edwards, for whom he won big races on such horses as Monsieur

Le Curé. In 1993 he teamed up with Kim Bailey, a partnership that reaped great rewards at Cheltenham in 1995. A succession of injuries meant that Williamson was restricted to the role of spectator the following year.

Williamson's class was very much in evidence on the opening day of the 1999 festival when he rode the second Irish winner, Generosa, in the Casino Hurdle Final. Generosa was a well-fancied 12–1 winner and claimed the race after jumping the last from Shannon Gale (the subject of a £100,000 each-way bet which paid dividends when the horse came in fourth) and the Martin Pipe-trained favourite Gallant Moss. For Clare-based trainer John Hassett it was a dream come true, as it was his first ever winner in England. Incredibly, with Tommy Treacy in the saddle, the following day Generosa ran a cracking race to finish third in the Coral Cup Hurdle Handicap.

Generosa was Williamson's second win of the day after taking the Kim Bailey-trained Betty's Boy to claim the William Hill National Hunt Chase. The next day he had the look of the winning jockey for the Millennium Gold Cup as he cruised to apparent certain victory on Nick Dundee – before his dreams crashed down. What was his own assessment of Cheltenham 1999 when he had been the envy of most jockeys with the quality of his rides for the meeting?

> It started off like a dream for me with my wins on Betty's Boy and Generosa. I thought it was going to be 1995 all over again for me. It was a great achievement for Johnny Hassett to have Generosa so right. Unfortunately I was already committed so I had to miss out on the ride on the horse in the Coral, though I would have loved to have had the ride. After the first day of the festival I was pretty certain I was going to have my 100th win of the season on either Nick Dundee or Teeton Mill but things could not have gone more wrong. Nick Dundee was travelling so smoothly but in an instant the dreams of a whole heap of Irish punters had gone down the tubes. I think everybody was really looking forward to the Gold Cup this year. There was so much hype about the clash of Florida Pearl and Teeton Mill – the best of Irish against what was supposed to be the best of English. This is what the magic of Cheltenham is all about. Again I really had my hopes up for the big one, but for the second day running things certainly didn't go according to plan. Life goes on, though, and a jockey can't afford to mope around feeling sorry for himself, so I put the disappointments of the festival behind me to win my 100th race of the season the very next day at Folkestone.

Sex Talk

Ted Walsh points out that Irish jockeys can sometimes find the post-race moments more hazardous than actually competing in a big race.

> An Irish jockey friend of mine, who shall remain nameless, was once invited to ride for the Queen Mother. It was very unusual for an Irish jockey to be granted this honour. The only snag was that he had false teeth and knew he would be introduced to her just before the race. Normally he would have left them in a safe place well before the race but there was no way he was going to meet her toothless. He met Her Majesty and did all the courtesies and everything beautifully. The problem was that the race was then about to start. He couldn't possibly compete with his false teeth in, so he gave them to some fella who put them in his back pocket without really looking at them. He went on to win the race but then his problems were only starting. He knew he would have to meet the Queen Mother again and he had a mad rush to track down his teeth. When he finally found his man, he popped in the teeth, not realising that the man's pocket was full of horse hair, cigarette ash and God knows what else. When he met the Queen Mother again he almost puked on her!

Cork-born jockey Mick Fitzgerald is as famous for his euphoric soundbite as he is for his victory on Rough Quest in the Martell Grand National in 1996. 'Sex will be an anti-climax after that,' was his description of the experience. He described the National as the best 12 minutes of his life. His fiancée Jane Brackenbury responded by saying, 'He's never lasted 12 minutes in his life!'

Another memorable comment had come the morning of the race when John Francome, ironically Fitzgerald's idol, had suggested on television that the only way the horse could make the trip was in a horse-box. It was only Fitzgerald's second ride in the National; the previous year he did not survive the first fence.

Fitzgerald's love affair with horses began when he was nine and his father bought him a pony to share with his brother and sister. Two more ponies quickly followed, even though his parents were far from affluent. Today, from their pub and bed-and-breakfast business in Kilfinane in County Limerick, the proud parents can share in some of their son's greatest successes – though usually in different locations, as both cannot afford to be away at the same time. Given the demands of their business,

Mick's father, John, goes to Aintree, while his mother, Alice, goes to Cheltenham.

After serving his apprenticeship with Irish trainers Richard Lister and John Hayden, Fitzgerald moved to England to John Jenkins's stable without ever riding a winner in Ireland. In 1988, Christmas came a few days early for the 18-year-old jockey when he rode his first big winner on Lover's Secret in a conditional jockeys' selling hurdle at Ludlow on 20 December. After a second winner in quick succession he thought the game was becoming easy, but he then went 18 months without a win and thought seriously about quitting.

Rough Quest gave him his second victory at the Cheltenham Festival in the Ritz Club Chase in 1995 and a month later his first victory on Irish soil in the Castlemartin Stud Handicap at Punchestown. The previous year he had won his first victory at the festival on Raymylette in the Cathcart.

Fitzgerald's own neat style of riding is in some ways akin to a flat style and can largely be attributed to his experiences on the flat. He cites the invention of the video as a major influence on his career because it enables him to improve by reviewing his own performances and then breaking down his mistakes and eliminating them as much as possible.

On the second day of the 1999 festival Fitzgerald landed the big race of the day on the classy grey Call Equiname in the Queen Mother Champion Chase. True to form, Fitzgerald reacted to his victory with a nice quip.

> There was one call I wanted above all others at this year's festival – Call Equiname. I'd been badgering Paul Nicholls to get the leg-up on this one and I count myself lucky to have succeeded – the trainer being my brother-in-law was only a tiny help! The first thing I said to him after the race was, 'Was that all right?' Obviously it was tough on his young stable jockey, Joe Tizzard, to have to miss out on the race.

As if to emphasise the vagaries of the sport, Fitzgerald fell at the second on the Queen Mother's Easter Ross in the following race. The next day, though, he was back in the winners' enclosure.

> It was a day I'll never forget. Cheltenham means an awful lot to me and I had not ridden a winner there for four years. When the Tuesday went by with no winner, I was getting a bit used to it. Then to win a Champion Chase, a Triumph Hurdle (on Katarino), a Gold Cup and the Cathcart (on Stormyfairweather) and to finish leading jockey at the meeting was fantastic. I felt as if I was on top of the

world. Earlier in my career, when I wasn't having success, I had almost gone to New Zealand, so I enjoy success all the more because of that.

Everything went right for me in the Gold Cup. See More Business was going so well I just had to steer. Paul [Nicholls] told me he was in great form when I rode him around Wincanton a few days beforehand and I said if the horse jumped he would finish in the top three. When Florida Pearl landed over the third last and emptied a bit, I looked beside me and saw Go Ballistic. I knew what he can do because I'd won six on him [he had also been Go Ballistic's jockey when favourite for the Grand National that never was] and I thought I'd win from there. I needed a long one at the last and I thought to myself, 'You're either coming up or you're going down.' I had schooled See More Business a few weeks before, once with blinkers and once without. The difference was almost like sitting on two different horses.

When Imperial Call won the Gold Cup in 1996 I finished second on Rough Quest. I was so gutted that I'll never, ever forget it. Everyone said I gave him a great ride, yet I still felt there was something wrong. I wanted to feel what Conor O'Dwyer felt on that day – and now I have! It's a feeling that will stay with me for a long, long time.

Mick's agent is Cameron McMillan of RBI Promotions Ltd, who represent the top ten flat and national hunt jockeys in Britain. Cameron offers a different perspective on the festival.

It's a very busy time for us: the zenith of national hunt racing. If there is a lot of pressure on our jockeys for those days, they certainly don't show it. Obviously the stakes are much higher because the horses are much better and the prestige of winning is much greater, but they take it all in their stride. They are all very philosophical about it and as far as possible treat each contest as just another race.

Our Irish jockeys are very diverse in their personalities but they all have one thing in common – they are all very professional. Richard Dunwoody is very intense, but a very decent man. Tony McCoy is much younger and has what you might call the hunger of youth. Norman Williamson is very, very professional. Mick Fitzgerald is probably that little bit more easygoing. He's certainly very at ease talking to people and is one of the most articulate jockeys you can meet.

We are the official sponsors for such companies as Guinness and Smurfit, so obviously we do a lot of corporate business and entertainment. Last year, for example, we brought down the Liverpool football team for lunch. Our task really is to integrate the giants of racing and the giants of industry for those three days. In that respect, the memory of one of our jockeys that stands out most was Tony McCoy's Gold Cup victory on Mr Mulligan, because Guinness were sponsoring him.

For top jockeys the corporate part of their livelihood is developing. Each day of the festival our leading jockeys act as corporate speakers for our guests by providing pre-race analysis. I think this aspect of a top, professional jockey's life will increase significantly in the years to come. For that reason, our most important job in a sense during the festival is to synchronise our jockeys' timetables so that they show up to the sponsors when they are expected but are also back with their horses whenever they need to be.

Inevitably, in this high-pressure environment, there can be the odd *faux pas*.

Sometimes things go wrong and there is a glitch in the arrangements. It is invariably an organisational slip-up. Although it can be a bit embarrassing for the jockey, it is never their fault.

A case in point was what happened to Mick Fitzgerald. Mick was due to address some of our clients in the corporate box before racing at Windsor. Through no fault of his own he arrived a bit late and had to go directly to racing. He had rides in the first two races and had a first and a second. As he was free until the last race, he rushed up to the sponsor's box and apologised profusely for having missed the pre-race analysis. For 40 minutes he launched into a masterly incisive and entertaining analysis of the day's racing. As he finished, he went around to everybody and again apologised profusely for missing the pre-race analysis.

Later, I asked the sponsor what he thought of Mick Fitzgerald. The sponsor said he had never turned up. Mick had been given the wrong directions and through no fault of his own had gone to the wrong box! I thought it was hilarious.

The Real McCoy

At the age of 12, Tony McCoy bought a bicycle so he could cycle the ten miles to Willie Rock's stables. It was there he rode his first racehorse and it was there that his interest in horses became an obsession.

At the age of 15 he signed apprentice forms for Jim Bolger, working on horses like Jet Ski Lady and St Jovite. There he worked with Sabrina Winters, a woman with a good way with horses who has since become Mrs Adrian Maguire. His first win was on Legal Steps at Thurles on 26 March 1991, but an accident when riding a Bolger two-year-old on the gallops saw his career turning a different corner. While he was sidelined for almost six months his weight rocketed from 7st 9lb to 9st 7lb. When he recovered, a return to the flat was not feasible. A new career in jumping beckoned.

In the summer of 1994, when he had won 13 races in Ireland, Toby Balding offered McCoy a job in England. Four years earlier Adrian Maguire had accepted a similar offer. That September McCoy began work with Balding and within 14 months he had ridden 154 winners. He won the conditional jockeys championship with 74 winners and in the process beat Maguire's old record. The following season, his first as a fully fledged jockey, he took the title with 175, a brilliant new constellation in an otherwise gloomy sporting sky. He was the fastest jockey to 100 wins in a season, the fastest to 200 and the youngest champion jockey since 1962. In 1996 he had his first win at the Cheltenham Festival when Kibreet won the Grand Annual Chase. In 1997 he took a 20–1 shot, Mr Mulligan, to win the Gold Cup.

The following year he dramatically illustrated the fine line between Irish victory and defeat when Meath trainer Noel Meade, after years of trying in vain, appeared to have claimed his first win in the festival after Richard Dunwoody's mount Hill Society seemed to have snatched the Arkle Trophy from the Martin Pipe-trained Champleve, with McCoy in the saddle. After an agonising ten-minute wait, the photo-finish gave the race to McCoy. It was a huge anti-climax for Meade, saved only by the melodramatic manner of the defeat. Later McCoy and trainer Martin Pipe secured an opening-day double with Unsinkable Boxer in the Gold Card Handicap Hurdle.

McCoy went on to clinch his leading-rider-of-the-festival prize with a dramatic treble in the last three races of the meeting, with Edredon Bleu in the Grand Annual Chase Challenge Cup, Cyfor Malta in the Cathcart Challenge Cup Chase and Blowing Wind in the Vincent O'Brien County Handicap Hurdle – equalling Jamie Osborne's record of five festival winners. In the opening race of Cheltenham 1999, McCoy made history by winning his fourth consecutive race at the festival on the Martin Pipe-trained 8–1 Hors La Loi III in the Supreme Novices' Hurdle.

Like Richard Dunwoody, McCoy's firm foothold on the ladder to success has not been accidental. A revealing insight into his mindset came when he asked Nick Jackson, Dunwoody's personal assistant who had previously worked for McCoy, to make a video of his races one day. Jackson duly copied his winners but neglected to include a narrow loser. McCoy was furious and barked, 'What's the good in that? How am I going to learn from that?'

Mercy Rimell, who successfully stepped into the breach after the death of her husband Fred, is a big fan of the real McCoy. 'Arkle was the best Gold Cup winner I have seen but I think two jockeys are head and shoulders above anyone else – Tony McCoy and Richard Dunwoody. Tony is the best I've ever seen; when he comes to the last his horse always seems to be balanced.'

TEN

I Rode Her Mother

'Riding is the art of keeping a horse between yourself and the ground.'

ALAN ADAMS

Ted Walsh has rewritten the lexicon of horseracing commentary, popularising such phrases as 'a great lepper', 'bits of chances', 'gutsy buggers', 'arse over tip' and, most famously, 'I rode her mother' – a reference to a horse whose mother he had ridden, lest there be any confusion.

Racing seems to lend itself to possible misinterpretations. *The Sporting Life* left itself open to similar misunderstanding in 1977 with its report that 'John Higgins fractured a bone in his left leg in a fall from Mrs Higgins at Edinburgh on Monday, and will be out of action for a month'. Peter Bromley once said on the BBC, 'The Game Spirit Chase, named after Game Spirit, a lovely horse owned by Her Majesty the Queen Mother, who dropped dead here after a long and distinguished career.'

Sport is now a serious business. In January 1995, a company who until then had had forgettable advertising became one of Britain's largest food brands after Gary Lineker started to endorse its product. Lineker was chosen by Walker's crisps as he shared Leicester roots with the company. Although the ads don't have the obvious brilliance of Nike's campaign around Peter Schmeichel ('The last time he dropped a ball was when his voice broke'), Lineker has proved such a successful spokesman that the campaign simultaneously helped him shed his wooden image and enabled Walker's to name a flavour after him – Salt 'n' Lineker.

Sport is a powerful weapon in the media ratings war. If one example illustrates this trend perfectly it is Paul Gascoigne's abrupt departure from Glenn Hoddle's World Cup plans a week before France 1998. Following market research, the BBC decided that it should drop its traditional élitism in its news agenda and opt for 'popularness', i.e. what the masses are really talking about. Accordingly, the day after the 'Gazza axed' story broke,

Radio 4's highly lauded *PM* programme devoted a lengthy item to the Gazza story. The reporter had 'doorstepped' Gascoigne's family in Gateshead but, getting no comment, had recorded their dogs barking inside the house instead – a 'scoop' which was proudly broadcast on air. Moreover, the local newsagent where Gascoigne's sister had bought the papers that morning was also quizzed and was able to confirm the astonishing fact that she 'seemed upset'.

As if this was not enough, the upmarket *Newsnight* illustrated part of its Gazza feature by having psychologist Oliver James sitting in London's Pharmacy bar, where Gazza had memorably got drunk, saying with profundity that such talents also have extreme personalities. This was the perfect cue to rehash the story of Gazza's assault on his wife and to pose the question so beloved of tabloids: should Shazza leave Gazza?

Most revealing, however, was the BBC's evening news treatment of the story. On the day the story broke it persisted with its traditional agenda and led with an earthquake in Afghanistan which had claimed thousands of lives. On the following day, after talk about Gazza had reached fever pitch, the *Nine O'Clock News*'s top story was not William Hague's first reshuffle of the Conservative shadow cabinet but Gazza. In marked contrast, on ITN's *News at Ten* Hague's reshuffle was the lead story. This led some critics to accuse the BBC of treating Gascoigne 'as though he were a great statesman'.

In this competitive television environment, sports personalities are cultivated carefully and selectively by television moguls. Ex-jockeys have not always comfortably made the transition to television personality. In an effort to boost its ratings for the Breeders (Some call it the Bleeders) Cup, NBC, amidst much hype, decided to get Fred Astaire's wife, ex-jockey Robyn Symth, to do interviews on horseback. She looked great galloping beside the breathless, mud-splattered winning jockeys. The sound effects were marvellous. The only fly in the ointment was that Robyn had virtually no idea what questions to ask.

It is no accident that Ted Walsh pops up frequently to elucidate matters intelligently on both Channel 4 and RTE. Revered by racing fans and a familiar name even to those who know nothing about the sport, Ted is a star performer with a unique popular appeal. He was Ireland's top amateur jockey for almost two decades, winning the Irish amateur championship title a record 11 times between 1972 and 1984. Given his success as an amateur, why didn't he turn professional?

> Basically I was a bit too heavy, although I'm quite small, only five
> foot eight. My father was six foot one and his brothers were all

around the six-foot mark and my mother's side were all big men but I stayed small. I'm the runt of the family! My son Ted is a big man and plays rugby for Naas, as did my other son Ruby, though I didn't play it and have only been to see one rugby match in my life. At the time there were a lot of top-class professional jockeys around and I suppose I didn't have the nerve. I'm sorry I didn't now, though. The only trouble when you are an amateur is that you can only ride one or two horses a day, whereas if you are a professional you can get right into the thick of it and get as many as five or six rides a day.

Saddle Up

Like Vincent O'Brien, Walsh learned all he knows about horses from his father. Not for them the fractious working partnership celebrated in *Steptoe and Son*. Many of Ted's most treasured memories are of his father, Ruby.

> Although most people seem to think I'm a Kildare man, I'm actually a native of Fermoy. Horses were always the topic of conversation around the table in our house. My mother's people were very involved in horses. She was a Kilkenny woman and her father was a blacksmith. My father was initially very involved in point-to-point and it was only later that he got involved in national hunt racing. He also trained a few flat horses.
>
> Horses were always knocking about as I was growing up. When I was about nine or ten I started going to fairs like Cahirmee and Tallaght on 4 September and the Puck fair. To a young fella like me they were like the Wild West, with all the horses. All those fairs are gone now. Nowadays all you get there is fellas selling stereos.
>
> I was always riding horses and never thought about anything else. When I was 15 or 16 I began riding horses in races. It took me a long time to ride a winner but once I got the first one I had a lot after that.

As a youngster Walsh had the great good fortune to grow up close to racing genius, which was an important influence on his early career.

> We grew up in Cork close to where Vincent O'Brien was born. He was someone I always looked up to because my father and my uncle Ted admired him so much. When he said one of his horses was a

115

good one it was taken as gospel. Although he had so many winners, I think the race I remember most involving him was the 1984 Epsom Derby. It was Ireland versus Ireland: David O'Brien's Secreto ridden by Christy Roche and Vincent with El Gran Señor, ridden by Pat Eddery. I think what really struck me was that although Christy Roche was the great champion jockey an Irish-based jockey had never won the Epsom Derby and the fact that he had done it in such dramatic fashion made it a unique occasion, although Mick Kinane went on to emulate Christy's achievement a few years later. It was like an all-Irish big victory at Cheltenham. Then you add in the fact that the father was beaten by the son, with David pipping Vincent. The only problem was that the Irish racing fans lost an absolute fortune because Vincent's horse had a massive reputation and had seemed home and hosed just 100 yards from the line.

In my teenage years in Kildare, Arkle was king. The great thing about Arkle was that Pat Taaffe only lived down the road from me. I'd go to Mass on a Sunday and I'd see him there. It was a treat just to be so close to him, and the fact that he was associated with Arkle gave me a great interest. I was lucky enough later to ride for Pat, and in actual fact I think I rode his first winner as a trainer. Funnily enough, Mill House was bred in Naas, very close to me, as well, and he was broken in by Pat Taaffe too. The papers in England were hailing him as the greatest horse since Golden Miller after he won the Gold Cup in 1963. Then Arkle came on to the scene and was our next Prince Regent. It was great to see the two of them going to war. Before they met in the Gold Cup in 1964, they'd been at the Hennessy in Newbury and Arkle had made a bad mistake at the third last, giving him five pounds. That vindicated what the English had been saying about him and Arkle didn't get a chance to redeem himself until the Gold Cup – and, boy, did he do a good job! I'll remember that race till the day I die.

The great thing about Arkle is that he is the horse that every other horse is judged by in the same way as footballers are judged against George Best or hurlers are judged against Christy Ring. When I was an impressionable young lad, you can imagine how glamorous racing seemed then.

A lesser-known fact about Walsh is that his father also excelled in another sport.

He was a good hurler. He played in the north Cork league. He played junior hurling with Cork and won an All-Ireland junior medal with them and a Railway Cup medal. He never made it to the Cork senior team because they were a side of all the stars at the time, with the likes of Christy Ring and Jack Lynch.

Ted put the lessons he learned from his father to good effect to ride over 550 winners. Asked what he most looked forward to at Cheltenham, Peter Scudamore once said 'going home in one piece'. For Walsh it is the thrill of victory, though he is not daunted by failure. Samuel Beckett's words from *Westward Ho* could be his motto: 'Ever tried. Ever failed. No matter. Try again. Fail again. Fail better.' He rode four winners at the Cheltenham Festival, most notably Hilly Way in the Queen Mother Champion Chase in 1979. He twice won the Kim Muir Chase, on Castleruddery in 1974 and on Prolan in 1976.

If Cheltenham provided Ted with some of the highlights of his career as both a jockey and a trainer, it also provided many low points. In the 1982 Champion Hurdle he was riding the favourite, Daring Run, trained by Peter McCreery. Daring Run slipped on the flat and the race went to another amateur jockey, Colin Magnier, on Michael Cunningham's 40–1 chance For Auction.

Fifteen years after his Cheltenham 'mishap', Ted was forcefully reminded of his embarrassment on live television by his Channel 4 colleague John McCririck. McCririck was smarting from Walsh's comment, 'John, we're up a very big height here, and if we weren't covered in with glass I'd probably throw you off the stand. You've come out with some dreadful statements . . .'

'Ted, you fell off the Irish favourite in the Champion Hurdle,' butted in the sartorially challenged one.

Quick as a flash Ted responded, 'Yeah, and I got a fortune for it!'

Was Daring Run his biggest Cheltenham setback?

> Definitely not. I was far from certain he was going to win it. I've had my disappointments there as a jockey with horses I was sure were going to win – that's a harder blow to take. Even worse is when you fall on a horse that you think is a sure-fire winner. I've done that a few times too!

He laughs when I cautiously enquire if Mount Prague, the Mick O'Toole-trained 11–8 favourite in the 1977 National Hunt Chase, might have been such an occasion.

> Yeah. You wouldn't be too far wrong there. There was a ditch going away from the stands in those days and I ended up making a right

mess of my collarbone at it! I really thought I was home and hosed but he stepped into the ditch and that was that.

Getting back to Daring Run, though, he indirectly gave me one of my worst moments in racing. Really when you're in a race it's a joint effort between the jockey and the horse. It's terrible, though, when you are solely responsible for a horse having a bad run. The sad part is that you as the jockey know half a furlong before everyone else that you have messed up. You've made the wrong move or followed the wrong fella or something. It's the worst feeling in the world.

I remember a few times after I'd given a really bad race to one of my father's horses, he'd be furious. He was a great winner but a bad loser. A few times when I had run a corker in Listowel, my father would say nothing as he drove me home. Sometimes he would speak after we went past Limerick, and he'd suddenly say, 'What were you at? Jesus, what were you doing?'

The good trainers wouldn't embarrass you in public but they might pull you aside afterwards. Usually if a jockey is worth his salt he'll say, 'I'm sorry, I gave that horse a bad ride and I'm to blame,' and that's that. Usually if a trainer's loyal he'll give you another chance. When I used to ride Daring Run the trainer, Peter McCreery, was very loyal to me. I had 13 or 14 winners out of 17 rides but I gave him a few bad rides and I was pulled out of him. It was pressure from the owners, I'm sure. No doubt plenty of other people were telling them that I wasn't up to the job. I felt as if my right arm had been cut off. By that stage I had learned to keep my trap shut so I said nothing, although I was devastated, especially because I was scared another jockey would have great success with him. In the end I got the ride back on him but racing is a tough game like that.

I always tried to think of Frank Berry at times like that. He was champion jockey about 13 times and he epitomises what national hunt jockeys should be. He always took his disappointments well and never said anything bad about anyone. His career lasted over 20 years and he made very, very few enemies in that time, which is very unusual for a jump jockey.

You have to take the swings and the roundabouts. It was Peter McCreery who gave me my first winner at Cheltenham, Castleruddery, owned by Mrs Harper, a lovely old lady from Wicklow. Then Eddie O'Grady gave me my second, on Prolan, a grey horse owned by Michael Cuddy and his late wife, two lovely people.

I was very lucky in 1979 with Hilly Way. It was the first time I rode a winner in Cheltenham against professionals. This was one of the feature races, not as good as the Champion Hurdle or the Gold Cup but still a great race. Tommy Carmody and Tommy Carberry both turned him down and Gerry Newman wasn't getting on so well with him so I was kind of fourth choice but I ended up winning.

To be truthful, I was always sorry I didn't get the chance to win a Champion Hurdle on Daring Run. He won twice in Aintree but he was second in a novice hurdle in Cheltenham as well. Cheltenham was a bit of a bogey for him. He got beaten a couple of times there even when I didn't ride him but he was a very good horse. Owned by Andy Doyle down in Wexford, he twice won the Irish Champion Hurdle. He was probably the best horse I rode.

If Ted was fortunate enough to have few altercations with his trainers, that was certainly not the case with the general public.

Cheltenham is unquestionably my favourite meeting but there are a lot of Irish meetings I enjoy. I love the Punchestown Festival and other meetings like Gowran Park and Limerick Junction. Leopardstown is a great place for atmosphere and it's a great place for punters. When I used to ride there fellas would be roaring at you 'cos they had lost their last few quid on you. 'Well, you wouldn't get a ride in a whorehouse,' they'd say. If you had been beaten on an odds-on favourite, some of those fellas were ready to dig your mother up out of the grave and throw her at you. I remember a friend of mine who was an amateur jockey defending me there one time. They turned on him and said, 'Look at him, he's only a pancake jockey. He only gets a ride every Shrove Tuesday.'

I remember once riding a horse for Jim Bolger and making every mistake in the book. We lost the race by three-quarters of a length and they nearly lynched me. Jim gave me another chance, though, and we won the second time. The same fellas were patting me on the back. If those guys have £40 on you and they lose it I suppose they're entitled to feel put out.

Although Ted's business is dependent upon gambling, he has some misgivings about it.

I know very few people who are professional punters. J.P. McManus has major interests. The only one I know is Barney Curley, though he owns horses as well. I rode a horse called I'm The Driver for Barney one year at the Galway Races. He didn't tell me exactly how much he had put on him. He just said, 'I've the price of a good Rolls-Royce on him.' A good Rolls-Royce was worth £50,000 to £60,000 then! The horse was good but he had one little kink – you couldn't really run free on him. Anyway, to cut a long story short, the plan I had to win the race didn't work because two other jockeys took up the pace early on – which was the last thing we wanted – and we finished fifth. Being a typical punter, he came back the next day and I rode a horse for him called Buck Me Off. We won and Barney got back all he had lost the previous day.

People go on about alcohol but at some stage a fella will get so drunk that he'll fall down, but the lad who is addicted to gambling will not fall down. A fella could gamble away his home and everything he owns but somehow he'll still want to keep going. I've known fellas, the nicest lads in the world, and they've lost everything. It's the saddest thing I find in racing.

Whiphand

Jockeys are a strange breed. Take the case of Cheltenham-born Frederick James Archer, champion jockey 13 times, who shot himself dead in a fit of delirium at the age of 29. Walsh battles for the mantle of greatest communicator amongst the ex-jockeys with the man Lester Piggott once said, in jest, couldn't ride a bike, Willie Carson.

Although Willie grew up in Stirling in Scotland, the Carsons are immigrants from Bray, County Wicklow. His father worked all his life as a Fyffes banana packer and his mother worked as a waitress in Dunblane. Like Walsh, Carson makes up for his lack of inches with a rapier-like wit. As a young man Carson literally bumped into Cassius Clay, who responded by turning to the diminutive jockey and pleading, 'Don't hit me! Don't hit me please!'

Carson was not afraid to use the whip in his days as a jockey. Neither was Walsh. Peter O'Sullevan was not always impressed by Ted's propensity for raising his arm. Normally Peter's voice has the effect of a warm brandy from a St Bernard, thawing you out and bringing you slowly back to life. For a moment, though, it takes on all the world-weary cynicism of a Tory cabinet minister's wife and his normal boyish enthusiasm evaporates.

In the course of my career as a commentator, one practice which developed, in both flat and jumping, which I found disturbing was the habitual misuse of the whip. I considered it unnecessary, unproductive and offensive. I know cruelty is relative and racehorses are among the most pampered of animals and there may be a case for giving a horse a crack or two. But when a 'crack or two' develops into a good hiding it is wholly unacceptable. I believe in Stan Mellor's dictum: 'Instead of hitting horses, jockeys should ride properly.'

It's a fine line when you think of Lester Piggott, who did both. Everybody knows, though, that when Lester struck, he hit a horse in the right place, in the right rhythm, persuading his mount to lengthen his stride. I remember talking to him once about his Derby wins on Roberto [1972] and The Minstrel [1977], asking him to account for the rapid-fire salvos, in double or treble time, just before the line. He agreed it was against all logic but pointed out that both horses were very lazy and that they hadn't been damaged by his use of the whip as both of them ate up clean that night and had improved performances in subsequent races.

As I see it, when routine application of the whip is more widely looked upon as an uncouth substitute for talent, it will be employed with far less frequency.

Ted Walsh was one of the best amateur riders in my time or any time. He had a fine record on a horse called Daring Run, who was a fine hurdler, but Ted had the habit of hitting him often down the shoulder in the latter stages of a race. Neither Daring Run nor his supporters appeared to gain anything from these attacks and finally, resisting the impulse to interrupt my commentary by yelling, 'Put that f**king stick down,' I wrote in my column, in rather forceful language, as I recall, that Ted's tactics were particularly unnecessary on such a willing horse.

Grand National Day, 4 April 1981, is a day I recall vividly for two reasons. Firstly because of one of the great fairytale results in steeplechasing's spectacular, in which Bob Champion, who had fought such a courageous battle against cancer, triumphed on another ex-invalid, Aldaniti, at the expense of gallant 54-year-old amateur John Thorne and Spartan Missile. When John put his arms around Bob, leaving no doubt that he was truly as happy over Bob's victory as he would have been if he had won himself, it encapsulated for me the Corinthian spirit which still lives in the National. My happiest memories of racing were the successes of my own horses, especially Be Friendly and Attivo, but Aldaniti's victory really moved me.

I remember clearly another incident before the race. I had just commentated on Ted winning the Sun Templegate Hurdle on Daring Run. Ted had given him a most tender ride. I was rushing down to the weighing-room for a last anxious view of the 39 big-race jockeys in colours when Ted, whom I had not seen face to face since severely criticising his conduct in the newspaper, strode across the weighing-room towards me. Ted was then the eight-times champion, and as my sole qualification, such as it was, consisted of being an honorary life member of the Jockeys Association of Great Britain, he had good reason to feel entitled to question my critical qualifications. In fact what he said was, 'You were right, Pete. There's no need to be that hard on that horse. It's a poor man who can't take advice and learn from his mistakes.'

I was thrilled by his reaction and I felt it said a lot about Ted. He has a small frame but he's a big man in the true sense of the term.

President Truman's comment about size readily springs to mind: 'When it comes to inches, my boy, you should only consider the forehead. Better to have a spare inch between the top of your nose and the hairline than between the ankle and the kneecap.'

False sentiment, though, does not figure in Ted's make-up. He once had a bad fall at Cheltenham, to be greeted by a female onlooker saying, 'The poor horse!'

'"Poor horse"! What about me? I've a wife and children to look after. What about my welfare?' replied an indignant Walsh.

I was champion Irish amateur jockey 11 times but my four victories at Cheltenham meant more to me than anything else I achieved as a jockey. I especially remember that in 1986 I had very little chance of winning on Attitude Adjuster in the Foxhunters. He was trained by Mouse Morris for Sue Magnier and was the sort of tough old horse who needs a lot of pressure. At that stage the English authorities were starting to clamp down on the use of the whip. I knew that would be a problem, so I gave him a few cracks of the whip before we got to the start so that he'd know in advance that I had the whip on me. In fact he was on song that day and took the initiative from the start, and he won easily without any need for me to put pressure on him.

It was funny afterwards to hear that Peter O'Sullevan had said some nice things about me about the restraint I had shown. He even said that I had demonstrated the correct approach to employment of the whip. The simple fact is that if the race had been run at home,

I'd have cut rashers off him. I had really let him have it in Thurles two weeks before.

I was in the twilight of my career at the time, and after winning the race I decided it was time for me to retire.

My Lovely Horse

Although Walsh's decision to become a trainer was inevitable, the timing was prompted by one of the saddest events in his life.

> My father died on New Year's Day, 1991. I had no intention of becoming a trainer until my dad retired or until the Lord called him. He was 71 years of age and it was very sudden. He had been at Tramore earlier that day and I had gone to Fairyhouse. We had runners in both places, none of them any good, but we'd had a good Christmas, a couple of nice winners, and he was in good form heading off. On the way home he got a pain and I was going to take him to the hospital in Naas but he collapsed and died in the hall. It was a nice way for him to go but a bit sudden for all of us. So I became a trainer after that. Luckily enough I won my first race. We hadn't a lot of horses but we had some nice horses.

His finest hour as a trainer came at Cheltenham in 1997, when Commanche Court was one of three Irish winners. The hero worship after the victory reflected Ted's virtual cult status, Commanche Court's triumph in the Elite Racing Club Triumph Hurdle provoking such hysteria that from the reaction you could have been forgiven for thinking that Danoli had just won the Gold Cup. It was a fitting compliment to trainer and racing pundit Walsh's popularity on both sides of the Irish Sea.

The horse stayed back in the early stages until the race sorted itself out. Under the careful supervision of Norman Williamson, he steered his way through the field as the leaders scaled the top of Cheltenham hill. Dermot Desmond's black-and-white colours were nicely placed as he came down the slope. As he rounded the home turn, Williamson appeared to have Commanche Court glued to the rails, saving the horse for a final charge before producing him to take control at the final flight. A combination of courage, class and speed did the rest and Ireland had another Cheltenham win.

Ted produced a magic television moment when interviewed by Brough Scott: 'Wonderful. Wonderful. Possibly the greatest racing day of my life.

123

Wonderful. All the family are here, the kids, and I'm sure my mum is looking in at home. I could kiss you too.' And he promptly did so, to Scott's surprise, eliciting a bemused 'Oh, lovely' in response.

Derek Thompson then nabbed jockey Norman Williamson for an immediate interview, saying, 'The popularity of this man is incredible.'

'Ted can train as well as talk, can't he?' was Williamson's instant reply.

> It was an unbelievable feeling to see my son Ruby lead him up. We'll never know if he'd have ridden him as well as Norman Williamson did.
>
> Any trainer will tell you it's everyone's dream to have a winner there. It's such a great occasion. I shed a tear or two. I suppose I'm an emotional old git at the back of it all. That was better than riding. There's no comparison. That win was f**king brilliant.
>
> I think it's better to have a winner as a trainer, though there is a lot more pressure in the build-up. I don't think anything in racing has given me more pleasure than my win in Cheltenham as a trainer. I'm the mixed farmer of racing. I've a lot of irons in the fire. That's probably a wise thing from the economic point of view. I must say I really enjoy working on the television and we have great gas. Plus I get paid to go to race meetings I would go to anyway. It's nice to be a commentator but it's nothing, and I really mean nothing, compared to having a winner there as a jockey or a trainer.

The Road Not Taken

Like Dick Francis, former champion jockey John Francome has become a millionaire as a result of a second career penning a racing thriller once a year. Is Ted Walsh likely to be introduced at future Cheltenham Festivals as a best-selling writer?

> I've got a few ambitions yet, but to become the new Dick Francis isn't one of them!'

What is so special about Cheltenham?

> Cheltenham is the big one. It's like if you are interested in the GAA [Gaelic Athletic Association] you want to get to Croke Park for the All-Ireland final. I'm glad to see Kildare winning in Croke Park again, especially 'cos they've been in the doldrums for so long. It's

great to be part of the great occasion that it is in Croke Park with the Artane Boys Band, the singing of the national anthem and the whole atmosphere of the big day. Cheltenham is racing's answer to that. It is the highlight of the year for me. From Christmas I look forward to it and the buzz that goes with it.

Cheltenham is about excellence. It is the place to win for any fella involved in the national hunt game. To even get a ride there is great, but to win there is unbelievable because of the fantastic reception you get in the winners' enclosure. I think as you get on in years you appreciate those days more.

For Ireland's most popular racing analyst, nationalism is very much at the heart of Cheltenham.

I've been to great race meetings all over the world from Punchestown to California and there's nothing to compare with Cheltenham. It's the biggest meeting of them all. Effectively you have two nations competing against each other and you can't get that anywhere else. A lot of reputations are at stake and people's judgements are on the line.

Apart from Ted himself, who are the Irish characters in Cheltenham?

Well, I'm not sure that I'm a character. I think all the Irish there are characters in their own way. It's a small ship in Ireland so I know everybody in the game, but I suppose if you push me I would have to say John Mulhern and Mick O'Toole. Like myself, their passion sometimes gets the better of them and they wear their hearts on their sleeves.

Not surprisingly, Cheltenham features at the top of Ted's list of ambitions.

I'm in love with racing and I'd love to train the winner of the Cheltenham Gold Cup, not because of the financial rewards but because it's the ultimate in national hunt racing. The Gold Cup is the quarest race, though. You need an awful lot of luck to win it and you have to be spot on for the day. When I was a child I thought you needed a wonderhorse like Arkle to win the Gold Cup, but then horses like Cool Ground and Norton's Coin came along to win there. You really need to be 100 per cent perfect on the day.

Ted was not the only member of his class in school to have been bitten by the Cheltenham bug. One of Cheltenham's most devout patrons is his former school pal, the Irish Finance Minister Charlie McCreevy. Mr McCreevy displayed his interest in racing in the 1999 Finance Bill not only by significantly cutting the betting tax but by introducing a special provision whereby the tax bill of £400,000 on the £1 million raised for Shane Broderick would be waived. The minister has not, though, gone so far as to compare himself with a horse, unlike former Chancellor of the Exchequer Norman Lamont, who once commented, 'Desert Orchid and I have a lot in common. We are both greys; vast sums of money are riding on our performance; the opposition hopes we will fall at the first fence; and we are both carrying too much weight.' Other Irish politicians with a penchant for Cheltenham include former Minister Michael Lowry.

Father Ted

In 1998 18-year-old Ruby Walsh emulated his famous father not only by winning the amateur championship but by taking his place on the Festival Roll of Honour on his debut visit. Willie Mullins took a remarkable third consecutive Wetherby's Festival Bumper when Alexander Banquet defeated the hugely backed favourite Joe Mac in a real dog-fight. The Irish roars assumed victory for Joe Mac when Conor O'Dwyer ranged alongside Ruby on the turn-in but Joe Mac couldn't get past and persistently drifted left on to Alexander Banquet.

The mob hysteria which had followed Norman Williamson landing the Triumph Hurdle the previous year for his father on Commanche Court was not repeated for Ruby on only his third ever ride at the festival. This can be attributed to the huge Irish money on Joe Mac, who had started at 6–4 after being 3–1 in the morning. In the winners' enclosure the proud father was purring. As he kissed his wife, Helen, Walsh the elder summed it up in one word: 'Brilliant!'

> The bumper was always a favourite race of mine but I never rode in one at Cheltenham because it wasn't introduced to the festival until after I retired. It was great for Ruby to win at Cheltenham so early in his career.

In 1999 all Irish hopes were on Ruby to write another chapter in the story of Irish success at Cheltenham on Alexander Banquet in the Royal and SunAlliance Novices' Hurdle, but the combination finished a disappointing seventh. Although the race was won by the English banker Barton, there was an Irish connection in the form of the winning jockey, Lorcan Wyer, winning his first race at the festival as a professional. It was a very popular win, as Wyer's career had been dogged by a succession of injuries. Ruby, though, did put in one of the Irish performances of the meeting when finishing second the next day on the Willie Mullins-trained Balla Sola in the Triumph Hurdle at 16–1.

Ted expresses cautious optimism when asked about Ruby's prospects.

> Ruby has a good future and he has the ability and the hunger. All he needs is the luck. You must have luck to make it to the top in this game. He's a big lad [five foot ten inches] so he'll have to watch his weight.

Willie Mullins was less cautious when asked his verdict: 'His finishes are excellent, as is his ability to get a horse jumping. He is very good at thinking a race out for himself and is also very willing to listen.'

To add to the family connection, Ruby's sister, Jennifer, is her brother's keeper after becoming his agent when he turned pro. Their partnership had begun when Ruby was still in school in Rathcoole, from where he used to ring her on Friday lunchtimes to see if she could organise spare bumper rides for him.

Ted has another reason to bask in his son's success.

> Ruby was named after my father and he would have got a great kick out of seeing his grandson do so well because it's an unusual name for a fella. My dad's older friends get a great kick out of Ruby's successes now because it keeps the name alive.

Holy Wit

Like Mick Doyle, Ted is one of the great storytellers of Irish sport. His sharp mind was evident on one of his first appearances on Ireland's best-known television programme *The Late, Late Show*. Asked to comment about fellow guest Mick Jagger's ex-wife Jerry Hall's exotic lifestyle, Ted replied with lightning speed, 'I wouldn't be able to say anything about that. I just spend my evenings at home drinking Bovril.' Ms Hall was fronting a massive advertising campaign for Bovril at the time. It was difficult to know whether the bemused look on her face was because she didn't get the joke or because she couldn't make out Ted's accent!

Enthusiasm is stamped emphatically on every facet of his personality. He tells the story of the three Irishmen at the World Cup finals in 1990. They were travelling outside Rome when they came upon the Popemobile overturned at the side of the road. They recognised it instantly, having seen the Pope driving in it when he said a special Mass at Galway racecourse in 1979. The Pope lay dead at the wheel. He had seriously breached protocol and slipped out of the Vatican for a quiet drive in the country. At that precise moment Vatican officials arrived on the scene and were anxious to cover up this indiscretion. They made the Irishmen swear a solemn vow never to reveal what they had seen. The Pope's death was not to be announced until the following Monday. The official line was to be that he had died quietly in his sleep after a few days of illness. As the men from the Emerald Isle were all former altar boys, they readily agreed to this request. After bidding goodbye to their new-found friends, the threesome quickly came up with a plot to make a killing. They would get great odds from the bookies on the Pope dying by Monday.

The following week the three men met up again. Two were deliriously happy, having made a fortune. The other was crestfallen. When asked why he looked so gloomy, he replied that he had made nothing. 'I doubled my bet on the Pope dying with one on the death of the Queen Mother . . .'

ELEVEN

Racing Certainty

'Anybody who finds it easy to make money on the horses is probably in the dog-food business.'

FRANKLIN P. JONES

Scientists have never unravelled the nature/nurture question, whether talent is inherited or can be instilled. Bill Shankly, the sage of Anfield, had no doubts: 'Coaches don't make great players, mothers and fathers do.' Aidan O'Brien's is a natural talent. Irish trainer John Fowler once listed his 'recreations' as 'mostly unprintable'. Veteran trainer Ken 'Benign Bishop' Oliver's slogan was 'Win or lose, we'll have a booze'. Aidan O'Brien, bespectacled and unassuming, is cast in a different mould. There is more to this man than meets the eye. He does his talking on the racetrack and in the record books. A non-smoker and non-drinker, O'Brien was presented with a magnum of champagne at Punchestown when he became the first Irish trainer to land 200 winners in a calendar year in August 1995. He declined a taste, claiming he would rather have a cup of tea!

Little wonder he was once compared to a Trappist monk. A more helpful comparison might be with Frank Williams, the Formula One magnate who has a passionate obsession to win and win and win again.

O'Brien lives a two-dimensional life with time only for work and family. His wife Anne Marie is a former model and amateur jockey. Her 18th birthday was a crucial date in her life. For that birthday, her parents offered her a choice: a party or a horse. She chose the horse, a filly called Lunalae on which she won two races. Irish racing's premier couple met when they were still in their teens and competing against each other in Galway. A scriptwriter could not have chosen a more fitting mount for O'Brien's race – a horse called Midsummer Fun.

O'Brien left school before doing his Leaving Certificate and had a variety of jobs, such as weeding strawberries and driving a fork-lift truck. Having learned his craft in Jim Bolger's training yard, O'Brien then switched his allegiance to his new wife, who had secured a trainer's licence. Anne

Marie's father, Joe Crowley, is considered to be one of Ireland's best judges of horses. From her base in Piltown, County Kilkenny, in 1993, Anne Marie became the first female champion national hunt trainer, but a new role was opening for her as a mother. Her husband stepped into her training shoes and the rest is history.

As in all sports, fresh blood is the lifeline of racing. In his first full year as a trainer in 1993–94, he registered an amazing 176 winners, despite being only 25. New shoots spring up every season but it was immediately obvious that the racing public was seeing the emergence of a full flower. It wasn't just because he had a lot of winners that he caught people's eye, but because he won so much with mediocre horses. This inevitably raised the question: if he can train ordinary horses to win, what heights could he reach if he were given good horses? One of the people to consider the question was John Magnier, who invited him to train at the legendary Ballydoyle establishment. The answers came fast and furious. A new master of Ballydoyle was born, with a determination, a single-mindedness and a passion that the previous master could only admire.

Like Cliff Richard, he does not look his years. Two years ago a prospective owner arrived in Ballydoyle for a scheduled appointment. O'Brien was doing casual work in the yard and was dressed like a stable boy. The stranger asked him, 'Where's the trainer?'

We reap what we sow. The turning of the world depends on countless unsung heroes going about their business of earning a quiet living. But the salt in the soup is provided by exceptional people who take risks for no more fundamental reason than it reminds them that they and the rest of us are alive. Aidan O'Brien is such a man.

Silken Skills

In 1996 O'Brien had his first victory at Cheltenham with Urubande. Istabraq (the name means 'silk' in Arabic) gave him his second the following year. Istabraq was a foal by Saddler's Wells out of Betty's Secret and a three-parts brother to Secreto, who famously won the Derby in 1984. With those genes he might have been expected to enjoy a career on the flat, but nature endowed him with his father's stamina rather than his mother's speed. In the words of Charlie Swan, 'Riding him is like driving a Rolls-Royce.'

He won only two races out of ten starts on the flat, though despite this was made ante-post favourite for the Cesarewitch Handicap as a three-year-old. Istabraq's first outing over jumps came at Punchestown, when he was beaten by a head following a mistake at the last. The 1998 Champion Hurdle was his ninth consecutive win. He made history by becoming the first SunAlliance winner to win the Champion Hurdle.

St Charlie's Day

In 1997 Istabraq had won the SunAlliance despite being saturated in a sea of sweat. Being the consummate professional trainer, Aidan O'Brien decided to do everything possible to keep the horse cool the following year. The horse was brought into the parade ring just seconds before the bell for jockeys to mount was sounded. Charlie Swan got on at the last moment and although the horse started to sweat then, it was nothing like the previous year. Swan was brimming with confidence: 'Four days before the race Aidan told me Istabraq would destroy them. I knew he had to be exceptional for Aidan to say that.'

It was an excellent opening day for Irish jockeys, with a double for Tony McCoy, Paul Carberry, a late substitute for the injured Tony Dobbin, winning the William Hill National Handicap Hunt Chase and amateur rider Séamus Durack, born in Perth but reared in Tipperary, winning the Kim Muir on Time For A Run. Durack's victory vindicated his decision early in 1996 to leave an equine science course at the University of Limerick after a year to work as a stable lad for English trainer Philip Hobbs.

The Smurfit Champion Hurdle brings a cheque of over £100,000 to the winning owner. It is indicative of J.P. McManus's wealth that this sum would hardly have been considered significant as he stepped up to collect his purse after Istabraq's 1998 St Patrick's Day triumph. Such was the Irish money on Istabraq, who started as 3–1 favourite, that top bookie Victor Chandler claimed it was the most costly race of his days in Cheltenham. Asked about the scale of his winnings, J.P. McManus would simply say, 'It should be enough to pay for the party.'

As had been the case the previous year when Charlie Swan had galvanised the horse to hold off the challenge of Fred Hutsby's Mighty Moss, the dividends were as much emotional as financial. The horse had been recommended to McManus by John Durkan at the Newmarket July sales for £40,000, when he was assistant to John Gosden. Almost immediately Durkan predicted that the horse would win the SunAlliance. In 1997 Durkan lay in hospital in New York fighting a brave battle against leukaemia while the horse he had trained fulfilled his prophecy. By the following year, as Istabraq went on to an even greater triumph, Durkan had tragically lost his battle. The John Durkan Leukaemia Trust Fund was set up to raise funds to establish an Institute of Molecular Medicine.

In 1997 Istabraq was the first Irish winner of the Cheltenham Festival. The importance of this, and the Irish dimension in general, for the festival was generously acknowledged in Brough Scott's comment on Channel 4: 'We have lift-off!'

That year O'Brien's growing self-confidence was apparent when he openly shared his high hopes for an unraced two-year-old colt named King Of Kings to journalists. The following year, when one of those journalists returned, he asked O'Brien if he had another King Of Kings. Without a second's hesitation O'Brien replied, 'We've got ten of them.'

There were occasional blips along the way. Plans for his 28th birthday celebrations that October were dampened at rain-soaked Tipperary when he was fined £500 by the stewards for using the racecourse as a training ground with the two-year-old Gentle Thoughts. The filly was suspended from racing for 30 days after finishing hugely impressively in third place after racing at the rear of the field at the two-furlong marker.

Attention to detail is central to O'Brien's success. On a trip to England where travelling horses were provided with two beds of straw, O'Brien brought four extra of his own, in addition to humidifiers, oxidisers and a 24-hour guard for the horses. Every horse sent abroad to a race by O'Brien travels under the watchful eye of his travelling head lad, Pat Keating.

Before Cheltenham 1998, Istabraq had not been very impressive in his narrow victory over His Song in the Irish Champion Hurdle at Leopardstown. The doubters were not assuaged when Aidan O'Brien said he was preparing the horse for Cheltenham and he could not afford to have him peaking seven weeks early.

Shortly before the festival, O'Brien temporarily surfaced from the cocoon of his meticulous organisation to take part in a revealing exchange with Ted Walsh. Walsh asked, 'How much is there between Istabraq and Theatreworld?'

'A couple of minutes,' answered O'Brien.

'A couple of minutes on the gallops or in the stables?'

'At least a minute on the gallops.'

'If that's the case, Istabraq will be in and hosed off before Theatreworld has crossed the line. John Magnier [owner of Theatreworld] won't be a happy man.'

Istabraq became the first Irish-based winner of the race since Dawn Run in 1984, and the result was confirmation not only of Aidan O'Brien's genius as a trainer but also of his abilities as a tipster, after he predicted that his other runner, Theatreworld, was the only danger. Theatreworld duly finished second, 12 lengths behind Istabraq – the greatest winning margin since 1932.

1999 saw almost a carbon copy of the previous year's event when Istabraq stormed ahead in the final two furlongs with a terrific burst of speed in glorious sunshine, although the horse had sweated badly in the paddock before the race. He cruised to the last and when Charlie Swan asked the question Istabraq answered emphatically, eventually winning by three and a half lengths from stablemate Theatreworld (finishing in the frame for the third year running) and French Holly. The 1–2 favourite was immediately made 7–4 favourite for the Millennium Champion Hurdle, though such was the manner of Barton's victory in the Royal and SunAlliance Novices' Hurdle the following day that he looked like he would provide Istabraq's sternest test.

Odds On

The only Irish eyes that weren't smiling belonged to the bookies. Ian Marimon of Paddy Power Bookmakers is dismissive of the story of a rich bookie, a poor bookie and the tooth fairy who are in a room with a £100 note on the table when the light goes out. When the light comes back on the money is gone. So who took it? It's got to be the rich bookie, because the other two are figments of the imagination. He winces at the memory of Istabraq's wins.

> Cheltenham is huge to us. There are two types of racing days for us: ordinary days and Cheltenham days. The difference between the two is like the difference between the FAI Cup final and the World Cup final! It's the focal point of racing for all Irish fans. I'd say our business goes up about 500 per cent for those three days.
>
> The Irish are very patriotic backers. They lay a lot of money on Irish horses. If you think back to Cheltenham 1998, we had to pay out a small fortune when Istabraq won the Champion Hurdle. There was also an incredible amount of money on Florida Pearl as well – after all, he was the Irish banker of the meeting. The only thing that saved us in that case was that Florida Pearl's odds were very low. The other thing that saved us that year was that Dorans Pride didn't win the Gold Cup. If he had, we would have had to pay out a seven-figure sum.
>
> I know people love stories about people making fools of the bookies. I think straightaway of Barney Curley. He had a stud farm

in Wicklow, populated it with moderate horses and began to place them in weak races where he knew he could make a killing. His most famous coup was with Yellow Sam at Bellowstown [in the two-mile-five-furlong Mount Hanover Amateur Riders' Handicap Hurdle] in 1975. The horse had odds of 20–1. Barney had men laying bets on the horse at shops all over the place. It was a simple plan really. The betting system worked by off-course bookies phoning through to the course to offset their potential liabilities, preventing fancied horses going off with big odds. By the time the horse ran, the odds should have been 1–2. The beauty of the situation from Barney's point of view was that there was only one phone line into the ground and this huge, fat guy got hold of it, claiming his mother was sick, and he wouldn't let go of it until the race was over. So nobody knew what was going on outside! It is said that Barney won £300,000, which is a lot of money even now but it was a massive sum back then.

Barney Curley is one of the most fascinating characters in Irish racing. Born in Fermanagh, as a young man he was training to become a Jesuit priest, but when he contracted tuberculosis at the age of 21 he was compelled to spend a year in a sanatorium and his life took a different direction. The clerical influence has obviously lingered, though, and not only in the way he still says the rosary every day. Years later, after John McCririck publicly criticised him, Curley confronted him and said, 'Never, ever mention my name on television again, or I'll defrock you in front of your viewers.' Curley had a number of careers which included managing Frankie McBride, who became the first Irish showband singer to chart in the British Top Ten.

In 1984 Curley tried a different form of gambling when he raffled his mansion in Mullingar in Middleton Park. Private lotteries were illegal, so to give it a veneer of respectability he enlisted a charitable cause, the local Ballingore GAA club, and all purchasers of tickets were enlisted as members and requested to answer three simple questions to introduce an element of skill. It was a complex scam and involved a promotional film featuring a voice-over by the most respected voice in Irish racing, Michael O'Hehir. The draw itself was televised by the BBC. Curley and O'Hehir were charged under the Illegal Gaming Act but the charges against O'Hehir were later dropped. On appeal, Curley escaped a three-month jail sentence and kept the proceeds of the raffle, a tidy sum of £1.8 million.

The Racing Post once asked, 'Who is Barney Curley . . . and why does he make such a bloody nuisance of himself?' Although he was unable ever to pull off the same scam again as he had with Yellow Sam, Barney found another way around the bookies when he paid a telephone engineer £1,000 to knock out all the phones in Thirsk for a short time to allow him to back an unraced three-year-old called Tralee Falcon at 14–1 – and enable him to pick up £80,000 in winnings.

Ian Marimon is glad that there is only one Barney Curley.

> There are a few other guys you want to keep a careful eye on. Of course everybody knows about Gay Future, when 'the Cork Mafia' famously, or infamously, depending on your point of view, switched a horse. Although people thought it was fishy, nobody was sure until somebody rang back to check in Ireland. It was the cleaning lady who answered and, not realising she was being probed, with blissful ignorance she spilled the beans. The boyos were convicted of fraud. If they hadn't been found out they would have made £200,000.
>
> My favourite story, though, has to be the story of the Trodmore Races – it must be the most brilliant fraud ever in the history of racing. Of course the most intriguing thing about the story is that it was found out – which raises the question of how many frauds there were which were never discovered.

This coup dates back to 1 August 1898. It was every punter's ultimate fantasy: managing to publish a racing card in the papers for a meeting that never existed and, the icing on the cake, publishing the 'results' the following day. The brains behind the scam were even considerate enough not only to arrange their own winners but to return their own SPs.

It all began with a letter in *The Sportsman*, a daily newspaper published in London, from a writer who signed himself as 'G. Martin, St Ives, Cornwall', enclosing a card for the six races at a meeting at Trodmore. The fraudsters shrewdly chose a Bank Holiday Monday, a particularly busy day in the racing calendar when overworked journalists were delighted with this generous assistance from an external source. The runners were duly published in *The Sportsman* and the schemers went into action. Betting shops would not appear on the scene for another 63 years, which left them with two alternatives: they could either bet on credit or try their luck with the street bookies that were commonplace in London. Betting on credit was effectively a non-runner, because they had to pick up their winnings and disappear before the truth was uncovered. Clearly they had to spread their bets thinly so as not to excite suspicion about their interest in a meeting no one had ever heard of. Their plan worked perfectly and Mr (or

Ms) Martin telegraphed the results to *The Sportsman*, which obligingly printed them the next day. The plotters were too shrewd to let greed get the better of them: the six winners featured four favourites and two 5–1 winners.

The Sporting Life were a little miffed by its rival getting exclusive news of this meeting and responded appropriately – by lifting the results and reprinting them the following day. That's when the careful planning went wrong. There was a typing error and one of the 'winners', 'Reaper', was listed at 5–2 although *The Sportsman* had stated 5–1. Inevitably the bookies wanted the discrepancy explained. Investigations into Trodmore and G. Martin revealed a spectacular swindle. It was not until 23 August that the general public learned of this breathtaking audacity, when *The Sportsman* published the following:

> Investigation has shown that there is no such place as Trodmore and that no race meeting was held on 1 August in the neighbourhood of St Ives, Cornwall. It is obvious, therefore, that 'Martin', by himself or in league with others, invented the programme and report in question for the purpose of defrauding bookmakers, several of whom have communicated with us.

The hoaxers were never caught, though the finger of suspicion was pointed at members of the Fourth Estate as rumours of an 'inside job' abounded. The chuckles quickly evaporate as Ian Marimon describes the other side of the story.

> Nobody sheds any tears when the bookies take a big hit at Cheltenham – or anywhere else, for that matter. Yet sometimes it's no laughing matter. I think back about ten years ago when Rotherfield Greys won the Stewards' Cup at Glorious Goodwood. The horse was owned by people from the West of Ireland and most bookies were caught out very badly when he won. I think about 10 per cent of the independent bookies in Ireland went out of business. I know of at least five bookies in the Galway area who went to the wall. Obviously it's not just a personal tragedy for them, it's terrible for their wives and families also.
>
> That said, even though we may have to pay out a lot of money over those three days, and although we might have mixed feelings when horses like Istabraq win, we all enjoy and look forward to Cheltenham.

How then did Istabraq's 1998 win affect ante-post betters?

> After Cheltenham we immediately offered odds of 7–2 for Istabraq to retain his title the following year and odds of 6–1 for Florida Pearl to win the Gold Cup. Immediately we had bets of £2,000 and £4,000 on Istabraq and a couple of £1,000 bets on Florida Pearl at those odds. Every working day for the rest of the year we got at least one phone call enquiring about their ante-post odds.
>
> Ante-post punters are a particular breed. You don't get people like J.P. McManus backing ante-post because he reckons too much can happen in a build-up to a race, like the wrong weather conditions or a slight injury, but there are always some who will give it a go.

Professional ethics preclude Ian from revealing too much about his company's client list.

> There are a few people who make us immediately sit up and take notice when they come in to put on a bet. Their track record is hugely impressive. In fact, when they come in to back a horse, some of us have been known to go around the corner and put a few quid of our own on the horse they fancy. Usually our confidence in their skills is well placed.

Best guesstimates indicate that Irish punters spent £15 million on the 1999 Cheltenham Festival, losing between £3 million and £3.5 million.

Champion Charlie

It is a curious irony that while his biggest threats at Cheltenham are Irish jockeys based in England, such as Tony McCoy, Adrian Maguire and Richard Dunwoody, Charlie Swan is of British stock, with an English mother and a Scottish father. In fact, his great-great-great-great-great-grandfather was Bonnie Prince Charlie's physician.

In 1993 Swan became the first jump jockey in Irish racing history to ride 100 domestic winners in a calendar year. He had had his first winner under Rules in 1983 on his first ride in a two-year-old race on the flat on Final Assault, a horse owned by his grandmother, trained by his father and broken in by Charlie himself. He went on to serve his apprenticeship with Kevin Prendergast at the Curragh, and rode 56 winners on the flat before increasing weight necessitated a change to the jumps.

Swan left a lasting impression on racing enthusiasts at the Curragh in 1984, when he briefly became Cheeky Charlie.

> I was riding a filly in a mile-and-a-half handicap. The valet gave me breeches which were too small for me. As I burst out of the stalls, the poppers they were done up with burst open. After half a furlong the bloody breeches were down my knees! I kept trying to pull them up. Christy Roche yelled at me, 'Leave them alone! You'll fall!' But I kept trying because I didn't want people in the stands looking at me in my underpants. It was completely impossible and I just gave up. I rode for the line with my breeches hanging loose below my knees, feeling a right fool. I finished a close third, and were it not for the breeches I could have won. Since then many people have said they saw me that day – which is not the memory I want people to have of me!

This, though, is the only time in Swan's illustrious career when he was left feeling a proper Charlie. He then moved to Dessie Hughes, hero of the 1979 Champion Hurdle on Monksfield, and became champion jockey in 1989–90. His first ride at the Cheltenham Festival was in 1987 on a horse trained by his father, Donald, called Irish Dream. It would be three years before he would notch up his first win there, in the Stayers' Hurdle. He struck gold with the Mouse Morris-trained Trapper John. But victory did not come easy.

> Cheltenham is a tough course to ride, especially if there are big fields. It's quite tight and you need plenty of luck if you are to get a clear run. You are on the turn most of the way. Especially down the back straight it seems as if you are always on a slight curve, and the hills make it even higher. I followed Mouse's instructions and kept the horse wide and it really paid off for us because he wasn't a great jumper. He was a really tough, genuine horse, though. Richard Dunwoody made the early running on Bluff Cove but I passed him after the final flight and we galloped to victory.
>
> There was a lot of pressure on us because there hadn't been an Irish winner at the festival for two years. The tears were coming down Mouse's face. When I pulled him up, he was lame and I had to lead him back to the winners' enclosure. This was a disappointment, because since my first ride at the festival on Irish Dream in 1987, I had dreamed of riding into the winners' enclosure in triumph.

After the race I was told the stewards wanted me. They told me I was guilty of excessive use of the whip and that they were suspending me for two days. To be honest, it didn't bother me at all. I had ridden my first Cheltenham winner and that's all that mattered.

In 1993 Charlie Swan won the Triumph Hurdle on Shawiya. That same day he claimed his fourth victory of the meeting to win the Bonusprint Stayers' Hurdle on Shuil Ar Aghaidh, having won by 12 lengths on Montelado and Fissure Seal on the opening day.

Swan won the Ritz Club Trophy as the meeting's leading rider in both 1993 and 1994. One of his most notable victories came in the '94 meeting on Time For A Run after the trainer, Edward O'Grady, famously told him to go out and ride 'with balls of steel'. What is Champion Charlie's attitude to Cheltenham?

There's that bit more pressure beforehand at this meeting but once you're out there on the horse it's just down to whether you're good enough.

It's a nice rivalry at the festival on the track and in the stands. When you look at all the trouble north of the border, it's good to see everyone so relaxed at Cheltenham, where the Irish and English thing is so good-natured. Cheltenham will always be *the* meeting for me. I just love it.

Aidan O'Brien is Swan's number-one fan.

To my mind, he is the best jockey in the world. I have seen plenty of rivals but I have no doubt whatsoever that he is better. None of the others have his racing brain. He also has a great pair of hands and, while he can be as hard as necessary when a horse is not doing enough, he is basically kind to his mounts. He has a gift for this game, and he is able to assess horses simply by riding against them. Even when he does not win a race, he picks up valuable knowledge that he can put to use to beat the opposition the next time. He would often ring me at midnight with ideas on how we might improve one of the horses' chances of winning. I'm glad he is so serious about his job because it helps me to do mine.

He's very good with owners and doesn't blame the horses when he loses. The way I work is that everybody is held responsible for their particular aspect of the job. It's the jockey's job to ensure that the horses jump properly. Although I usually know how he plans to run a race, I don't give him instructions because plans often have to be changed. He doesn't like to lose.

Ted Walsh too is a big fan of Swan's.

I've always admired him a lot, not just as a jockey but because of the way he treats people. It doesn't take much for some young jockeys to lose the run of themselves when they get a bit of success, but Charlie was never like that. If a lesser-known trainer with a few horses engaged him, Charlie always gave more than value for money. He's not just a great rider but a class race rider – which can't, I'm afraid, be said for all jump jockeys. He's also a great judge of a horse's abilities, and if he told you yours needed a shorter trip, or a longer trip, or how it should be used in a race, he wouldn't be wrong very often. That advice is worth a good bit. Especially for owners or small trainers, he would always try and find something encouraging to say. He'd always leave the fella feeling good, so that he could tell his mates, 'I had Charlie Swan riding for me today and he tells me that horse of mine could be a nice horse in a year's time.' A lot can happen in a year, so the owner has something to feel good about the next morning.

Trainer Spotter

Aidan O'Brien is one of racing's apostles of specialisation. In 1998, as his haul of classic wins rocketed, he announced that he would devote most of his energies to training horses for the flat. It has been said that the movement to flat from national hunt is preferable because it is a quicker death. Unlike the situation in 1959 when Vincent O'Brien bade his sad farewell to Cheltenham, however, the new master of Ballydoyle is maintaining some of his top jump horses like Istabraq.

Keeping it in the family, most of Aidan O'Brien's national hunt horses were switched to his sister-in-law, Frances Crowley, a former successful jockey at the tender age of 25. Not all sisters in this extraordinary family have careers in racing; one works in graphic design and another in an art gallery. But armed with a B. Comm from University College, Dublin, and a postgraduate degree in equine studies from the veterinary college in Ballsbridge, Frances took out her training licence in June 1998. Although she professes to suffer from Vibrating Binocular Syndrome during big races, as would have been expected she was an immediate success both on the flat and in national hunt, notably with Golden Rule's triumph in the Cuisine de France Handicap in the Curragh that same month.

O'Brien is a very self-effacing man, perhaps too much so for his own good; yet this is a restraint passing unrecognised as a hidden strength, intended for the good of others. Even so, there are times when his friends see that observant eye register just a faint shadow of irony. He can be quick enough to smile dissent with a tiny curl of his lip. He does not heed any rumours; he does not care for gossip; he is too busy tending his horses and pursuing his ambitions to worry about what others think. What is the source which creates and drives this man? He is accommodating to the question but is unable to conceal the merest hint that he has taken on board George Bernard Shaw's advice not to 'waste time on people who don't know what they think'. The mystery remains deep within the man.

Given O'Brien's astonishing progress up the ladder of success, who said the past alone has heroes? When Ted Walsh is asked the secret of Aidan O'Brien's success, the answer comes with lightning speed: 'Youth.'

What do you mean by that, Ted?

> Well, he's very young, and because of that he's got the hunger. That drives him to work very, very hard and that's why he is such a success. He's been lucky in one way in that part of the benefit of our so-called Celtic tiger is that we can keep our best young horses here now. If you think back to 1989, when the Irish had a blank in Cheltenham, our economy was in a bit of mess so a lot of good horses had to be sold. That doesn't have to happen now. If you think of Archie O'Leary, he could have sold Florida Pearl for £300,000 and yet he's only a stride away in any three-mile chase from being worth nothing. I know this is straying off the point a bit, but I think the late Mrs Hill too was a brave woman because she could have got a fortune for Dawn Run and we all know what happened there. Aidan has the benefit of having a lot of owners holding on to their promising horses and not selling them when there's the first sign of a few bob profit – and he even has J.P. McManus importing some from France for him!

Walsh is more circumspect when asked about Istabraq.

> It takes time before you can make a proper evaluation of a horse. You can only really do it after a horse's career has finished. Istabraq is a wonderful horse but I think it's too early yet to have the last word on him. He's a class act and is a lovely ball of a horse. He has

stamina and speed. J.P. McManus has a lot of horses in training but Istabraq is the sort you only get once in a lifetime, and then only if you are very, very lucky. He likes jumping and runs as straight as a gun barrel. Think of the way he won at Cheltenham in 1998 – he absolutely trounced the opposition. I've heard people saying that he didn't have to face the same calibre of horse as Monksfield did when he won his Champion Hurdle. But you can only beat the best that is around at any given time. We are always looking for heroes and Istabraq is definitely a hero. Whether or not he would have beaten Hatton's Grace or Sir Ken at his best is another question, and ultimately a pointless one. Mind you, for the first time since Arkle they're betting at Cheltenham in the Champion Hurdle without Istabraq because everybody's expecting him to win. The only betting is about who's going to be in the places. He's got everything you would want a great horse to have, allied to a great jockey and a wonderful trainer. I would rate him right up there with the great Champion Hurdle winners.

TWELVE

A Pearl Beyond Price

'Remember – Lady Godiva put all she had on a horse.'

W.C. FIELDS

It is a tribute to steeplechasing's ultimate champion that through the years there have been a number of Irish horses prematurely labelled with the tag of 'the new Arkle'. Any Irish horse who attacks from the start reducing opponents to routed cavalry provokes comparison with 'Himself'. Hail the new Arkle. The most recent equine talent to be laden with the burden of comparison is Florida Pearl, after his Royal and SunAlliance Chase victory in 1998. Despite doubts about his stamina, he was the Irish banker at Cheltenham.

Bankers don't always win at Cheltenham. A case in point was Jim Dreaper's gentle giant, Harcon, owned by Patricia Conway. The Irish banker for Cheltenham in 1995, he only came second to Brief Gale in the SunAlliance Novices' Chase. Florida Pearl, though, did not disappoint. With Richard Dunwoody in the saddle, the six-year-old gelding, the 11–8 favourite, beat Escartefigue, piloted by Adrian Maguire, by a length and a half. The Cheltenham crowd hardly knew where to begin its paean of praise. Odds as low as 6–1 were quoted by William Hill for the horse to win the Gold Cup the following year, while the Tote went 10–1.

Florida Pearl had been the first of 14 Irish horses to arrive on Saturday afternoon at the green patchwork of fields which constitutes the backdrop to the festival, with another 30 due to be stabled at the course the following night for the annual three days of ecstasy.

The Life of Brian

Another web was spun in the lush Irish tapestry of Cheltenham that same day by Brian Harding from Castletownroche in County Cork. He deputised for the injured Tony Dobbin, who had been hospitalised after injuring his thumb in a fall on the opening day of the festival, as One Man finally laid his Cheltenham ghost to rest in the Queen Mother Champion Chase. This victory followed a year on the sidelines after a serious head injury.

On previous visits to the Cotswolds, One Man had always fallen victim to the final, unforgiving ascent to the line. Abysmal performances in the Gold Cup suggested a flaw beneath the horse's buoyant racing style and the decision to drop the grey back to two miles had an air of desperation to it. However, he dominated throughout, jumping with easy fluency, as Or Royal vainly pursued him up the hill.

The media attention on the day was chiefly on Top Cees, well ridden by Barry Fenton to claim the Coral Cup. The previous month the horse had entered racing's hall of fame, not because of his exploits on the track but through events in the courts. The High Court had upheld a libel action brought against *The Sporting Life* by Lynda Ramsden, his trainer, her husband Jack and Kieren Fallon, the champion flat jockey, and awarded them £195,000 damages plus costs. In an editorial, the newspaper had unambiguously accused them of deception in their running of Top Cees before he won the Chester Cup at Newmarket in 1995. After the race at Cheltenham, Channel 4 presenter Derek Thompson, whose evidence had formed the keystone of the defendants' case, was subjected to much unsolicited advice and to the chant of 'Tommo, Tommo, where are you now?'. Not surprisingly, he did not seek an interview with anyone connected with the winning horse. Although the odds were 11–1, Jack Ramsden's comment attracted many chuckles: 'He has always been a good earner, one way or another.'

The Bumper King

Willie Mullins went on not only to confirm his place in one of the great Cheltenham dynasties but also to save the bookies' bacon. Florida Pearl and Istabraq had rubbed salt into their wounds; French Holly and Unsinkable Boxer had also cost them dearly. In the Wetherby's Champion Bumper, he preserved them from the *coup de grâce*, as Alexander Banquet bravely denied the white-hot favourite Joe Mac. Mullins's horse looked like being a good second to Joe Mac turning for home but, when push came to shove, he kept pulling out a bit extra up the hill, thriving on hard work.

It was the Bagenalstown-based trainer's third consecutive win in that race, earning him the sobriquet 'the Bumper King'. His first had come with Robert Sinclair's Whither Or Which in 1996, when he doubled up as jockey. His previous wins in the saddle at the festival had come on Hazy

Dawn, the horse owned by singer Roly Daniels, in 1982 and Mac's Friendly in 1984. Both wins came on horses trained by his father and in the National Hunt Chase. Willie's first win as a trainer at the festival came in 1995, when Tourist Attractions won the Supreme Novices' Hurdle, and that year he also rode Skehanagh Bridge to get third in the bumper. Although his 1999 runner, Alexander Banquet, had impressed when beating Malabar on his introduction over two miles at Navan in February, he was unable to make a major impact at Cheltenham.

Ted Walsh explains the appeal of the bumper for the Irish.

> Well, they're always very competitive. At Cheltenham it's always a great spectacle because it rides very tight and it's pretty bunched, 'cos everyone's looking for some daylight. I suppose the fact that they go at a fair old pace helps the spectacle. The bumper is a big part of the Irish racing culture but it's not so in England – especially because they normally don't pay decent prize money for it. That's probably why the Irish do so much better than the English at the bumper in Cheltenham.

Florida Pearl's owner Archie O'Leary is a big admirer of the trainer of one of Irish racing's hottest properties, who is famous for minimising risk and maximising potential. His association with Willie Mullins began in 1993. Almost immediately he thought he had unearthed a real star in the shape of Afghani, but the attrition rate amongst the equine athletes ensures that the shadow of failure will always dog even the most successful stride. Injuries turned the dream sour.

> I bought Afghani one week before he won at Listowel and I told Willie if we won he would have half the prize money. A week after Listowel, the horse got a tendon injury. Willie rang to tell me and told me he'd torn up the cheque. Not many trainers would do that. It was a shrewd move on his part too, though.

A replacement, Florida Pearl, was purchased from Tom Costello for £50,000 after only one point-to-point run.

> If he had turned out to be useless, I'd have looked a complete arsehole, but there's no point being like so many others who are paying peanuts and expecting a new Arkle. Willie just said, 'It's your money,' and I said, 'Go.'

Since Florida Pearl's career started to take off, O'Leary has turned down a number of lucrative offers for his star horse.

> What am I supposed to do with that kind of money? Count it every night? Have two steaks instead of one? Maybe if some wealthy sheikh offered £500,000 and then added a few noughts I might consider it, but this horse is all about enjoyment and the buzz. Having said that, if I was a younger man with a younger family I might have done things differently.

Training national hunt horses is an exact science but Mullins is the embodiment of thoroughness.

> Willie is ultra-conservative but very honest and utterly dedicated. I couldn't say enough about him. I just hope he doesn't get too big! He's got tremendous attention to every detail. He worries a lot about small things. An hour before we ran in the P.J. Moriarty Chase, Willie came to me and said, 'His blood isn't right.' I said, 'F**k it, Willie, I don't want to hear it.' We won anyway.
>
> Willie believes that we're too slow in Ireland about sending our horses jumping. He feels that's why we don't have a better record in the Gold Cup.
>
> I asked Willie once about running the horse in the King George. He said a few things. Kempton mightn't suit him. Leopardstown and Cheltenham, with their rangy hills, suit him. A lot of horses are trained to peak for the King George but if you do that you can't peak again for Cheltenham. As far as Willie is concerned, Cheltenham is the one that matters. Plus if you go to Kempton you are at the mercy of the vagaries of the English weather. Also if you go to Kempton you have to cross the sea and you don't want to be doing that too often. Willie is a great believer in bringing a horse fresh to Cheltenham.
>
> Having said, though, that Willie is very cautious, it was a brave decision on his part to put Florida Pearl straight to chasing without even one run over hurdles in public. His judgement was pretty quickly shown to be spot on when he won by 20 lengths on his debut over fences at Leopardstown.

Mullins's head girl and assistant Tracy Gilmore is also greatly admired by O'Leary.

Tracy is wonderful. She imparts an awful lot of TLC to all the horses, and our horse seems to be a particular favourite.

Gilmore had arrived in Carlow from Pennsylvania to get a bit of experience but the arrangement turned out to be less temporary than envisaged. Mullins seems to have a hypnotic effect on foreign women. In 1980, a young woman from Essex came to Doninga to buy an event horse. Jackie, formerly a leading amateur jockey in her own right, ended up marrying Willie and is now work rider for Florida Pearl.

The Trying Game

In the foyer of the Berkley Court Hotel, Archie O'Leary is in his natural habitat. By accident, our appointment coincided with the AGM of the Irish Rugby Football Union. Rubbing shoulders with an assembly line of Irish rugby greats, he pauses for a warm greeting with former Lion Ronnie Dawson.

A thrice-capped Irish second-row forward, O'Leary toured Argentina and Chile with Ireland in 1952. Former Irish captain Jim McCarthy, a close friend of Archie's, remembers this tour with affection.

> It was a total success off the field and a disaster on it! We were the first international team to be beaten by Argentina. When we got there we were told we couldn't play any rugby because Eva Perón had just died. They sent us down to Santiago, Chile, to teach the cadets how to play. After eight days they beat us!
>
> The players didn't take the playing side very seriously. At one stage Paddy Lawler went missing for a few days and nobody had a clue where he was. When he returned, a team meeting was hastily called. The team manager solemnly announced that he had been talking to Dublin, which was a big deal in 1952, and then looked around menacingly and said, 'I'm deciding whether or not to send some players home.' Paddy stood up straightaway and replied, 'We've been talking among ourselves and we're deciding whether or not we should send you home!'

O'Leary loved the rivalry between Cork and Limerick rugby, and also enjoyed the social side of the game.

> Rugby was more fun then than now, although it was pretty tough on the pitch. In fact one of my clearest memories of my Ireland

career is going down on a ball, getting kicked and breaking two ribs and having to play on because Mick Lane had already gone off. That was bloody painful. But on the Monday afterwards, I had an X-ray done which cost £1 11s 6d, so I sent the bill to the IRFU. In return I got a snotty reply which said this was an amateur game and that there was no way in hell they were going to pay for it.

Rugby was good for my business life. It opened doors for me and was a great introduction to people. People feel they know you if you get a name for yourself in sport. It all helps in business. Florida Pearl is a big help to me. He doesn't draw a wage packet but he certainly makes his contribution. I'm amazed that people come up to me in the street and ask me about the horse. We have a very wide following in Ireland.

Natural Born Thriller

Not everyone welcomes having a microphone stuck under their face. The legendary Kerry footballer Ger Power was once asked a question in the build-up to a big match. He replied, 'Whatever I said last year, put me down for the same again this time.'

Like Tom Foley, O'Leary is a natural when it comes to the media. With his vitality and youthful appearance, he would make an ideal star of a Viagra ad – though he gives no indication of needing it! He possesses a decency and warmth that overshadows his great physical powers. He is the Sharon Shannon of racing. He smiles a lot.

He is also an insurance mogul, employing over 100 people in his business. Apart from his headquarters in South Mall in Cork, he also has offices in Mallow, Galway and Dublin. He is proud of his achievements: 'I started off on my own in 1961 with one fella and a girl. As if that wasn't scary enough, the fella wouldn't even talk to me!'

When The Thinker won the Gold Cup in 1987 for trainer Arthur Stephenson, he was so unperturbed that he watched it on television from Hexham racecourse. Archie O'Leary is not so stoic. As he speaks, he gives glimpses of a blindingly bright future for his charge, a vibrancy and irresistibility that seems as though it might sweep all before him.

He is a huge fan of Richard Dunwoody.

> It is an education just to watch him. I think he is a great jockey. He's probably the best of the national hunt jockeys around. He's been a big fan of Florida Pearl from the start. I think it's the horse's athleticism which appealed to him. Although he takes instructions

from Willie, in the final analysis Willie lets him run his own race because it's impossible to plan for all the unexpected things that can happen in a race. He's got a few good years left in him and I intend to get the full benefit of those years!

He has one main wish for his horse.

All I'm hoping is that he will stay free from injury. You think of the tragedies that can happen to a horse in a race. I think back to French Ballerina, a Cheltenham winner in 1998 but a few months later it was all over for him. To win any race at Cheltenham the only luck you need is to avoid bad luck. The first important thing is just to get him there.

On and Off the Rails

Cheltenham is an enormous logistic operation on the ground but the festival represents three of the most popular and most successful days of the whole sporting calendar. At its heart it obviously revolves around horses locked in competition, but what is it about the meeting that makes it the anvil of Irish dreams?

Leopardstown is very good but Cheltenham has a particular Irish buzz because we're taking on the enemy. The days of us having inferior horses are over, so we can keep our best horses at home now, with the Celtic tiger and all that. That's the way it should be. We are competing against them on an equal footing. The Irish trainers are sending better horses to Cheltenham – I certainly wouldn't send a horse to the festival unless he had a good chance of winning because the Irish punters always back Irish horses. Irish farmers breeding a horse or two a year are constantly dreaming that they've found a new Arkle to win at Cheltenham, so the festival and national hunt racing in general are very close to the hearts of the Irish people.

Cheltenham has its own mystique. I've been going there since 1961 and I still get a great buzz. I think it's the best national hunt meeting in the world. The Irish are made to feel very welcome there and they contribute greatly to the economy – in more ways than one!

In 1986 I was lucky enough to have a box on Gold Cup day and to have it halfway between the last fence and the winning post. It was a tremendous finish. Dawn Run won and lost the race three times.

To see the welcome the Irish give when one of our horses wins at Cheltenham is unbelievable. The social life is excellent. In 1998 we weren't sure whether we'd win or not, so when I was arranging a special dinner in advance I called it a win-lose-or-draw dinner.

To win twice at Cheltenham was great, but having won the second I started dreaming about winning the Gold Cup. The mind starts to wander about who the threats might be, such as Escartefigue. On Gold Cup day, though, horses you've not heard much of run the race of their lives.

Anatomy of a Winner

What's so special about Florida Pearl?

> He's a very kind, gentle soul. My nine-year-old granddaughter went up and rode the horse around the yard and he didn't bat an eyelid. He's very photogenic, so that may explain why people have taken him to their hearts. He's very lovable. You saw that at Cheltenham when Dunwoody had him in the ring under his arm. He's an exciting horse, he jumps terribly well and he obviously has the speed. Before his Cheltenham win in '98 people had worries about him staying but Willie never had any doubts.
>
> As favourite he was expected to run well in the Royal SunAlliance Chase, but you need a little luck in novice chases around Cheltenham. Willie's basic plan was to avoid trouble and ensure he got around safely, knowing that there would be enough there for a final big push. We had a couple of anxious moments in that race but Richard Dunwoody kept us out of trouble. Willie's plan worked out perfectly, though I think he might have felt we hit the front a little too soon.

So is his feverish optimism justified and is Florida Pearl the new Arkle?

> Arkle was a star. Florida Pearl is a potential star. He's still a young horse. Come back and ask me that question in a few years!

With his passion rising with every syllable, Ted Walsh has one concern about Florida Pearl.

He's a great horse. He's won over two miles and three miles up the hill at Cheltenham. He's got great speed, ability and potential. People, though, are going to judge him on his ability to win the Gold Cup or not. The only thing that is going to do him down is the media. They have hyped him like mad and then if he doesn't deliver the goods they'll crucify him. Journalists who don't have a bull's clue about racing but have made a good living writing and talking about it had turned him into 'the new Arkle' at a ridiculously early stage in his career. You have to judge a horse on his own terms and not any other horse's – let alone Arkle. Look at the way they hyped up horses in the past, like Carvill's Hill. Florida Pearl is a great horse and if all goes well he's got a great future, but it's not fair to the horse to compare him with the likes of Desert Orchid and Dawn Run.

Even now he's got relatively little experience. Apart from his talent, though, he has two great advantages. He's got a wonderful man on his back. Richard Dunwoody is the best national hunt jockey I've ever seen in my life. He's stood the test of time. The horse has also got a great trainer. What more could any horse want? The Irish racing public love him.

Spectating is no sport for the unfit. At best it leaves you shattered; at worst it could kill you. How thrilled was Archie O'Leary when Florida Pearl won his first race in Cheltenham in 1997?

I didn't enjoy it. I normally don't get overexcited before a race once I see the horse is settled down, but that day I was so nervous my glasses were shaking. Ted Walsh said after we won that having a winner at Cheltenham is like losing your virginity to Kim Basinger. It's all downhill afterwards. Mind you, when I heard that, I had to ask my wife who Kim Basinger was!

In 1999 Willie Mullins was visibly very tense before the Gold Cup. His horses had not run to form, notably Alexander Banquet in the clash of Ireland versus England against Barton, though Balla Sola's excellent performance behind Katarino in the Triumph Hurdle had raised hopes that all the hype about 'the new Arkle' was justified. In the best Gold Cup field of the decade, Florida Pearl, the 5–2 favourite, finished third in the race, 18 lengths behind See More Business at 16–1, although the foremost Irish challenger had looked a big danger at the third last.

A serious injury to the King George and Hennessy winner, the Venetia Williams-trained Teeton Mill, did help everyone to keep a sense of perspective about Florida Pearl's defeat. The race proved the unique power of the sport, which can both crush the spirits and elevate them like nothing else. Ironically, See More Business had only been purchased by his owner when one of his favourite horses, See More Indians, had to be retired because of injury.

The plan for Florida Pearl, still only a seven-year-old, is to go for two more Gold Cups. See More Business, having started second favourite the previous year only to fall at the seventh, has proved that disappointment in the Gold Cup one year can be replaced by triumph the next. Despite the frustration of not winning at the festival for a third consecutive year, Florida Pearl will be back.

PART TWO

The Punters

THIRTEEN

The Sundance Kid

'I backed the right horse, but the wrong horse went and won.'
H.A. JONES AND H. HERMAN

Racing has always had people who were a thorn in the bookies' side. Lord Wigg once said, 'It is frequently asserted in bookmaking circles that my mother and father met only once and then for a very brief period.'

In the 1970s J.P. McManus established himself as a legendary figure with his successes in the betting ring at Cheltenham and elsewhere, to such an extent that top sports journalist Hugh McIlvanney wrote a piece about him in *The Observer* in which he called him 'The Sundance Kid'. The name stuck, and McManus was catapulted to an élite status in Irish sporting folklore.

His Roscommon-born father, Johnny, moved from Dublin to Ballygar before eventually settling in Limerick in the early '50s. Johnny always kept a few young potential showjumpers and also liked to bet on the horses – always a pound at a time. It rubbed off on J.P. The earliest bet he can remember was at the age of nine, on Merryman II when he won the Grand National in 1960 at 13–2.

His punting was a handicap to his academic advancement. He tells a story from his schooldays about a history exam which was due to start at 2.30 p.m. He knew that after 45 or 50 minutes a Brother would come to stand at the door to ensure that no one slipped out early. He fancied a horse very much at Limerick, managed to get out of the room before the Brother took up duty and cycled like mad to the racecourse, only to arrive at Greenpark just as his fancy was passing the post – a winner!

After he left school he moved into his late father's plant hire business. One of his duties was to clear the site for the house that he subsequently lived in. Realising at an early age that the path to fame and fortune was not to be found driving a bulldozer, he decided to become a bookmaker, having dabbled in betting since his schooldays. A lot of his time during his teenage years was spent in Alf Hogan's betting shop in Limerick, when the tax was a shilling on single bets and nothing on multiples. Income tax is the mother of invention.

He went broke twice shortly after he started as a bookie and had to return home. The second time he went back, his mother loaned him a few hundred pounds. He told her, 'If I take it and Father gets to know about it, he won't be too pleased,' as the last thing he wanted J.P. to be was a bookmaker. She told him, 'He won't know anything about it.' J.P. took the money.

> I suppose I had more respect for it than for any money I ever had in my pockets. The odd thing is that I've never been broke since. Sure, I was often, very often, very short of money, but there is all the difference in the world between having a little money and having no money at all. Once you've been flat broke and somehow come through it, you certainly come to respect money and you certainly never want to be skint again.

He considered himself a professional gambler whether he is punting or making a book, but not an addictive gambler. In 1975 he purchased his first horse, the Con Collins-trained double Irish Cesarewitch winner Cill Dara. Since then he has supported many trainers like Eddie O'Grady, Christy Roche, Arthur Moore, Enda Bolger and Donald Swan. Asked how many horses he owns, he replied, 'Too many slow ones!'

The raising of the betting tax from 5 per cent to 20 per cent in the early 1970s prompted McManus to stop betting in bookies' offices and concentrate on the course. He later became a tax exile and moved to Geneva to head a currency-dealing operation. His close friends include Dermot Desmond and John Magnier, and the three have been described as a 'super-rich holy trinity'. All three were rumoured to have made a killing in correctly anticipating the Mexican peso devaluation in 1995 and in July 1999 they were reported to be seeking a 10 per cent share in Manchester United. Desmond was also one of the Sundance Kid's partners in the reported £38 million purchase of the Sandy Lane Hotel in Barbados. Estimates of his wealth vary, but an indication of the depth of his pockets came in October 1998 when he offered a £50 million donation to the Irish Government towards the cost of a new national sports stadium. Little wonder, then, that he is considered the richest man in racing circles, outside the sheikhs and Robert Sangster.

With Godd on our Side

His first Cheltenham winner came in 1982 with Mister Donovan in the SunAlliance Novices' Hurdle at 9–2, trained by Edward O'Grady and ridden by T.J. Ryan. In an interview after the race he said, 'I didn't have a very good day the opening day but I wasn't too bothered, as I was pretty confident I would get it all back on the Wednesday. I expected we might get up to 14–1 but the word got out about Mister Donovan's ability and I had to take far less than those odds.'

The following year he won again with the Edward O'Grady-trained Bit Of A Skite. The Sundance Kid's largesse in the betting ring is in inverse proportion to the volume of his words in public. The following he admitted in a rare interview:

> I didn't have a bob on him. A fortnight before the race one of his feet got a bad infection and the blacksmith had to cut a large hole in the front of his hoof. For 11 days the horse just worked in Joan Moore's equine pool. In fact the morning of the race the hole was filled with Polyfilla, just for cosmetic purposes. We couldn't back him. Sure, who cares now anyway?

The winning jockey was Frank Codd but according to the racecard his name was Frank Godd. One Irish punter, blissfully unaware of the injury, was tempted by the odds of 5–1, saying, 'How can we get beaten with God on our side?'

It took more than eight years for McManus to win his third race at Cheltenham, this time with Danny Connors. He seldom bets on his own horses: 'Once the bookies think I'm having a cut with one of my horses, the odds they offer are quite restrictive.' He made an exception, though, for Danny Connors at 9–1 in a very competitive race with 29 runners, the 1991 Golden Handicap Hurdle Final. With Mark Dwyer in the saddle, he provided Jonjo O'Neill with his first festival winner as a trainer.

In 1994 he won the Coral Cup Handicap Hurdle with the Eddie O'Grady-trained Time For A Run. In 1997 the same horse had a near miss at the festival after being warm favourite in the Fulke Walwyn/Kim Muir Chase. With Philip Fenton in the saddle, he travelled well throughout the race until making a bad mistake at the second last. Although he rallied heroically and gradually closed the gap on King Lucifer, the line came a neck too soon. To compound the disappointment, Fenton was given a four-day ban for his use of the whip.

The First Cut Is Not Always the Deepest

While amateurs tend to scale back when on a winning streak, professionals tend to double up. Love hurts – and so do heavy losses at Cheltenham. The Sundance Kid has had setbacks along the way, notably a bad Cheltenham in 1976, especially the failure of Brown Lad to win the Gold Cup.

There were other disappointments too. Two years later he had the 8–11 favourite, the Eddie O'Grady-trained Jack Of Trumps, in the National Hunt Chase, only to see him fall at the 17th. In 1999 he was supposed to provide Noel Meade with his first win at Cheltenham after 23 years of trying. In 1981 Meade's Batista had been short-headed in the Triumph Hurdle. Eleven years later the Meath-based trainer had shattered the windscreen of his car with his fist after his red-hot favourite Tiananmen Square had lost the festival bumper. Seventeen years later, in the colours of J.P. McManus, he had had one of the Irish bankers for the festival in the Supreme Novices' Hurdle with Cardinal Hill. This tends to be a strong race for the Irish, with 31 successes to date, but Cardinal Hill fell at the second last when travelling well. To compound the Sundance Kid's disappointment, the other leading Irish challenger, his own Joe Mac, did not atone for his defeat in the bumper the previous year, finishing second again.

Cliff Noone, journalist with *The Irish Field*, feels that J.P.'s popularity with racing fans can probably be attributed to his capacity to handle both victory and defeat in the same manner.

> Down through the years there have been great Irish characters at Cheltenham. The late Tom Dreaper, with his great successes at the festival, was obviously one. Of course, anybody in the business will think straightaway of Mick O'Toole and the fact that there was an awful lot of money pocketed in the betting ring after Davy Lad won the Gold Cup back in 1977 – and Mick would have taken great pleasure in that!
>
> Arthur Moore is another that springs to mind, especially the day when he led one of his horses into the winners' enclosure and put his hat on the horse's head between his ears. The English punters had never seen anything like it and were gobsmacked! It had the same sort of impact as when Frankie Dettori first burst on the scene and brought a new style of celebration.
>
> Of course, when you talk about characters today, you must think of J.P. McManus. Like most Irish people, J.P. loves national hunt racing with a passion and Cheltenham is the biggest event in the national hunt calendar – though obviously we would like to think

that Punchestown can rival it, and in recent years it's come very close. For people like J.P. and, indeed, anyone interested in national hunt, from about Christmas onwards all the focus is on Cheltenham and all the big meetings like the Christmas one at Leopardstown are viewed primarily for what hints they offer for Cheltenham. Given the deep-rooted rivalry between the Irish and the English racing folk, everybody here wants to see the best of the Irish horses take on and beat the best of English. Cheltenham is magical because this is where this competition happens, and the festival feeds on this rivalry.

Irish fans support J.P. in Cheltenham because they hope they can share in his success if they follow his lead. The only thing is that in recent years J.P. has become very much more discreet about his punting habits. Everyone knows he will be there having a cut, yet except for a few who are close to him, they have no idea who he is betting on!

Over the years J.P. has put together a very strong team of horses – and not just in Ireland, but with a great Cheltenham hero, Jonjo O'Neill, in England. He has now also started buying top French horses to strengthen his hand at the festival, and that says a lot about how much winning at Cheltenham means to him.

Like most punters, McManus loses as well as wins. He just does it on a larger scale. One example of this is the story about his fortunes during the festival in 1994. He was said to have lost £30,000 after backing one of his own stable, Gimme Five, to win the Gold Card Handicap. The seven-year-old plunged from 10–1 to 4–1 favourite on the day, only to finish 20th. The next day J.P. returned to back Danoli to the tune of £80,000, which saw him take in double that amount. With characteristic understatement, he was widely quoted as saying, 'That put the wheels back on the bike!'

To date, Istabraq's Champion Hurdle victories have been J.P.'s biggest wins in Cheltenham. Given his penchant for naming horses after Limerick hurlers, a number of people speculated that a man named Istabraq must have played for Limerick in their All-Ireland success in 1973! Apart from his Cheltenham triumphs, a particularly satisfying Istabraq win for McManus was his victory in the £50,000 James McManus Memorial Hurdle in Tipperary in October 1997, a race named after the winning owner's father.

Aidan O'Brien, though, is not a man to let the horse's success go to his owner's head. A month before the 1999 festival, McManus went to Ballydoyle to see his star horse – but his visit coincided with Istabraq having a little sleep and O'Brien refused to let him be disturbed. McManus joked, 'So we know who the boss of Ballydoyle is!'

On the second day of the 1999 festival, J.P. was back in the winners' enclosure after the Coral Cup Handicap Hurdle, with Khayrawani, who had finished second in the race the previous year, winning in a photo finish from the John Mulhern-trained Miltonfield. The Irish had the first five horses home, with Generosa, Darapour and Fishin Joella finishing behind the front two. The Irish 13–2 favourite Archive Footage, trained by Dermot Weld, burst a blood vessel during the race and made no impact.

McManus's horse was trained by former Derby-winning jockey Christy Roche, who had been a great help to Aidan O'Brien in the early days of his training career. Another Irish Cheltenham dynasty looked to have been spawned in the shape of the winning jockey, 18-year-old Fran Berry. His father Frank had won six times at Cheltenham, including winning the Gold Cup in 1972 on Glencarraig Lady.

J.P.'s commitment to national hunt was evident when he purchased Le Coudray in France in December 1998 for an undisclosed sum. The four-year-old hurdler, trained by Chantilly-based Marcel Rolland, had proved a major money-winner in his native country, having been the champion of his age group. His victories included the prestigious Prix Renaud du Vivier at Auteuil. This was a major breach of conventional practice; historically, Ireland has always been an exporter of exciting equine talent. The horse was immediately sent to Ballydoyle to the stewardship of Aidan O'Brien. In January the hurdler announced his arrival with an impressive win over Ladbroke winner Archive Footage in the Stayers' Hurdle at Naas with Charlie Swan in the saddle.

Le Coudray started 2–1 joint favourite for the Stayers' Hurdle at Cheltenham, only to be beaten by a neck in the dying strides by Richard Johnson, having his first win at the festival on the 40–1 shot Anzum. In fact, so late did they leave it that the winning horse's trainer David Nicholson had already walked away from watching the race, satisfied that the eight-year-old had earned a place, and Charlie Swan was only aware of the winning horse's presence in the final three strides. Swan felt that he was denied the race by Norman Williamson, the rider of third-placed Lady Rebecca, who had moved across to the stands side turning into the home straight and taken Le Coudray with him. The stewards investigated the incident and agreed that Lady Rebecca had interfered with Le Coudray but found that it was accidental.

Another second came to McManus in the Foxhunter Chase with the veteran Elegant Lord. The 3–1 favourite, trained by Enda Bolger and ridden by Philip Fenton, was beaten by 13 lengths by Castle Mane. There was further disappointment for McManus in the Triumph Hurdle on the same day when his Christy Roche-trained Afarad, who had been travelling well turning for home, ran out of steam to finish third behind Katarino and Balla Sola.

McManus looked to have his hand strengthened with the once-joint favourite for the 1999 Cheltenham Festival bumper, the Christy Roche-trained gelding Youlneverwalkalone, who had jumped to the head of the festival bumper market following an impressive win at Leopardstown over Christmas. However, injury prevented the horse from competing at Cheltenham and deprived McManus of the chance to claim a hat-trick of victories.

You've Got a Friend

McManus paid £13,000 to charity for the racecard of the 1997 Hennessy Gold Cup, a race which saw his great friend Peter O'Sullevan's final BBC commentary. O'Sullevan is uniquely qualified to answer the question 'What makes Cheltenham magical for punters?'.

> In a word, it's about class, or in two words, it's about class and quality. Nothing can take the place of quality. You get the best from Ireland taking on the best from Britain and sometimes France. The true champions come out for the Cheltenham Festival. You never see bad horses winning there. Owners and trainers aren't inclined to send them there unless they have a fair indication that they will be able to compete at this level. So when you've a bet there, you set your judgement and your know-how to the task of deciding between the merits of horses you've seen live or on television. When it works well and you win, then it's pretty great.
>
> Another thing about Cheltenham is that you get a very strong ring, perhaps the strongest you get anywhere in national hunt racing. It's very appealing to bet there because you can have a serious punt without the bookies panicking. Once you've done your homework properly and chosen the right horses, then you will reap the rewards.

Peter O'Sullevan is ideally placed to give a rare insight into the Sundance Kid.

> He's a great friend. He's poured me many a glass of Haut-Brion! I

have to say that I had the great good fortune in the early years of our friendship to get on well with his mother, which is very important for a journalist ringing his home and trying to eke out an interview from him! I admire him enormously for his capacity to take defeat and success equally well. He has a marvellous approach.

He does a lot of things on the quiet to help people. Of course, he's not the only Irish racing personality to be interested in the welfare of others. I've been very impressed to hear about the charity [Direct Aid for Africa] which Barney Curley and Frankie Dettori have set up for the poor in Zambia.

J.P. told me once that the trouble with Cheltenham and jump racing is that you wish half your life away. From September or October you're wishing it was Cheltenham time, and the travelling is usually better than the arriving. Anticipation is the keenest pleasure.

Of course, things don't always go according to plan. One of his Cheltenham winners was Bit Of A Skite. J.P. had been talking with great confidence about the horse for most of that season and I had planned to have a sizeable wager on him, but then the horse got injured and he dissuaded me from having a bet. The next time I saw him was in the winners' enclosure with the horse he had convinced me not to back! In fairness, he felt worse about that than I did.

So where does J.P. stand in terms of the Anglo-Irish rivalry?

What really ignites Cheltenham is the unique partisanship between the Irish and the English. Mercifully it's a friendly rivalry between the two countries. The English and Irish meet on common ground with a shared appreciation of the horse. The English applaud with equal enthusiasm when the Irish win.

There are no other days in the jump-racing calendar which celebrate the jumping horse the way Cheltenham does. Of course, the fact that the festival takes in such a wonderful theatre is a big bonus. The big thing, though, is that it has got such drama. Before it begins there's a great build-up. It attracts a happy obsession, where racing people are expressing their opinions about the odds. If you contrast that with what happens in France for their big national hunt races there's no build-up to them at all. Nobody is talking about them until the actual day of the race.

J.P. McManus is not patriotic when it comes to betting. He makes his decision on who is most likely to win. Okay, if it's an Irish horse it's a bonus, but in betting terms it doesn't make any difference.

Remember that J.P. is not betting for fun. He's not in the business simply for the thrill of having a go. If he doesn't keep ahead of the field, then it's all meaningless. The business is about picking winners at the right odds. That is why reading the form book is so important. You must be able to weigh up the race, take the conditions into consideration and, most importantly, feel you are getting value for money. If he fancies a horse sufficiently it won't bother him that he is not the favourite, though he'll obviously be very keen to find genuine reasons why a horse can drift in the market. You can't put any faith into rumour.

Things go wrong when you lose the run of yourself. Cheltenham generates a buzz all of its own. You can get mentally worn out over the three days. It's not unusual to see men who are normally very cool and who do everything properly doing the right thing for the first day and most of the second day but then losing the run of themselves. If you are to survive in Cheltenham you must be disciplined. Otherwise you'll lose your shirt.

Another trap he generally avoids is ante-post betting. He's got to know the state of the ground before he really makes up his mind. He told me once that, as a rule of thumb, punters usually do better when the ground is soft. When it's fast at the festival meeting, you've got to be extra careful. The records show that, he tells me.

Of course, for the bookmakers Cheltenham is a great luxury. Everybody wants to bet because the festival has an enormous amount of atmosphere. Cheltenham inspires the likes of J.P. McManus. It draws him like a magnet. The trouble with English racing for people like J.P. is that there aren't enough bloody non-triers. Personally, I blame the Jockey Club!

The laughter in his voice betrays his own membership of that august body.

FOURTEEN

The Voice

I have seen flowers come out in stony places,
and kind things done by men with ugly faces,
and the Gold Cup won by the worst horse at the races.

JOHN MASEFIELD

Peter O'Sullevan has it. Dan Maskell had it. Bill McLaren has it. Michael O'Hehir had it. Micheál O'Muircheartaigh has it in abundance. The 'it' is hard to define but it has to do with their power to make the sport they love accessible to all. The ingredients are in-depth knowledge, a love for the sport that knows no limits and an unfailing ability to convey the flow of a sporting event to equally satisfy the needs of the *cognoscenti* and those at the opposite end of the spectrum of sporting knowledge.

Broadcasters and journalists are not universally loved. Hence the story of the traveller wandering on an island inhabited entirely by cannibals and coming upon a butcher's shop which specialised in human brains. A sign in the shop read: 'Scientists' brains £20 per lb; economists' brains £40 per lb; philosophers' brains £60 per lb; and journalists' brains £200 per lb.' The traveller asked why it was that journalists' brains were so expensive. The butcher replied, 'It's because you have to kill ten times more journalists to get a pound of brains.'

Micheál O'Muircheartaigh, though, is completely free from the pretension associated with many of his colleagues. Not for him the nickname given to one of his peers: 'The ego has landed.' Micheál has carved out a unique place in the affections of Irish sport lovers over the last 50 years. The most mundane of matches come alive through his commentary. Everything he says into his microphone is informed by a passion that is as basic to him as breathing. His commentaries are famous for the richness of their texture, abounding with references that delight and surprise.

Last year's Kerryman of the Year was born in Dún Síon, near Dingle, in Kerry. He paints a picture of an idyllic childhood growing up on his parents' dairy farm. The fourth of eight children, the young Micheál loved riding horses, bringing the milk to the creamery and being by the sea.

> I was pretty old when I went to school, nearly six. I remember putting up a huge fight to be allowed to go to school. I am sure I couldn't actually read then, but I actually liked going to school.

At the age of 15, he left Dingle for the first time to attend a college in West Cork, which was the first step towards a career in teaching.

> It wasn't a conscious decision for teaching then. As far as I was concerned, the preparatory exam could just as well have been fishing. I had never been to Tralee, let alone Cork, and had never travelled on a bus or a train.

Was it a huge cultural shock for him?

> I would say it was more exciting really. I've never forgotten when we got into Cork City hearing the young people selling newspapers and shouting out 'Echo'. We didn't know what they were saying, and it was coming from all corners.

After qualifying as a teacher, he took up a post with the Christian Brothers in a Dublin school. With a complete lack of experience, his story is the broadcasting equivalent of *Roy of the Rovers*. He was only 18, training to be a teacher and still adjusting to life in Dublin when a friend saw a notice on the college noticeboard for part-time Irish-speaking commentators. The auditions were at Croke Park, a club game was in progress and each applicant was given a five-minute slot.

> A group of us went. We knew that it would be great fun, we knew we'd be in Croke Park, a place we revered, and, most importantly, we knew we would get in for free. It was an adventure.
>
> They had to pick somebody and they picked me. It is still a very vivid memory. Naturally, none of us knew the players, but I knew one who'd gone to school in Dingle, Teddy Hurley, and another player in midfield. I just talked away at random and people I knew featured very prominently, even though they were not involved in the action at all! I then moved into the big-money league and was offered a massive contract – all of £6! The important thing, though, is that I still enjoy it as much now as I did then.

What is perhaps less well known about Micheál is that he has a passionate interest in racing.

> I love to go horseracing. I've been involved in a syndicate owning part of a horse for a bit of fun. I think fun is what all sport should be about.

Twin-Track

Ireland's best-known voice speaks in twin-track. Gaelic-games analogies are woven into every conversation. This is particularly evident when he speaks about Cheltenham.

> Cheltenham is like the All-Ireland final. Everything leads up to the All-Ireland final. You look at players and teams all year to see how they are developing. It's the same with horses. Owners and trainers will always be measuring the worth of the horse in terms of the way they would perform in Cheltenham. If you like, it's the All-Ireland final of jump racing.
>
> Big crowds go there. Every horse is trying to win. There's a great atmosphere. It's run perfectly, but while it's very well organised, there isn't too much order there. You can enjoy it and move around and meet people and have a bit of fun. I'd say most people there lose money. People don't go to win money. It's a bonus if they do – but it's not everything. The casual punters will only watch the horse they've backed but professional punters will watch everything. They know the colours backwards.
>
> It's like Gaelic games. You know the difference straightaway between the casual fan and the real thing. The casual fan will ask, 'Who will win on Sunday?' The serious fan will ask, 'Who was the greatest player you ever saw?' or, even more tellingly, 'Who is the greatest player never to win an All-Ireland?'

Calling the Colours

Micheál's passion for sport is matched, if not surpassed, by his love of the Irish language. He is currently serving his second term as cathaoirleach of Bord na Gaeilge. He is keen to see young people in particular taking an interest in their native tongue.

I think the Celtic tiger is rubbing off on the arts. There is a new pride in Irish, which, I think, explains why people now use it when they come up to me, in Cheltenham, Croke Park, wherever.

Micheál has himself gone boldly into the world of racing commentary.

I am very involved in Bord na Gaeilge and we sponsored a race at Leopardstown. Given my involvement, I was asked to provide the on-course commentary and RTE also used it in their coverage of the race. It was different and a bit of fun. Both Danoli and Dorans Pride were in the race, though it was a small enough field. I had no problem with Dorans Pride because he wears the Mayo colours. He won and I've been backing him since out of loyalty.

I wouldn't be able to commentate on a big race because I wouldn't be able to call the colours, even though I've watched people like Tony O'Hehir and Des Scahill commentating.

In his broadcasting career Micheál has found evidence that if horseracing is the sport of kings, greyhound racing is the sport of princes. One of his coups was to become the first person to interview a British royal, Prince Edward, on RTE radio. As joint owner of Druid's Johnno, Prince Edward was celebrating his semi-final victory in the English Greyhound Derby at Wimbledon.

It didn't matter to me whether he was collecting the dole or he was a prince, he was the joint owner of the dog. I felt he enjoyed being there and that he would love to come there as an ordinary person and move around and enjoy the proceedings. Maybe go down and have a bet – not that he needed the money, but to be part of the excitement. I had told him that I wouldn't try to catch him out. I assured him we would be talking about sport, and that there would be no politics.

His coup provoked jealousy on the part of the other journalists present who insisted that they hear the tape, but Micheál deftly refused on the basis that he had to get his producer's permission.

A Licence to Thrill

Micheál's trips to Cheltenham have been purely as a fan.

> I think the festival is something special. The cream of horses go there. That's the Mecca. That's where the trainers and owners are aiming at. Followers go there to see the best of horses from Ireland and England compete against one another. I think part of it is that there is some sort of secondary competition going on between Ireland and England. The international aspect is absolutely terrific.
>
> They take care not just of their horses but of the course itself and the fences. They are very stiff fences for the horses, and to stress the care they take, the track they use for the Gold Cup, the race of the meeting, is not used during the year. It's kept exclusively for the Gold Cup, and they dry it and water it and cut the grass and make sure everything is right for the big race.
>
> Some of my favourite Cheltenham moments are Danoli's win and Florida Pearl's great win. I tend to link horses with people, and even though most people know about Archie O'Leary's career in rugby, I remember him as a promising golfer, so it was great for me to talk to him in Cheltenham last year after Florida Pearl's great win. I love it when an Irish horse wins from the smaller stables, in the same way as Derry's All-Ireland win in 1993 and Donegal's victory the previous year are among my most memorable sporting moments because of the emotion they generated. Both were the first senior All-Irelands for the respective counties.
>
> My favourite part of Cheltenham is when the winner is led in, especially if it's an Irish winner. If it's an Irish winner, all the Irish punters think they own the horse. He's not Tom Foley's, or whoever's. He's our horse. Everybody wants to be a part of it.

Two names loom large in Micheál's analysis of the great characters of Cheltenham.

> You'll meet a lot of people there – the same people you'll see at a Munster final or in Croke Park. I think Irish sports followers have changed. You had a particular audience for GAA 30 years ago, a particular audience for rugby. Nowadays you've a generation of sports followers who will go anywhere that they think they will get value. I think that's the way it should be. I think Ted Walsh is a great character and he's become a central part of Cheltenham. If you don't meet him, you'll hear him whether he's near or far away.

J.P. McManus is from Limerick and he loves Limerick hurling. He's very friendly with people who used to play for Limerick. He's called his horses after famous Limerick hurlers, such as Joe Mac, named after Joe MacKenna – the horse that didn't win in 1998! Another horse is called Grimes, after the last Limerick man to captain an All-Ireland winning side, but someone told me he does best on fast ground. A third gets his name from Limerick's great full-back Pat Hartigan, a man whose playing career was sadly ended by an eye injury. McManus's horses race in green and gold colours after his beloved South Liberties club. Cheltenham wouldn't be Cheltenham without him.

The Master

A mild heart attack in 1986 forced Ireland's top sports broadcaster to realise he had to slow down. Yet his mind is as agile as an Olympic gymnast. In fact, Micheál is much more than a sports commentator. He is a national institution. As we march, not always successfully, to the relentless demands of a faster, more superficial age, just to hear his voice is to know that all is well with the world. Although he has dabbled in television, his real forte is radio, as he paints pictures with words like a master craftsman. Irish sport would not be the same without him. He is irreplaceable.

FIFTEEN

The Boss

'Owning a racehorse is probably the most expensive way of getting on to a racecourse for nothing.'

CLEMENT FREUD

Whatever this indefinable thing called presence is, Charles J. Haughey has it in abundance. Such is the force of his personality that even the briefest of meetings with him can be memorable. Early on a November Saturday morning, the sun, appearing on the horizon, throws long streaks of blood-like red into the splendour of his James Gandon home in Kinsealy. Although he is not a tall man, he has the most marvellous eyes which give him a presence disproportionate to his physique. In the decades when he dominated the Irish political landscape, he could control everyone in the most crowded room with a steely glare but with a friendly nod could just as easily evoke great warmth.

His mind is as sharp as an executioner's axe. To listen to him talking about racing is both a pleasure and an education because of his penetrating scrutiny of facts and events, his astute evaluation of personalities and horses and his wry discernment which means that he never resorts to a clutter of common clichés. His love of horses began at an early age.

> When I was young we lived in Donnycarney, which was on the edge of the city then, and there was open farmland around us and there were always plenty of horses nearby. Particularly when we came home from school we used to skip across the fields to try and ride them. It could be very tricky but that was my first experience on horseback.

The spell horses cast on him in his childhood has never been broken and his interest intensified once he became an owner.

> The first few horses I had was back in the '50s. I didn't really own

many horses, though very often friends of mine would run horses in my name. I suppose it really began when a friend of mine, Major Laurie Gardener, who was very interested in racing and had some horses, was going abroad. He had one or two horses on his hands and he just gave them to me, saying, 'Well, I won't be able to race these for a long time so you might as well run them in your name and see how you get on with them.' That was my introduction to racing, and it has continued as a hobby off and on, though never very intensely, right up to the present day.

For all owners, winners are the magic lamp. The anvil of dreams. Racing can bring untold wealth and glory, but it is often expensively and riskily bought, young promise often yielding too quickly to despair. Does Mr Haughey make his own decisions about which horses to buy?

Certainly with regard to racehorses, I would rarely buy. I would usually have an arrangement with somebody who would own them to lease them or something like that. If I were actually buying a horse I would only do so on advice. I wouldn't have the expertise or the judgement to do the selecting myself.

Which of his horses stands out in his affections?

They all do. You develop a relationship with each horse in terms of getting to know their temperament. If racing is to provide you with the fun and the sporting interest it should, you certainly have to get to know the horses well, all their characteristics and foibles and whether they like soft or good going, and gradually you get to know an awful lot about them. It would be very difficult to single any one out because it is very easy to love horses. When a horse loses but gives of its very best, you may have a greater feeling for it than if it had actually won.

I had a horse once called Miss Cossie who was a great sprinter and she won a lot of races for me. I remember that the legendary Michael O'Hehir in his commentaries always pronounced her name as 'Miss Cosy'! I also had a great old servant called Vulforo. He came from Tom Costello in Clare, the famous Tom. Vulforo never hit the highlights but he kept on winning races. In fact, he won over 20 in all, including the Power's Gold Cup at Fairyhouse.

I had the honour of having a horse trained for me by Vincent O'Brien called Aristocracy, who won a race with the King, Lester Piggott, in the saddle. Winning is where the ultimate satisfaction comes but there's infinitely more to racing than that. It's really about knowing your horses.

Wonderhorse

Photos of his horses adorn his elegant home, as do pictures of the former Taoiseach and a *Who's Who* of world statesmen. If great horses can thrill people from afar, they are also sources of wonder to those closest to them. Mr Haughey had the good fortune to own a horse who symbolised the soaring athletic courage that makes jump racing more than a mere spectator sport.

> Flashing Steel was exceptional. He was the sort of horse that comes along once in a lifetime for most people, if at all. He was a wonderful character of a horse, very, very lovable and a brilliant performer: honest, faithful, gallant. He would never, ever not try his best. The finish of Flashing Steel's Grand National in 1995 is the race that definitely stands out for me, and I think a lot of people who were there on the day would agree. It had everything, that finish. It had Flashing Steel's courage and determination, carrying the top weight, coming over the last and putting in that final, storming sprint under Jamie Osborne's inspired guidance. The ultimate credit for Flashing Steel's success, though, must go to his outstanding trainer, John Mulhern. It was he who first identified that the horse had an exceptional talent and it was he who nurtured it and made him the great champion he was. I would regard winning the Irish Grand National as the greatest thing you can do in racing, with the possible exception of winning the Cheltenham Gold Cup.

Much of the media attention centred on the fact that Mr Haughey received his trophy from his former political foe, the then Taoiseach John Bruton. Neither man was in the least bit phased.

> It was an historic occasion – a racing event not likely to be repeated.

Festival Fervour

In 1993 the Queen Mother, Vincent O'Brien, Fulke Walwyn, Fred and Mercy Rimell, Golden Miller, Arkle, Sir Ken, Dick Francis, Dawn Run,

Jonjo O'Neill and Fred Winter were inducted into the first racing Hall of Fame at Cheltenham's Prestbury Park. It is right and fitting that Irish horses and personalities are so well represented. With the passing years, their names have obtained an even stronger evocative power.

Cheltenham is the Mecca of the jumping world. As sensation is to the tabloids, as Lourdes is to the sick, so Cheltenham is to the national hunt fellowship. It is a theatre of equine dreams, stirring abiding memories in its devotees. It has unlimited potential for excitement, drama, tension, spectacle, elation and bitter disappointment, all packaged together – though never neatly.

Charlie Haughey too worships at national hunt's highest altar.

> The Irish are addicted to national hunt racing. They tolerate the flat, I think, but their primary love is national hunt. Anybody would have to admit that Cheltenham is the ultimate where national hunt racing is concerned. Punchestown is really developing and it probably won't be too long before it becomes another Cheltenham. But the Irish love the Cheltenham Festival because it's the best racing. It is a sort of pilgrimage for them, as well as an established tradition.

Cheltenham is the temple, but it demands its sacrifice. Many owners are unable to come up with the goods. Mr Haughey, though, knows what it's like to be a winner in Cheltenham.

> Flashing Steel did very well in Cheltenham. He had an astonishing finish in the Gold Cup to finish fourth. He was nowhere until the final stages but he came up with an amazing spurt. He was always a terrific finisher. He could always come up with a phenomenal burst of speed at the end of a race. Once he was in the leading group he was a formidable presence in any race.

Put not your trust in horses. The 11th commandment is totally ignored for the three days of the festival. Chesterton claimed that the Gaels are the race that God made mad, 'for all their wars are merry, and all their songs are sad'. No fight do the Irish take on with such relish as their war with the English bookies at Cheltenham. Charlie Haughey believes, though, that the Anglo-Irish rivalry is of secondary importance.

> The Irish love the element of rivalry in it but that's not the primary attraction. It is because it is a great calendar of racing. They love a

good horse. The Irish would go just as readily to Cheltenham to see a great English horse and be delighted if it won. They are going for the excellence of the racing. Of course, the major reason the Irish love the Irish horses to win is simply because they have backed them! They are the horses they know best and so they back them and want them to win.

Racing is the iceberg sport. Only a tiny part of the story, the bit on the racecourse, is above the waterline. There are a huge number of people working in the racing industry who are in the main hidden from public view. Eimear Haughey inherited her father's passion for horses. She competed as a jockey in a number of charity races, but her commitment to horses goes much further.

> Eimear is very much into bloodstock breeding. That's her career and she is very good at it. From the very start that's all she wanted to do. She knows it very well. Her knowledge, judgement and expertise would be appreciated by people in the bloodstock-breeding industry who know what it's all about.

He is amused when asked if he ever gives her or her husband, John Mulhern, advice about horses.

> I would never dare do that to either of them because I wouldn't have the capacity. They have between them an almost encyclopaedic knowledge of the bloodstock-breeding industry and racing. So they don't really need, nor I think would they really appreciate, anything other than a mere suggestion from me.

Renaissance Man

Clement Freud once argued in *The Sporting Life* that if the politicians of the two parts of the country behaved to one another with the same *bonhomie* as the racing folk, there would be no troubles in Ireland. Racing personalities figure prominently in Mr Haughey's most admired list.

> One of the most attractive things about bloodstock breeding and racing is that there are so many wonderful people in it, and wonderful characters like bloodstock agent Jack Doyle. I think that if you are in any way involved in it you have to be a character of some sort. Of all the great characters I met down the years, Tom

Dreaper would also be up there with the very best of them. He trained for me and he was a good personal friend and a very lovable man. He was a farmer as well as a trainer. He had an outstanding record and his achievements speak for themselves.

I also have a special affection for Vincent O'Brien. He is still a very close personal friend of mine. He would have to be seen as one of the real greats, not just of Irish sport but of Irish life generally. He taught us all to pursue excellence and not to settle for anything else, only for the very best. He proved that not just in terms of national hunt racing but also when he went on to excel on the flat. Both Tom and Vincent were exceptional people. Dick McCormick on the Curragh was another, and I had a very satisfactory spell with John Oxx.

There have been a number of great Irish jockeys down the years. Eddie Wright and Johnny Roe won a lot of races for me. More recently I am fond of and have great admiration for people like Jamie Osborne and Richard Dunwoody. And you couldn't possibly talk about national hunt racing in Ireland without referring to Ted Walsh, the doyen of them all. I'm very glad that he rode a number of winners for me, but much more important to me has been his friendship.

Mr Haughey is very proud of having a wide circle of faithful friends in every aspect of Irish life. In fact, the day I met him he had just received a letter from one of their number. It included a poem which he thought particularly pertinent given the prevailing tide of media comment about him. It was written in 1923 by Brian O'Higgins, a Republican prisoner in an internment camp known as Tintown in the Civil War, and recently discovered in an old photograph album.

The world will strip your failings
And hide the good you do
And with its sharpened thorns
The ways you walk bestrew;
You'll toil for men - they'll curse you;
'Twas thus, and thus 'tis yet,
And thus 'twill be forever -
But god does not forget.

Brian O'Higgins
Tintown 3
12/12/23

Mr Haughey remains a keen horseman, though he did have a few famous falls during his career. He was once alleged to have said that he chose black and blue as his colours because he was black and blue so often following riding mishaps. He laughs when quizzed about the veracity of that remark.

'I think you'd have to take that as apocryphal!'

SIXTEEN

Patriot Punters

'A mug is born every minute of the day, and thank Gawd some of them live.'

BOOKIE FRED SWINDELL

George Bernard Shaw divided the world into two classes: the equestrian class and the neurotic class. Irish history shows ample evidence of both. Records of early races can be traced back to pre-Christian Ireland, and the mysterious bond between the Irish and their horses continues to the present day. Films like *The Commitments* and *Into the West* popularised the notion of Dubliners keeping horses on the top floor of their tower blocks in places like Ballymun, occasionally taking them down in the lifts for exercise and a spot of lunch in an obliging neighbour's back garden.

Cheltenham's popularity is as difficult to explain to those who have never experienced it as the lbw rule in cricket. For some the festival is a fatal attraction. In 1994, Lord Vestey, Chairman of Cheltenham, said, 'We lose one or two customers each year. It's the sheer excitement that the racing brings to everyone. They die of a combination of factors. But everyone's adrenalin and pulse rise at the moments of high drama at Cheltenham, and I'm not surprised one or two keel over.'

Of course, the Irish represent a bonanza for the local economy, particularly as the licensing hours in the town are extended during the festival. But the gambling fever that overtakes the Irish during the festival is not restricted to betting on the horses. Card games too are a big business, though in the last decade, thanks to the watchful eye of the police, the massive poker games have, allegedly, moved from the bars to the bedrooms.

The Sporting Life once argued, 'The simple truth is that some of our racecourses are poorly run and unimaginatively managed and couldn't attract extra customers if Arkle, Desert Orchid, Nijinsky and the Archangel Gabriel all appeared on the same card.' Cheltenham certainly does not fall into that category. The festival is an adult version of Disneyland. Normal living is magically suspended for a state of communal bliss. It is a licence to thrill and be thrilled – except when the betting arm goes out of control and the annual family holiday has been recklessly squandered. Elation can quickly yield to bitter disappointment.

In this corner of the Cotswolds, punters experience more ups and downs than the Emperor Charlemagne. It's not so much for whom the bell tolls as for whom the wheel of fortune turns. 'Horses don't bet on people. They have too much sense,' sang Tom Lehrer. People don't return the compliment. At Cheltenham, the devil makes work for Irish hands. Even the wisdom of Solomon and the wealth of Croesus would be insufficient to combat the Cheltenham temptations. In this hotbed of frenzy, there is no room for dispassionate reasoning and the previous year's forays with those bookie chappies alter so much in the recollection that history is rewritten to the point of fiction.

Beware the Ides of March

Some Irish punters disagree about the most appropriate adaptation of Bill Shankly's famous line about football. Is it the joy of winning or the joy of beating the Brits that is more important than life and death? Patriotism can be an expensive quality at Cheltenham, however. Many Irish punters have lost their shirts backing fancied Irish horses that have failed to deliver despite the nation's great expectations.

A good start for the Irish always electrifies the meeting. A classic example came in 1998, when four of the first five home in the opening race, the Citroen Supreme Novices' Hurdle, were Irish-trained. The Pat Flynn-trained mare French Ballerina, in the colours of Mrs John Magnier and ridden by Graham Bradley, trounced the favourite His Song by seven lengths in only her third race over hurdles. It was the Carrick-on-Suir trainer's second win in the race, having won with Montelado in 1993. Asked to compare the two winners, Flynn replied, 'If they raced, the photo would take half an hour and the winner would be the one who stuck its tongue out!'

Little wonder, then, that in the old days, when the Irish always seemed to win the first two races, an Irish wit would always turn around to his English hosts and say, 'Sorry lads. When exactly will the English horses start running?'

In 1998 Irish-trained horses won four races (French Ballerina in the Supreme Novices' Hurdle, Istabraq in the Champion Hurdle, Florida Pearl in the SunAlliance Chase and Alexander Banquet in the Champion

Bumper) but 23 others took home prize money amounting to a record total of £430,324 (524,785 punts). Irish jockeys won 13 of the 20 races and were placed on 26 others, with Tony McCoy as the top jockey.

Patriot punters wryly recall stories of the might-have-beens. In 1983, Irish outsider Boreen Prince (50–1) almost snatched victory in the Champion Hurdle when the winner Gaye Brief (7–1) made a mistake at the last flight and threatened to fall. Boreen Prince finished three lengths behind. Gaye Brief made history by becoming the first winning horse in the Champion Hurdle to be trained by a woman, Mercy Rimell, widow of Fred, who had himself both ridden and trained Cheltenham winners.

Rumours of who made what from the bookies go forth and multiply. Estimates of owner Noel Furlong's earnings when Destriero won the 1991 Cheltenham's Supreme Novices' Hurdle vary from £1 to £3 million. And 1977 saw a bonanza day for lucky punters in Cheltenham when a 400–1 outsider, Zulu Gold, emerged victorious. Irish and British backers missed out on a windfall, though, because it was Cheltenham, Adelaide.

Divine Inspiration

The crowd at Cheltenham produces a unique atmosphere unmatched by any other sporting occasion on the planet. The Irish are always at the forefront of the action and intent on having a good time, making every post a winning post, raising the roof as well as their glasses and betting boldly. Horses are to Cheltenham what films are to Hollywood: an obsession that has a pecking order, is discussed endlessly and by everyone and comes complete with its own arcane laws and rituals. The churches of this strange sporting religion are anywhere two or more racing fans are gathered, and its gurus are anyone who can hold an audience.

On festival Tuesday, the stylish Golden Valley hotel in Cheltenham is transformed into a monument of pilgrimage, abuzz with visitors from across the Irish Sea who have come to pay homage at the shrine of national hunt racing. In this case there is no doubt as to what the majority of the faithful are praying for – Irish wins and plenty of craic.

The religious symbolism is increased by the *de facto* chaplain to the Irish congregation, Fr Sean Breen, who has made this unique pilgrimage over 30 times. During Mass for Irish punters at the Cheltenham Festival he once said, 'I know it's difficult for you, Lord, we have so many runners.' Some unkind souls have speculated that Fr Breen's assiduous attendance at Cheltenham is part of a shrewd career move. In 1994 Fr Donal Bambury launched Doncaster's trial Sunday meeting with a service. Almost immediately he was promoted to Monsignor. His cousin, Irish bookie Pat Bambury, responded to this development by saying, 'We had him at 10,000–1 to be the next Pope. I suppose we will have to adjust the odds now.'

Although he does not hide his tendency to pray for Irish successes at Cheltenham, Fr Breen does not partake of what some see as the pagan practice of blessing horses. Whether or not it transgresses the boundaries of theological orthodoxy, it did no harm to Danoli in 1994.

Other semi-religious strands to the proceedings include the fact that from time to time groups of Irish racing fans have walked up to the course carrying an urn in order to scatter a loved one's ashes at the final fence. And rumour has it that some rural communities organise a whip-round to send a representative to Cheltenham in the same way as their Muslim counterparts might sponsor an individual to go on the Haj to Mecca. Finally, according to legend, with each of the great Arkle's three victories in the Gold Cup, the sky was turned black with triumphantly tossed priests' hats.

The Mighty Quinn

Some of Ireland's wealthiest men such as Michael Smurfit are also part of the green invasion, as is former teen idol, style-setter and sometime Irish resident Ron Wood of the Rolling Stones, who has his horses trained in Ireland.

Charles Greenville once said, 'Racing is just like dam-drinking: momentary excitement and wretched intervals; full consciousness of the mischievous effects of the habit and equal difficulty in abstaining from it.' Irish soccer international Niall Quinn, who in 1983 played in an All-Ireland minor hurling final with Dublin, would agree. He is a regular visitor to the festival. His World Cup goal against Holland during Italia 1990, the crucial equaliser in response to Ruud Gullit's goal which secured Ireland's passage into the knockout phases of the competition, earned him a place in Irish sporting folklore. Nowadays Niall also gets goosepimples from owning horses.

Niall had a dream introduction to racing. His first horse, Cois Na Tine, won his first race.

> It's funny the way things work out. I hadn't much of an interest in racing until I bought the horse. Some years ago I was at the Texaco Sports awards and I got talking to trainer Jim Bolger. When I woke

up the next morning I owned a racehorse. We were so lucky to win our first race, but Jim warned me straightaway not to get carried away because you can't win every time.

I became completely wrapped up in racing. I get all the papers and magazines and read up on every horse going. It's always been in my blood but it really gripped me once I became an owner.

Niall sold off the horse to a new owner in America (for £250,000, according to *Raceform Update*, 23 April 1994). Why did he sell a winning horse?

I would have had to win about five League Championships and three European Cups to earn the same money. It was put to me that by refusing the offer it would have been like putting on £40,000 or £50,000 to win, every time it ran, should it fail in the future.

He shipped the horse home when he became injured, saying he was determined he would not be turned into horsemeat.

Apart from being a successful owner, Niall is heavily involved in racing syndicates. In fact, one of his syndicates has been lauded for the way they celebrated – even though they didn't actually win the race!

Really it's a much better day out if you're part of a group or share a horse. The syndicates I'm part of are just great – if we have a winner, that's it, you can count the best part of two days gone. At one stage one of our horses, Hopping Higgins, came second in the Norfolk Stakes in Royal Ascot. We celebrated, though, as if we'd won. I can remember parish priests drinking champagne in the owners' enclosure and a whole gang of us travelled back to Ireland and continued the party at Lillie's Bordello.

Quinn speaks glowingly about his passion for Cheltenham. But sporting success can be a rose with thorns. The demands of Sunderland's push for promotion forced Quinn to miss out on the festival in 1999.

It's the ultimate racing experience, particularly when Irish horses like Florida Pearl or Istabraq are doing well. It's every race fan's fantasy. The Irish bring so much to the meeting. They are there for the sport and for the craic and for the love of the game. Most are happy just to be there. If they win, that's a great bonus.

Like former English international Mick Channon and former Newcastle and Coventry star Mick Quinn (no relation), Niall plans to go into racing once his soccer days are over.

> The racecourse offers similar surroundings and a similar
> atmosphere, and it is also a profession that requires a lot of hard
> work, but the rewards are great.

By Royal Appointment

In the halcyon days of 'amateurism', Wimbledon's strawberries and cream were the preserve of the upper class. One incident illustrates this. The three-times winner in the mid-1930s, Fred Perry, was from a working-class background. He later recalled that, while taking a shower after his first victory, he overheard a leading official of the All England Club referring to his triumph as a 'catastrophe'. The real tragedy, murmured another official, 'is that because he's English we're going to have to pretend to be pleased'! Cheltenham melts away the class boundaries and is a great leveller. One person ideally equipped to give a dispassionate view of the egalitarianism of Irish racing is HRH Princess Haya Bint Al Hussein, daughter of the late King Hussein of Jordan. She was introduced to this world by one of its biggest names.

The 1977 Grand National made history by allowing the first woman jockey to take her place at the start. However, it was an Irish jockey, Tommy Stack, who had the day of his life by steering home Red Rum to win his third Grand National. Stack was born in Moyvane, County Kerry, on 15 November 1945. Initially he worked as an insurance clerk in Dublin, but his interest in racing was triggered by his old school pal Barry Brogan, and after spending some time at Barry's family yard he decided to make his name in the sport. In 1965 he moved to England to join forces with trainer Bobby Renton and began to ride as an amateur, his first victory coming in a handicap hurdle at Wetherby on 2 October 1965 on New Money.

Following two years in the amateur ranks he turned professional, and in 1971, after Renton's retirement, he spent a short period in a dual role as jockey and trainer. In that capacity he briefly trained a six-year-old horse called Red Rum, but later that year he passed on his training duties to Anthony Gillam. In 1974 he became first jockey to W.A. Stephenson. He became champion jockey in the 1974–75 season, clocking up 82 winners. Two seasons later he repeated this achievement with 97 winners. In 1977 he had his finest hour when he won the Grand National on Red Rum, the combination having been narrowly beaten by Rag Trade the previous year.

It was the 12-year-old bay gelding's fifth consecutive attempt at the fearsome Aintree fences – winning both in 1973 (itself one of the great sporting moments when Red Rum pulled back a seemingly impossible lead from the Australian 'wonderhorse' Crisp to snatch victory over the last few lengths) and '74, coming second in '75 and '76 and winning in '77 by 25 lengths. The darling of racegoers, trained by Ginger McCain on the Southport sands, had become the first horse to win this most demanding of steeplechases three times.

Stack retired as a jockey in 1978 and after a career in the Irish bloodstock industry he took out his full licence as a trainer in 1988. He went on to taste success as a trainer, notably when his young chaser Gale Again won at Cheltenham and, 24 hours later, when he claimed his first English classic with Las Menias in the 1,000 Guineas.

It was Stack who introduced Princess Haya to the unique excitement, drama and unpredictability of Irish racing. While she was successfully completing her honours degree in Politics, Philosophy and Economics in Oxford, Stack brought her over to compete at a number of Irish race meetings like Killarney. Her political textbooks and her Irish terrier, Pooky, travelled with her. Her welcome in Ireland was much warmer than her introduction to England had been when she started school there at the age of 11. A dead rabbit was put into her bed a couple of nights after she arrived, and she suffered a severe cold-shouldering later on during the time of the Gulf War. In 1995 she moved to Ireland to learn the ropes of international showjumping with Paul Darragh, although she had competed in her first junior international at the age of 12. For some inexplicable reason she was refused permission to ride in the Dublin Horse Show that year. Her face wreathed in smiles and full of youthful enthusiasm, Princess Haya has no difficulty talking about her impressions of the world of Irish racing.

> Being a princess in Jordan is very different from being a princess abroad. At home I am respected because I am my father's daughter, but in Ireland I am treated the same as everyone else.
>
> The only time I've ever been conscious of my status is when I made a major mistake. Thankfully that didn't happen so much to me in Ireland, but I remember jumping in Japan and having a really bad fall right in front of the press corps. Within seconds I was bombarded with zoom lenses flashing two feet away from me. I wasn't sure whether to get up and walk away or play dead!
>
> The only other time I've made a fool of myself was in Lisbon. All top jumpers when they are walking the course go right up to the

fence and look at it in a deep and meaningful way. I decided to do that too, so I went up to a fence and put my hand on top of it. Immediately the whole fence came crashing around me!

Irish people are very like people in Jordan. They are both very easygoing. I see my country as a poor country surrounded by rich ones, and Ireland is in a similar position in Europe. A sense of humour gets us both by. It may explain why I feel at home in Ireland – people are welcoming and friendly, as in the Arab world. One thing I learned very quickly is that Irish people have a great love for horses. It's the same thing in Jordan. One of the great things about horses is that they bring people together and the barriers between people, whether they be class, religion, sex, skin colour or whatever, don't matter so much. It's not who you are but your love for horses that matters. That's why I loved competing at Irish race meetings so much. There was always a wonderful atmosphere. Of course, people like to win, but it's not the be-all and end-all and everybody really knows how to enjoy themselves.

Lives Less Ordinary: 18 March 1999

A racing fan believes that there are 362 days in the year and then Cheltenham; a racing fanatic knows that there are really only three days in the year and the other 362 are simply a breather until the next festival. Many of these modern-day Irish pilgrims travel with Carlow-based Tully's Travel Ltd, racing-travel specialists. Frank Tully, founder and owner, is celebrating his company's 50th anniversary. How did his association with Cheltenham begin?

We became interested in Cheltenham because we have clients who go every year and one of them said we should charter an aircraft, which we did. We now carry between a thousand and twelve hundred people a year to the festival and we provide packages for all the top meetings: Aintree, Ascot, Prix de L'Arc, York and so on.

The national hunt people are the very best and nicest people to travel with. They are all extremely helpful. To take one example, during a long postal strike one year in the run-up to Cheltenham, one of our clients, who had a few newspaper shops in Dublin, told us to send all the tickets to him and he would hand them out for us. He had no idea of the number of tickets involved so we did not accept his offer and instead delivered them by courier all over the country, but we appreciated the kind gesture very much.

At Dublin Airport the sight of trainer Michael O'Brien in his wheelchair is a sobering reminder, if one were necessary, that racing is a serious business. A number of punters wish him well, as he has Knife Edge, one of the fancied runners, in the opening race of the day, the Elite Racing Club Triumph Hurdle, having previously won the race with Shawiya. Inevitably puns abound about our hopes being on a knife edge. Confidence is high because Knife Edge is unbeaten in four starts, though that afternoon it will be shown to be misplaced.

The plane seems to take an inordinate length of time to take off, prompting barbs that, 'It can't make it up the hill!' The man beside me shakes his head at my stupidity when informed of my intention to go for Florida Pearl. He spends the next 20 minutes trying to convince me to switch to Teeton Mill. As he is from Dundalk I deflect his attention by speaking about my passion for the Corrs, and we spend the rest of the flight in pleasant conversation about the new 'fab four'.

The Irishness of the group is highlighted by the fact that on the bus on the way to Prestbury Park six people are conversing in Irish. As the gates open at 10.30 a.m., Irish glories of yesteryear are almost immediately recalled as Imperial Call's Gold Cup is replayed on the giant video screen.

For the jockeys, as for Cheltenham manager Ed Gillespie, this is a week for business. The mobile phones in their hands are no fashion accessories. They exchange quick pleasantries with the true fans who have been out very early in the morning to scrutinise the form of the horses. The archetypal grandfather is the first to ask the question that is on everybody's lips: 'Will the weather hold?' He scratches his head as he looks up at the sky. 'Be Gawd, I think it will,' he says cheerfully. When his companion looks doubtful, he revises his opinion as he scrutinises the heavens for a second time. 'Then again it mightn't,' he says, anxious to cover all the options.

Media types abound, scurrying frantically. A very busy Mark Pitman buys a steak sandwich from one of the many fast-food outlets and eats it with a speed that would give an ulcer expert ulcers. Deadlines wait for no man or woman. One wonders if this curious breed are appreciated. Having retired from the BBC in 1997, Sir Peter O'Sullevan, for so long the voice of Prestbury Park, lost his nameplate in the Cheltenham press room with almost immediate effect. The following March he entered the course's press centre to find that the place where he had prepared for his commentaries had been given over to the *Irish Star*, a change achieved with a piece of card and some Sellotape. 'I went in to see if I was still alive. Apparently I'm not!' he said with a rueful smile. The room itself is like a college library the day before the final exams. There is barely elbow room along the rows of benches. Equality of opportunity does not seem to be a reality here, as there is only one female in the room.

'Isn't that Clare Balding?' whispers a star-struck fan outside with the sort of hairdo that could cause a hole in the ozone layer all by itself.

'Yeah. She's better looking in the flesh than she is on television!' replies her boyfriend in a voice that would make a Leonard Cohen song seem cheerful.

'Isn't she the one who said on Radio 5 that she was high on coke?'

'Something like that.' (She later explained that she drank too much Coke in the car on the way to the race.)

Although the meeting is all about Anglo-Irish rivalry, in broadcasting it's a story of Anglo-Irish collaboration. The BBC and RTE are sharing facilities. Although there are over two hours to go before the first race, RTE Radio's senior sports producer Noel Coughlan has his preparations almost complete. His is a sacred trust: to bring the thrills and spills of this auditorium of wonder to the vast legion of Irish people who can't afford the time or the money to be at Cheltenham but to whom it remains a matter of passion. That morning, as he breakfasted in his hotel with popular broadcaster Des Cahill, a man had approached their table and asked Des, 'Excuse me, sir. Are you J.P. McManus?'

'No,' replied Des, 'but I wish I had his money!'

On the fifth floor of the stand, BBC commentator Peter Bromley is already in position for his afternoon's work. He has a breathtaking view of this equine shrine. Can there be a natural arena to match it in any sporting venue? The secret of his success as a commentator is revealed – meticulous research. Beside the runners for each race are three pieces of information about each horse in neat handwriting. For extra emphasis, key points are stressed in different-colour pens. The ex-army man is in sombre mood.

> I was very sad to see Nick Dundee falling yesterday. It was a terrible event, not just for the connections but for all the Irish. That's a very difficult fence, especially for novices who have probably never run as fast in their lives as they do coming down that hill. Because it's downhill you have to take that fence just right. It's a real problem. I've seen a lot of runners falling there and a lot of good jockeys like Mick Fitzgerald have had their problems at it. I remember three horses falling at it once. You've got to approach it like dressage and hold back. The best jockey I've ever seen at handling that fence was Stan Mellor. He always had his horse spot on for it.

> Looking down from here, it's easy to get a misleading view of the course. It looks wonderful, but what you have to realise is that it's a

very tight course. The horse is nearly always twisting or turning or going uphill or downhill. You've got to have your wits about you all the time as a jockey and if your horse has any flaws this is the place where they will be painfully exposed.

The corporate boxes are on the lower floors, with J.P. McManus's box on the fourth floor. Outside the betting ring, Sean Ban Breathnach is conducting an interview as Michael Fortune walks by with his recording equipment under his arm. Star of *Après Match* Colm Murray is interviewing Ted Walsh in the centre of the deserted parade ring. A dedicated few are watching the empty pre-parade ring, with an unmistakably Irish voice speaking into a mobile phone and boasting of having had the first three winners the previous day.

In the Hall of Fame a man of mature years is availing himself of the chance to have a ride on the mechanical horse as the Irish Sports Minister Jim McDaid acquires his race card on his way to netting a cool £75,000 from the festival, mostly from bets on Istabraq and See More Business. Later, Minister for Agriculture Joe Walsh takes his place in the stand not far from where former Tipperary hurling great Pat Fox is holding court. And after helping Manchester United defeat Inter Milan the previous night in the Champions' League, Andy Cole is upbeat about Dorans Pride's chances in the Gold Cup.

As the time of the first race approaches, a steady stream of helicopters arrives. In the Tattersalls Grandstand a highly strung girl, Heidi on magic mushrooms, comments caustically on a jockey's bum as the first horses appear on the course. An anorexic figure with long hands and the kind of exuberant nasal hair from which it is difficult to tear one's gaze studies the form. Someone whispers that if he sneezed, bats would fly out of him. He is like a sponge; he says little but absorbs everything. The phrase 'not much to look at' might have been coined with him in mind, but when it comes to the action, he is a reputed 'hoor to work'.

Two men discuss the form like lovers: arguing one moment, intimate the next. One whispers conspiratorially, as if it were a state secret, that in 1992 it emerged that Cheltenham had been staging races over the wrong distances for almost 20 years. The Gold Cup and the Champion Hurdle had both been run over half a furlong longer than their official distances. The mistakes had been uncovered in a full remeasurement of Cheltenham and other courses carried out the previous year. Another gripe they share concerns the new winners' enclosure. While it does allow more people to see the winning horse, the old winners' enclosure had a magic atmosphere because it generated a deafening noise.

As the racing unfolds, nerves are soothed by frequent trips to the bar. Drink is used to soften the blow of a heavy loss, proving the veracity of A.E. Housman's pithy comment that 'Malt does more than Milton can, to justify God's way to man'. Any quarrels are quickly nipped in the bud. The barman is an old man but still vigorous enough. He has a way of mollifying awkward customers; he is as silent as the empty glasses which surround him. A cheery customer praises the restrained brilliance of Mick Fitzgerald. Sporting ecumenism breaks out as two young men share soccer jokes: 'What's the difference between George Graham and Tim Henman? When Tim Henman returns a backhander he's considered a hero.' A security guard looks very busy without doing anything. A bit like an election agent.

Bookies, pickpockets who let you use your own hands, get a battering. To many they're just debt collectors. A disillusioned punter mutters that the main reason why a chap becomes a bookmaker is because he is too scared to steal and too heavy to become a jockey.

It is said that there is nothing in the world that can make such a fool of a man as a horse. A beer-bellied man with an uncanny resemblance to David Mellor is comparing a little-known horse to Arkle. Before the excitement reaches its climax, this horse lives down to expectation and falls at the third fence.

Weather is a huge factor in deciding which punters are successful. Over 20 years ago, Ireland's favourite racing commentator Dessie Scahill stood to make a small fortune on an ante-post double on Decent Fellow to win the Sweeps Hurdle and Brown Lad (a horse that with luck on his side could have won three Gold Cups) to win the Gold Cup. The morning of the Gold Cup he was woken up by Ted Walsh, who was staying in the next room, saying, 'There's no racing today.' As Dessie enquired why, Walsh opened the window, stretched out his hand and gave him the answer – by pelting snow at him. The race was rescheduled for April but by the time it was run the ground was hard and Midnight Court went on to claim the ultimate prize.

Ted Walsh claims, 'When the gambling men get to Cheltenham, something happens. Their blood is up and they just plough in. They can go blindly and even bet on something at ridiculously short odds that they would never accept on their home ground.'

The day is a catalogue of disappointment for Irish punters with the notable exception of Space Trucker's win in the Grand Annual Chase, the oldest chase in the racing calendar. Although two years previously he had finished third to Make A Stand in the Champion Hurdle, Irish punters had reservations about backing him, despite his fine win in a prep race over hurdles at Leopardstown, because of Irish horses' poor record in the handicap chases at the festival. With the ground coming right for the

Jessica Harrington-trained horse and off a low weight, he stormed to victory, giving both Harrington and jockey Shay Barry their first wins at the festival. The trainer's instruction to her jockey had been, 'Whatever you do, don't appear until the last.' Barry followed her instructions to the letter and won with a burst of speed.

Despite the best efforts of Space Trucker, the mood on the last flight to Dublin is much more subdued than on the way over. The only consolation is that the millennium festival is just 362 days and 20 minutes away: same time, same venue, same magic.

Culture Club

Sport has always been inextricably linked with the wider culture and has always had massive cultural implications in Ireland. Witness John Montague's incisive observation: 'The Protestant boys played cricket, or kicked a queer-shaped ball like a pear. According to my Falls pal, Protestant balls bounced crooked as the Protestants themselves.'

Neville Cardus, perhaps the greatest sportswriter of them all, as is evident from his magical evocation of the fabled Test match between England and Australia at Lord's in 1930, incisively remarked that 'a great game is part of the nation's life and environment'. His game was cricket. His country was England. Yet, like all great writers, his uniquely personal experiences have universal applications. His observation forcefully reminds us of the prominence of a great game in the tapestry of national life. Cardus's basic insight has to be significantly modified for the Cheltenham Festival, given its unique Anglo-Irish composition.

Different countries have different national characteristics. In France they are passionate about ideas. If you shoot a man for disagreeing with you about the intricacies of philosophy, then that is a tremendous compliment to the life of the mind. The French, though, do not share the Irish passion for horses. When the Pope visited Ireland in 1979 he celebrated Mass on the racecourse in Galway. However, cynics might say that since the details of the private lives of the two other main celebrants of the Mass, Bishop Eamon Casey and Father Michael Cleary, have become public, French and Irish passions have more in common than we might have suspected.

There is not much justification for having a country that has nothing distinctive to contribute to the wider world. Mindsets are crucial to that distinctiveness, and Cheltenham exhibits the Irish distinctiveness at its best.

A crucial difference between the English and the Irish is the way they react to victory. The English tend to temper their celebrations with some of their hallowed reserve and aloofness. The Irish, on the other hand, let their emotions run wild and there are no inhibitions.

For years Danno Heaslip was at the heart of the Galwegians rugby team, playing in the scrum-half position. Danno and his brother Mick provided Ireland with another Cheltenham win when their horse For Auction won the 1982 Champion Hurdle at 40–1 under the stewardship of Colin Magnier. Part of racing folklore is the story of their special bet for the champagne money, which resulted in them netting £2,000. On arrival back at their hotel, Danno is said to have instructed the manager to open 100 bottles of champagne. His second instruction was for the manager to fetch a piano.

'But we don't have a piano here,' the manager replied.

'Then buy one,' said Danno.

Although the prize money was £40,000, the owners won more from the bookies, having backed their pride and joy at 50–1 on the course.

Probably the only Irishman with mixed feelings about the victory was Danno Heaslip's friend, former government minister Des O'Malley. He had been all geared up to attend the festival, but then a general election had intervened and he found himself back in office at the start of March, and at the last minute he had to cancel his trip to Cheltenham. He instructed Danno to put £25 each way on the horse for him. Danno went to Cheltenham on the Sunday but before leaving posted a letter to O'Malley's home in Limerick, saying that so many people had asked him to back the horse that he couldn't possibly get it all on, particularly as he was backing the horse heavily himself. He told O'Malley, therefore, to back the horse himself. The only problem was that O'Malley had left for Dublin before the post arrived on the Monday morning and didn't get the letter until after the race – having calculated that he had just won £1,250 on his investment!

Irish society, both before and after independence, has been perceived as having to contend with being on a periphery politically, economically and geographically. Cheltenham provides Irish punters with an opportunity to reverse that situation and take centre stage in the equine world.

According to Emile Zola, the purpose of democracy is to make people feel less different from one another. Cheltenham achieves this task admirably.

SEVENTEEN

History

> 'We have before had occasion to compliment the sagacity and intelligence displayed by Mr Cartwright's horses. They never win when they are favourites, but always when long odds are to be obtained about them. The public ought to be grateful to him.'
>
> *SPORTING LIFE*, 1865

The rich wells of sentiment play a huge part in the Cheltenham Festival, as Ted Walsh knows from first hand experience.

> I won my first race there in 1974 on Castleruddery. The horse was owned by Mrs Harper. She was a real old gent. At the end of every race you rode for her she'd come over and give you one of the old, red ten shilling notes and say, 'Get yourself some sweets'. She'd really wanted to run a horse in that particular race because her son had fought and died in World War Two and was killed with a man called Kim Muir. Kim's parents had put up a trophy for that race which was called the Kim Muir Memorial trophy. It was a fairytale ending and very nostalgic and a special thrill to win for such a lovely woman.

Given his history it was inevitable that Istabraq's third consecutive Champion Hurdle in the Millennium Festival was going to attract an outpouring of sentiment. No one could have foreseen, though, the drama in the 24 hours leading up to the big race. It was like the plot of a Dick Francis novel. So confident were they that Istabraq was going to romp home that Paddy Power bookmakers announced days before the race that they were going to pay out all bets on Istabraq to win.

The day before his date with destiny Istabraq had arrived at the Festival. All the omens were favourable. Then panic. Shortly after the wonder horse had been loaded into his box, Pat Keating, Aidan O'Brien's travelling head lad, spotted a trace of fresh blood on his nostril. Istabraq's aura of invincibility, the product of only three defeats in 24 races and each time on heavy ground over a longer trip than two miles, was momentarily shattered. It was easy to imagine the Irish racing fans who had gone on to their eternal reward leaning over the bannisters in heaven watching the drama unfold.

The feeling of uneasiness was accentuated by the fact that Istabraq was facing perhaps the best Champion Hurdle field of his career, with the impressive talents of Hors La Loi, Blue Royal and Ashley Park ready to pounce on any unexpected opportunities. Those punters grasping for straws recalled Istabraq's great heart and toughness when he won the SunAlliance in 1997.

From his home in Ballydoyle, a name synonymous with Cheltenham glory from the days of Vincent O'Brien, Aidan O'Brien was immediately on the phone to Charlie Swan and J.P. McManus. Neither could have ignored the concern in O'Brien's voice. The media got wind of the unexpected development and it immediately became a major news story. Was this going to be a case of paradise lost? Istabraq started to drift in the market to evens instead of the 8–15 he started at.

The previous month O'Brien had had two strokes of bad luck when he was forced to withdraw his two other strongly fancied horses from the Festival. Le Coudray had been 4–1 joint favourite to go one better than his second the previous year in the Bonusprint Stayers' Hurdle. Yeoman's Point had been a 14–1 chance for the Supreme Novices' Hurdle and was also entered in the Club Triumph Hurdle. Who was it that said bad luck always comes in threes?

Had it been any other venue, or any other race, O'Brien would have refused to let Istabraq run. Indeed, up until 11 a.m. Istabraq wasn't a certain runner. With a nation's expectations on his shoulders O'Brien took an unaccustomed gamble. It would be a brave man who would forego the opportunity for immortality. Istabraq did not disappoint. Paradise regained. In the process Swan shaved almost half a second off Make a Stand's three-year-old track record. The first prize of £108,725 took Istabraq past the £1 million mark in earnings after the Sterling differential is factored in.

Patrick Kavanagh once backed a horse at the Phoenix Park which led all the way and was fifteen lengths clear at the end. He declared it the most thrilling finish he had ever witnessed. In the circumstances J.P. McManus might have echoed the same sentiments about Istabraq's comfortable victory. He admitted his heart was in his mouth and his vision was not too good throughout the race.

The Festival had begun badly for the Sundance Kid. His heavily-fancied favourite, Youlneverwalkalone, was beaten in the opening race. Trainer Christy Roche had always held out great hopes for this horse a half-brother to Galmoy, who upheld Irish honour by winning twice at the Festival in the dark days of the 1980s when Irish horses were not making their customary impact. A so-called third world country would have been overjoyed to receive all the Irish money wagered on Youlneverwalkalone.

Top racing journalist Hugh McIlvanney has written humorously about a previously unidentified condition known as GOS, 'Groundless Optimism Syndrome'. This affliction is a delusional condition which strikes for the three days of the Festival, whereby people who have lost the family silver on previous visits to Cheltenham become convinced that they have new mystical powers of prophecy which enable them to bet with certainty. Inevitably, when they leave Prestbury Park three days later their wallets are very anaemic. J.P. McManus is not afflicted by GOS.

When Irish entertainer Brendan Grace strode up to the microphone to extol Istabraq's virtues in song at the victory presentation, a plummy accent was heard to marvel at the Oirishness of it all. The song may not have had the musical quality of the theme from *Black Beauty*, but the sentiment was right. J.P. received his trophy to an accompaniment of the well-known Irish traditional song, *Olé, Olé*. One of the banners in the crowd stated, 'Istabraq for President'. Nobody was disagreeing.

McManus went on the record to state that no amount of money would have tempted him to back Istabraq. This news was music to the ears of Victor Chandler, with whom J.P. has put his money on the line many times during the Festival in the past, as Vincent O'Brien had with William Hill a generation earlier. McManus is famously reported to have said of Chandler, 'he has the face of Mother Teresa and the mind of Al Capone'. Their epic tussles have been the stuff of myth, with J.P. cast in the role of a modern day Robin Hood. There is justification for this association, as J.P. has been the source of countless charitable donations and his golf classic has been a successful fund-raiser.

Istabraq's win was yet another triumph for Aidan O'Brien, who admitted that he had endured the most anxious 24 hours of his life. Although he has no blood relation with the greatest of them all, Vincent O'Brien, the two men seem to have similar genius, life-force and exacting standards. Both have shown an equal aptitude for winning big races on the flat.

The new master of Ballydoyle's fan club extends to Sir Alex Ferguson. Their bond of friendship was strengthened in June when O'Brien trained a first runner, Red Coral, to win at Naas for the Manchester United Racing Club.

O'Brien's excitable horse Istabraq joined an elite group: Hatton's Grace

(1949–51), Sir Ken (1952–54), Persian War (1968–70) and See You Then (1985–87), each of whom won the Champion Hurdle three years in succession. Can Istabraq go one better and become the greatest hurdler of all time? Even Arkle couldn't manage to win at the Festival five years in a row. Istabraq was immediately installed at a best priced 6–4 to return victoriously next year. The experience of the bloody nose should caution us about making rash judgements. Injury can prematurely disrupt, even end, any career – human or equine. Nonetheless, age is in Istabraq's favour. Hatton's Grace was nine years old when he won his first Champion Hurdle.

Here's to history in the making.

Oh, What a Perfect Day

It was a story to warm the heart. Noel Meade has had cruel luck at Cheltenham down through the years with Heist, Hill Society et al. He went to the Millennium Festival never having had a winner there, and a succession of near misses suggested that Prestbury Park had a jinx on him. Yet he brought 11 runners there, the biggest team of any Irish trainer.

After two decades of training, Meade was entitled to celebrate his first victory at the Festival in the Capel Cure Supreme Novices' Hurdle. Although most Irish money was on 5–4 favourite, the Conor O'Dwyer mount Youlneverwalkalone, there had been good interest in Meade's Sausalito Bay, who was backed from 20s into 14–1. The horse is owned by the five-man High Street Syndicate, who had also suffered 'the slings and arrows of outrageous fortune' as Meade went close in previous Festivals.

From the outset Sausalito Bay imposed himself on the race, helped in no small way by an inspirational ride from Paul Carberry. For a fleeting moment he looked in danger coming to the second last, but he found a new gear, and up the hill was too good for the fast-finishing Best Mate and the third-placed Youlneverwalkalone.

Meade's good fortune did not last long. In the very next race, the Irish Independent Arkle Trophy, his horse Frozen Groom was travelling strongly in the lead before falling at the third last.

The only surprise about Sausalito Bay's victory was that the winning jockey, Paul Carberry, was untypically restrained. This could be attributed solely to the back injury he sustained three weeks previously. Carberry rejoices in the nickname of Alice, given his penchant for singing a unique rendition of the well-known Smokie hit as his party piece. Stories of his high spirits are more common than showers in April.

Two out of Three Ain't Bad

Big wins are no novelty to Paul Carberry. On 10 April, 1999, Ireland secured its first win in the Aintree Grand National for 24 years, when the 9-year-old Bobbyjo cruised to a 10 lengths victory, with Carberry in the saddle. Paul began his victory parade about fifty yards from home. He celebrated in a unique way – grabbing a beam in the low roof of the enclosed unsaddling area, before pulling himself like a monkey from the saddle and landing down beside his mount as if he were the best known Romanian since Dracula, Nadia Comeneci, in boots.

The previous Irish jockey to win the Grand National was Paul's father, Tommy on L'Escargot, upsetting the favourite Red Rum. L'Escargot was trained by the late Dan Moore, whose daughter Pamela married Tommy. Tommy was the trainer of Bobbyjo. In an interview for RTE, Mrs Carberry put her finger on this intricate web of family connections. 'I used to be known as the daughter of Dan Moore, then as the wife of Tommy Carberry, and I suppose from now on it will be as the mother of Paul Carberry.'

The Carberrys were the first father and son combination as trainer and jockey to win the Grand National since Reg and Bruce Hobbs with Battleship in 1938. Ironically, they won only by beating Dan Moore's mount, Royal Danieli, by a head. Tommy became part of an elite group to both ride and train a National winner. The party continued in their native Ratoath for weeks. Having scaled the heights at Aintree, Carberry experienced the flip side of the racing coin shortly after when he was injured at a schooling session at Noel Meade's stables. Initially it seemed only a minor injury, but turned out to be a ruptured spleen, discovered only when Carberry collapsed and was rushed to Cashel hospital. His condition could have been fatal. The top jockey returned to action at Tralee, but another fall put him out of action again until Listowel.

In the Gold Cup the great new rivalry in Irish sport was in focus, with both Carberry, on Florida Pearl, and Ruby Walsh, on Rince Rí, going for glory. Because of his problems with his back, Carberry had to be declared fit by the course doctor before being permitted to ride in the Blue Riband of steeplechasing.

After disappointing at the 1999 Cheltenham Festival, and a subsequent 14 lengths defeat in the Punchestown Gold Cup Chase by Imperial Call, many had cast doubt on Florida Pearl's stamina. Violet O'Leary's horse showed signs of a return to form with a commanding victory over Dorans Pride in the inaugural running of the £100,000 James Nicholson Wine Merchant Champion Chase at Down Royal in November, running on strongly at the end of the three miles and one furlong race. However it was the manner of his victory in the Hennessy Gold Cup at Leopardstown in February that suggested he was really in peak form. He took the lead a full mile from home and with a convincing display of jumping had a most emphatic win over Dorans Pride and Rince Rí.

Despite Florida Pearl making mistakes at the third and second last, Carberry finished second in the Gold Cup. Indeed, Ireland's top chaser had passed Looks Like Trouble and taken the lead after Gloria Victis's tragic fall at the second last. It was a case of so near yet so far for Carberry. The blow to national pride was as keenly felt as the damage done to countless overdrafts.

There was a major Irish connection with the Gold Cup winner. Looks Like Trouble was trained by a 49-year-old native of the North Circular Road in Dublin, Noel Chance. The horse's victory the previous year in the SunAlliance had been tarnished because the favourite, Nick Dundee, had suffered a horrific fall. It was Chance's second victory in the race, having first won it with Mr Mulligan in 1997. Amazingly, Chance's fortunes went into decline after winning his first Gold Cup. Michael Worcester, owner of Mr Mulligan and Chance's main client, dramatically pruned his racing interests, and Chance was left with less than a dozen horses. By the Millennium Festival the number had risen again to 30. He resides at the famous Saxon House Stables, home of the 1973 Gold Cup hero, the Dikler, whose box Looks Like Trouble now inhabits.

The Irish connection with the winner would have been extended had not Cork-born Norman Williamson been sacked as the horse's jockey by its owner. A 'bad ride' in the King George at Kempton was believed to be the reason for this decision. Instead, it was Richard Johnson who was the winning jockey. Ironically, Johnson had suffered a similar fate when he was jocked off Mr Mulligan and missed out on his Gold Cup triumph. Although he looked crestfallen after the big race, Williamson did receive some measure of consolation in the very next race when he rode the novice and favourite, Samakaan, to victory in the Grand Annual. In the process he provided trainer Venetia Williams with her first Festival success. Such was the enthusiasm of Williamson's celebration as he passed the winning post that one could have been forgiven for thinking he had just won the Gold Cup.

For Paul Carberry a return of a winner and a second out of three Festival rides was pretty impressive. With a young horse, a young trainer and a young and hungry jockey, what are the odds of Paul Carberry and Florida Pearl going one better next year?

An Equine Fairytale

The final day of the Festival was a blank for Irish winners, despite the hopes of the nation resting on Limestone Lad in the Stayers Hurdle. Hans Christian Anderson would have struggled to imagine a fairytale like Limestone Lad's. All that was missing at Cheltenham was the perfect ending.

A succession of injuries had led Danoli's star to wane. Although Tom Foley's horse will never lose his capacity to generate mass dewy-eyed nostalgia, the Irish racing public needed a new 'people's champion'. Enter Jim Bowe, a man whose involvement in racing stretches back to the 1940s, and his son Michael. From their small yard on the Kilkenny–Tipperary border came Limestone Lad, a radiant new star on the equine firmament. In the autumn of 1999 he exploded onto the national consciousness with a string of victories. Then, on live television Limestone Lad announced his arrival to the big time in the most memorable way possible, with an emphatic win in the Hatton's Grace Hurdle at Punchestown over – Istabraq! People sat up and took further notice at Navan six days later when the popular seven-year-old defeated Le Coudray in the Navan Racecourse and Golfcourse Hurdle by 20 lengths. This horse embodies the incomparable appeal of National Hunt Racing, at once generating blood-stirring excitement and displaying the innate democracy of ambitions of the sport.

At all levels racing involves sacrifice. When Frankie Dettori was marrying the daughter of a Cambridge professor, Catherine Allen, his boss set the date. As he was riding for Godolphin, the wealthiest racing operation in the world, owned by the Maktoum brothers, Godolphin's racing manager told Dettori he would have to marry on a Sunday because of race commitments. Subsequently Sheikh Mohammed al-Maktoum 'requested' that Dettori give up his newly acquired passion for fox-hunting lest he sustain an injury. In both cases Dettori meekly accepted their 'suggestions'.

The sacrifices faced by the Bowes have been of a different order. Bill Shankly's famous 'life or death' quote doesn't even begin to describe their bond to their trade – or, more accurately, vocation. They have been forced to sell off their good horses. When Limestone Lad struck gold, Irish racing rejoiced in their long overdue good fortune. The inherent egalitarianism of National Hunt racing was confirmed once again.

Immediately punters were eloquently describing Irish racing's newest sensation like a Greek God. Their comments about how Limestone Lad was going to 'pulverise' the English opposition in Cheltenham were instructive – a linguistic structure enabling us to peer through the looking glass darkly, as it were, and glimpse at the Anglo-Irish rivalry that goes to the heart of Cheltenham. The Bee Gees were profoundly wrong. It is never 'only words'.

It was, though to be another story of Irish gallant failure at Cheltenham. For days beforehand there was constant speculation about whether or not Limestone Lad would even run in the race because the good ground might not suit him. Although, true to form, he burned off most of the field from the front, Mick Fitzgerald's mount Bacchanal proved to be too strong. Having been headed on the turn-in, Limestone Lad rallied heroically to lose by a length. An objection from jockey Shane McGovern failed to yield a change in the result. Better days will come. As of now this dream machine has to be judged as much in terms of potential as achievement. Yet even the most sceptical find it difficult to restrain the swelling of hope he engenders. The Millennium Festival, his first trip overseas, is just the prologue in the Limestone Lad story.

Saddle Up

Although the number of Irish winners at the Festival was disappointing, Irish jockeys rode 13 out of the 20 winners. On Wednesday Jim Culloty rode Lord Noelie to victory for his boss, Henrietta Knight, in the SunAlliance Chase. It was the 26-year-old from Killarney's first win at the Festival. Two other Irish jockeys, Paul Flynn and Tony Dobbin, also had their first victories.

The thriller of the Festival was served up by two Irish jockeys on top form. On Saturday, 11 December 1999, Tony McCoy had got into the spirit of the millennium early by riding his 1,000th career winner and shattering the previous best effort for that feat by almost five years. Fittingly, the honour came at Cheltenham on the 5–2 joint favourite, Majadou, trained by Martin Pipe, when winning the Wragge & Co Handicap Chase by 21 lengths from Dantes Cavalier. In the Champion Chase, McCoy on Edredon Bleu slugged it out with Norman Williamson on Direct Route, before McCoy claimed his only winner of the meeting. Williamson had the not-inconsiderable consolation of riding one of the stars of the Festival, the Tom Costello protegee, Monsignor, and another win on Samakaan.

Although Mick Fitzgerald was unable to repeat his major wins of the previous year, his sublime skills were there for all to see despite the disappointment of See More Business's failure to regain the Gold Cup. On the Tuesday his genius was evident on Tiutchev in the Arkle. If that was good, better was to follow for his trainer Nicky Henderson, on the error prone Marlborough, in the William Hill Handicap Chase when he waited until the second last fence to make his move and snatched the race at the last fence from Carl Llewellyn on Beau. He went on to regain his title of leading rider with Bacchanal in the Stayers' Hurdle, and again with Stormyfairweather in the Cathcart.

Legendary Irish jockey Jonjo O'Neill was back in the winner's enclosure at the Festival. With Tony Dobbin in the saddle, and despite a very late challenge from Danegold, he had his third win as a trainer with J.P. McManus's French acquisition, Master Tern, in the final race of the Festival, the Vincent O'Brien County Hurdle. It was time for a trip down memory lane. Memories of his win on Dawn Run were retold with gusto. Other stories surfaced as well.

Jonjo was a very focused competitor and, as such, was the last person anybody in the weighing room would have imagined likely to play a practical joke – unlike his celebrated rival John Francome, who was famous for his pranks and gags, even during races. One day as Francome walked into the weighing room, Jonjo approached him and told him to give one of their colleagues, Alan Brown, a ribbing about his mother's musical talents, because she had been featured in the local paper playing the piano. True to character, as soon as Francome walked in he began slagging Mrs Brown about her piano playing. A tense silence fell on the room. Alan looked as if he was going to burst into tears as he said in a muffled voice, 'My mother has no hands.'

Francome wished the ground would open up and swallow him. When he regained his composure he rushed in rage over to O'Neill and was about to thump him when all the other jockeys present burst into laughter. There was absolutely nothing wrong with Mrs Brown's hands!

Francome was not used to being the butt of such a joke and decided he would have to take revenge on his colleagues by setting up another jockey in the same way. His target was Bob Champion, famous for coming back from cancer to win the Grand National on Aldaniti in 1981. Francome set Bob up beautifully, and was brimming with pleasure at the thought of the look of horror on his colleague's face when they reached the punch-line. The problem was that the joke went completely over Champion's head. Far from showing embarrassment, Bob asked in all earnestness, 'Does she want to sell her piano then?'!

The peculiar kinsmanship between jockeys was starkly highlighted in June when Irish Jockey Ray Cochrane, despite suffering burns and a hand injury, risked his own life to save the housewives' favourite Frankie Dettori. After their private plane lurched wildly out of control soon after take-off,

Cochrane helped Dettori away from the shattered light aircraft and then went back to try, ultimately unsuccessfully to save the pilot, Patrick Mackey, despite the imminence of an explosion.

Shakin All Over

One of Ireland's leading writers, Joe O'Connor, once posed the question: Is football better than sex? Joe's witty argument could readily be transposed to the world of National Hunt Racing. At first glance this might be considered a highly contentious statement, as the two activities are so remarkably different. One involves the complete engagement of the senses, wild abandonment, heart-stopping elation and, above all, orgasmic bliss.

The other is sex.

Few know the sheer toe-curling ecstasy of winning and the adrenalin rush of having the small hairs standing on the back of the neck at Cheltenham better than Willie Mullins. His apparent stranglehold on the prestigious Festival bumper was continued when Charlie Swan won on Joe Cullen.

Edward O'Grady's Ned Kelly had been well fancied after two wins at Leopardstown and would probably have been a hot favourite had he a professional jockey on board, rather than the young amateur Tom Magnier. Instead, Mick Fitzgerald became the strong favourite on Inca and appeared to be in control until Swan made the decisive move, switching his mount to the outside as the gap on the rails closed. Race over. The war-whoops of victory told their own story, providing yet another endorsement of Willie's unique dominance of this race. Ironically, Mullins had made a number of efforts to sell the horse in the previous months, but had found no takers.

Mullins went into the race with a very strong hand because no less than four of his horses faced the tapes. BallyAmber was rated because of his staying power. Like Joe Cullen, Be My Royal had won first time out. However, Mullins had consistently tipped one of his other horses in the race, Tuesday, in the Florida Pearl colours to give him his fourth win in the race, joining Wither or Which, Florida Pearl and Alexander Banquet in the Mullins' hall of fame.

Mullins had other great performances at the Festival, notably when his 20–1 shot General Cloney, with Ruby Walsh in the saddle, finished third in the Triumph Hurdle.

The People's Pundit

It was no fluke that Ted Walsh was a winner of the prestigious Jacobs award for his broadcasting prowess. The job of a racing pundit, to steal shamelessly from Robert Frost, is to provide what is demanded of a good poem, 'not necessarily a great clarification . . . but a momentary stay against confusion'. As a television racing pundit, Walsh goes much further, never ceasing to inform, enthuse, entertain and to extend the boundaries of the English language. He has an empathetic relationship with every Irish racing fan because he is someone with whom even the most beleaguered punter can have a rapport.

His skills as racing analyst were showcased on the opening day of the Festival when he was asked to evaluate Richard Dunwoody's success as a jockey on the occasion of the first post-Dunwoody Festival – following the Irish jockey's enforced retirement.

> He was the most complete National Hunt jockey in my time. I've been knocking around this game a long time and for me the two great heroes of the game are Arkle and Dunwoody. He had no weaknesses and his record speaks for itself. The three most important things in a jockey are courage, a smart racing brain and commitment. Richard had all of these in abundance. None of the jockeys of today could find a better role model than him. That's not to say he was a saint. He certainly wasn't, as Adrian Maguire knows. He had that edge that all sportspeople must have. He wouldn't go out of his way to 'do' another jockey but he was tough. I suppose he'll need those qualities now as he starts his own business.

It is his obvious humanity that also makes Walsh such a favourite with Irish racing fans. In 1996 he raised £86,000 for People in Need when riding from Cork to Dublin.

Walsh went to Cheltenham with reason for confidence in his Gold Cup contender. After victory in the Power Gold Cup, Rince Rí had emerged as Ireland's top novice. He faced his first major pre-Cheltenham test over gluey ground in the Ericsson at the Leopardstown Christmas meeting. The competition was provided in the shape of the ante-post favourite for the Gold Cup, Florida Pearl. Although Florida Pearl seemed set to win after the last, he was unable to match Rince Rí.

Misadventure, in the form of serious injury, had dogged Ruby Walsh's season. With three fences to go in the Gold Cup, Ruby seemed to have Rince Rí ideally placed, out wide and going well. Then, disaster struck. The horse met the fence wrong and Ruby was dislodged. In media interviews immediately afterward Ruby was heard to say that the horse might have won had he not fallen. With the wisdom of age, his father was more circumspect and speculated that he might simply have been placed.

A month later it would be a different story for the Walshes. After an indifferent winter the Ted-trained and Ruby-ridden Papillon won the Aintree Grand National. To add to the occasion, Ted had just a few days previously wagered a 'modest sum' on the horse at odds of 40–1. Within weeks, father and son had pulled off an incredible double when a former Cheltenham hero, Commanche Court, owned by Dermot Desmond, won the Irish Grand National at Fairyhouse.

It is difficult to know if it is harder to breed a jockey than to breed a horse. There are already signs that Ruby has inherited his father's legendary wit. When asked how he performed in his Leaving Cert exams, Walsh the younger quipped, 'I rode three winners!'

The year 2000 will forever be remembered as the year of Ted and Ruby Walsh. A partnership like this can only make the good times better.

Money, Money, Money

Ireland had not done as well as people hoped for at the Millenium Festival, with three winners. The wild optimism of the start of the week was seriously misplaced. Ted Walsh was not surprised.

> I'm constantly stunned by just how many people believe what they want to believe when it comes to Cheltenham. It's virtually certain that every year we'll have fellas hyping up how many winners we're going to have. 'We'll have at least seven and maybe nine.' Its crazy stuff a lot of the time. What people still don't get is that Cheltenham is a very tough place to win races and just as tough to back winners.

In the bars following Istabraq's victory, Irish eyes were smiling. The post-mortems were not the most objective the racing world has ever heard. The experts catalogued his achievement as belonging in a long line of great Irish heroes, warriors and miscellaneous feats of Celtic courage. No metaphor was too layered in hyperbole, particularly as the drink took effect. Strong men came dangerously close to blubbering. A few got so emotional that they did the unthinkable; they hugged without embarrassment.

Cheltenham is the best of times. To have a runner worthy of even going to the start is an 'experience', and to win or to be associated with a winner is absolute heaven.

It can also be the worst of times. Cheltenham savagely exposes any discrepancy between hype and reality. One of the most striking examples dates back to 1992, when Carvill Hill came to the Gold Cup classed by some experts in the same bracket as Golden Miller and Arkle. Yet after the contest the same people were left eating large portions of humble pie as their delusions of grandeur were painfully shattered. Carvill Hill's inadequacies manifested themselves as early as the first fence with an incredibly clumsy jump. There followed another horrific mistake at the ninth and a series of ragged, hazardous jumps one after another. By the final two fences he was virtually pulled up. The way was apparently set for Adam Kondrat on The Fellow to claim the ultimate glory. It was then that the cream rose to the top in the shape of a 20-year-old Irish prodigy, Adrian Maguire. His characteristically furious challenge on the run-in gave the Gold Cup to the Toby Balding-trained Cool Ground.

Carvill Hill is one of the most spectacular illustrations of a truth revealed at every Festival: that there is all the difference in the world between a great racehorse and a racehorse with the ability to rise to some great performances.

Many Irish punters were to relearn that lesson the hard way at the Millennium Cheltenham Festival. A forlorn Irish punter of high intelligence, mature wisdom and with a sophisticated social sense was slowly making his way through customs at Birmingham airport. The customs officer asked, 'Anything to declare?'

After a dramatic pause the Irish man replied in a voice as miserable as a flooded meadow, 'Nothing but empty pockets.'